Organizing Modernity

To the men and women of Daresbury SERC Laboratory

Organizing Modernity

John Law

BLACKWELL
Oxford UK & Cambridge USA

First published 1994

Blackwell Publishers
108 Cowley Road, Oxford OX4 1JF, UK

238 Main Street,
Cambridge, Massachusetts 02142, USA

British Library Cataloguing in Publication Data
A CIP catalogue record for this book is available from the British Library.

Library of Congress Cataloging-in-Publication Data
Law, John, 1946–
    Organizing modernity / John Law.
        p.   cm.
    Includes bibliographical references (p. 196) and index.
    ISBN 0–631–18512–7 (acid-free paper). – ISBN 0–631–18513–5 (pbk.: acid-free paper)
    1. Sociology–Philosophy. 2. Social structure. 3. Organizational sociology. I. Title.
    HM24.L357 1994   93–15413
    301'.01–dc20   CIP

Typeset in 10½ on 12 pt Goudy Oldstyle by Apex Products, Singapore
Printed in Great Britain by T. J. Press, Padstow

This book is printed on acid-free paper

Contents

Acknowledgements

Like life, research is the outcome of interaction. During the three years of research and writing that led to this book I was helped by hundreds of people. I've pondered about whether I should try to acknowledge everyone individually, but in the end I've chosen not to do so for three main reasons. First, the list would be exceedingly long. Second, I am afraid that I might unwittingly exclude some who should be on it. And third, more so than is usual, I've tried to refer to individuals in the text. Here, then, I'd like to acknowledge my debt to four groups of people, together with the sponsors of the study, but I will mention only a few names.

First, there are those who work at, or are connected with, Daresbury Laboratory. These are the people who answered my questions, let me sit in on their meetings, and hang around their experiments. Throughout the long drawn-out process of fieldwork, they were vastly tolerant, supportive and helpful, giving up time and exposing their daily routines in ways that went quite beyond any call of duty. I'd like to record that though I found that fieldwork at Daresbury was sometimes nerve-racking and tiring, it was also one of the most precious and rewarding experiences of my life. So, though my debt to the people of Daresbury cannot adequately be put into words, I owe them a huge debt of gratitude, and would like to thank them all.

Second, I'd like to thank the sociologists (and members of allied trades). Thus, over the period, I wrestled with the arguments in the book with colleagues at Keele, and also with sociologists in the many other institutions who were kind enough to ask me to present aspects of the study. Often the suggestions or the awkward questions that arose either in seminars or informally turned out to be pivotal to the study. These were conversations crucial to the process of organizing and shaping the book. Accordingly, I'd like to thank all those whom I have talked with in sociology over the last three years, and in particular my colleagues in the Department of Sociology and Social Anthropology at the Keele University.

Third, I want to mention that the argument is also the product of long-term conversation and collaboration with a smaller number of academic colleagues and friends. Indeed, more than anything else, it is this continuing conversation with a few kindred spirits which has given point to the academic way of life during a time when it often seemed that the Universities were not such a good place to be in. But, more directly, these friends and colleagues have helped to shape my particular form of sociology. Commentators, critics, supporters, interpreters – these have been the friends on whom I have most depended. I owe them a huge debt, and I'd like to thank them all, but in particular I'd like to mention Michel Callon, Bob Cooper, Annemarie Mol and Leigh Star.

Fourth, I want to thank those who have had no direct academic connection with the study itself, but who have nevertheless played a crucial role in its form. Their work, as the symbolic interactionists would say, is largely though not entirely invisible in the present text. Though an acknowledgement is a fairly nominal form of undeleting, I'd nevertheless like to thank them, and in particular Sheila Halsall.

Finally, I should observe that since ethnography takes time it also costs money. Accordingly, I'd like to mention that the study was only possible because of the generous financial support of the Economic and Social Research Council, and the Science Policy Support Group. Their grant (Y 30 52 53 001), for a study of scientific accounting and the use of indicators, was made available within the Changing Culture of Science Research Initiative. I am deeply grateful to both organizations for their support.

As we move from a dualist theory of agency, notions of responsibility become progressively less clear-cut. Nevertheless, I'm still sufficiently humanist to feel the need to say that I take responsibility for errors and infelicities in the present text!

John Law,
Market Drayton

1

Introduction

1 TALES OF ORDERING AND ORGANIZING

And so each venture
Is a new beginning, a raid on the inarticulate
With shabby equipment always deteriorating
In the general mess of imprecision of feeling,
Undisciplined squads of emotion.

from East Coker by T. S. Eliot, *The Four Quartets*

Modernity was a long march to prison. It
never arrived there (though in some places
... it came quite close), albeit not for the
lack of trying.

Zygmunt Bauman, *Intimations of Postmodernity*

This is a book about organizing and ordering in the modern world. It is about ordering in formal organizations. It is a book about the social technologies of controlling. It is a book about the materials of the social, about what I call relational materialism. It is also, though to a smaller degree, about unfairnesses, inequalities and hierarchies. But, most fundamentally, it is about the oldest problem of them all – the problem of the social order. So the basic problem of the book is this: what on earth is the social order?

In response to this question I find that I have to refuse its terms. Thus as I see it, first the notion of order goes. Perhaps there is order*ing*, but there is certainly no order. This is because, as Zygmunt Bauman implies, orders are never complete. Instead they are more or less precarious and partial accomplishments that may be overturned. They are, in short, better seen as verbs rather than nouns. So it is that the first term is reshaped.

Second, the idea that there is a *single* order ('the' social order) goes. This is the dream, or the nightmare, of modernity. But there never was a root order, so we have to replace this aspiration by a concern with plural and incomplete processes of social ordering.

And finally, the notion that social ordering is, indeed, simply social also disappears. Rather, I argue, what we call the social is *materially heterogeneous*: talk, bodies, texts, machines, architectures, all of these and many more are implicated in and perform the 'social'. So it is that the question is reshaped. The problem of the social order is replaced by a concern with the plural processes of sociotechnical ordering. And this is the subject-matter of the book.

What, then, can one say about the character of sociotechnical ordering? Here, I argue, we should be modest. And the reason for modesty is very simple. It is that *we're caught up in ordering too*. When we write about ordering there is no question of standing apart and observing from a distance. We're participating in ordering too. We're unavoidably involved in the modern reflexive and self-reflexive project of monitoring, sensemaking and control. But since we participate in this project, we're also, and necessarily, caught up in its uncertainty, its incompleteness, its plurality, a sense of fragmentation.

What should we make of this? This is one of the great questions of contemporary social theory, the problem of the status of our writing in the self-reflexive world of high modernity. Do we continue to pretend if only for heuristic purposes that we are different? Do we therefore insist that social science can tell a reasonably ordered story about the world? Or do we wrestle with the uncertainties of our *own* implication in ordering, with the network of theoretical, epistemological and political questions that this acceptance entails?

When I've written in the past I've put these questions on the back burner. However, in this book I choose to do otherwise. Thus, though the argument is driven in large measure by theory and data, I explore the character of sociotechnical ordering, by weaving several more or less conventional stories together. One is an organizational ethnography. Briefly, the story is that for about a year I became a fly on the wall in a middle-sized formal organization, a very large scientific laboratory. I listened to participants, I watched them and I asked them questions. I was present as the managers wrestled with an increasingly intractable set of financial and organizational problems. So I watched them trying to throw an ordering net over the activities within the organization. This, then, is the first story. It is a small part of a tale about the management and organization of a world-class scientific laboratory, one that tells us something about management, something about formal organizations and something about science and technology.

The second story is more abstract. It has to do with what we can learn from *others* about the character of sociotechnical ordering. These others fall into at least two groups: 'subjects' on the one hand, and social theorists on the other. For instance, I learned a great deal about ordering from my 'subjects', the managers. I *saw* them ordering. And I heard them *talking* about ordering and organizing. But knowledge about ordering was everywhere in the Laboratory. Thus the technicians also ordered in their own distinctive ways: ordering is certainly not the preserve of those who give the orders, though it may be sometimes the latter's wish that this were so.

The knowledge about ordering in social science is, in part, more 'formal'. This is the tip of the ordering iceberg that is everywhere about us, the part that makes it into political and social theory. As one would expect, some parts of this are more helpful than others. Indeed, for reasons that I've touched on above, I'll argue that parts of it are not only wrong but immoral too. In particular, in this story – the tale of social theory – I'll suggest that theories which claim exclusive rights to social analysis are both wrong and harmful. Nevertheless, there is much to learn from social theory, even if it sometimes seems obscure. This, then, is the point of the second story – a story about social theory.

The third story has to do with politics. There is a (possibly apocryphal but) well-worn Chinese curse which says 'May you live in interesting times'. Regrettably, times are interesting. They are, it is true, much more interesting for those in the East or the South than they are for those of us who live in the developed West. None the less, they are interesting enough even here in middle-class England. For politics is not simply or primarily something that takes place in Whitehall, on Capitol Hill or in the European Commission in Brussels. As we have lived through a period of liberal economics triumphant, politics and political changes have reached deep into our lives. For instance, they have reached deep into the life of the Laboratory. They have shaped the lives of the managers and everyone else who works there. And they have affected my life, and no doubt your life too. So there is a political story to tell, to do with ideals, values and their limits – a story that forms an essential part of any account of social ordering.

Finally, there is also a personal story. Like C. Wright Mills (1959) I don't believe that 'the social order' or 'social organization' is something outside there, beyond our personal experience. If we feel this then something has gone wrong and we have been robbed of something that properly belongs to us. So a part of the personal story has to do with the way in which we are *all* social philosophers. The managers in the Laboratory are social philosophers. The technicians and the shop-floor workers are social philosophers. I'm a social philosopher, and so too are you, your children and your neighbours. So, like Sherry Turkle[1] who wrote about the debates that take place between six-year-old children about whether computers are alive or not, I believe that social and political theory is much too important to be left to Very Important Philosophers.

This, then, is one aspect of the personal story that I want to tell. But there is another part that has to do with the *process* of ethnography and writing, a process that is, as I have suggested above, just another form of ordering. Let me put it this way: as I describe the Laboratory *I do not always want to make myself invisible.* Thus I could offer an impersonal description of events in the Laboratory. I could talk of ethnographic research methods as if they were clear-cut, fixed and impersonal. I could pretend that there was no inter-action between what I observed and myself as observer. But, as I've indicated, I believe that this would be wrong because ethnography is also a story of research – and in some measure a tale about the conduct of the ethnographer as well. And, though perhaps in a smaller way, it is in addition about the way in which the ethnographer acts upon her subject-matter.

Sharon Traweek, an anthropologist who studies laboratories writes: 'I want to begin by telling a few tales.'[2] My object is to emulate Sharon. I want to tell tales about the Laboratory. I want to tell tales about processes of ordering and organizing. I want to tell tales about the very important but very local social philosophies which we all embody and perform. I want to tell tales about politics, morality and inequality. And I want to tell personal tales about research. For research, too, is a process of ordering. And, like many processes of ordering, research is hard.

2 THE PURITY OF ORDER?

Many of us have learned to want to cleave to an order. This is a modernist dream. In one way or another, we are attached to the idea that if our lives, our organizations, our social theories or our societies, were 'properly ordered' then all would be well. And we take it that such ordering is possible, at least some of the time. So when we encounter complexity we tend to treat it as distraction. We treat it as a sign of the limits to order. Or we think of it as evidence of failure.

Sherry Turkle has some very interesting things to say about purity, power and distraction. Watching and talking with people – mostly men – playing computer arcade games she found that the latter often represented an obsessive fascination. For some they were highly addictive, though they were certainly not mindless. For instance, she describes the way in which David, a lawyer in his mid-thirties, plays for an hour or two in an arcade after work before going home to his wife. David says:

> You're totally absorbed and it is all happening there. You know what you are supposed to do. There's no external confusion, there's no conflicting goals, there's none of the complexities that the rest of the world is filled with. It's so simple. You either get through this little maze so that the creature doesn't swallow you up or you don't. And if you can focus your attention on that, and if you can really learn what you are supposed to do, then you really are in relationship with the game. (Turkle 1984: 86)

Sherry Turkle is talking about computer arcade games. In effect, she is saying that if we build a thoroughly artificial world then it is possible, at least for a time, to cleave to a single order. It is possible to pretend that there are no distractions. But this *is* possible only for a time. At the end of his game David goes home. He talks to his wife. He starts, once more, to deal with complexity. One lesson, then, is that computer games are exceedingly odd. And, of course, they are artificial. They do not last for long, and they are only possible if an elaborate infrastructure is put in place, an infrastructure which has the effect of concealing complexity.

This lesson is to do with computer games, but I also think that it can be generalized. For one of the most important arguments of this book is that the social, all the social world, is complex and messy. Indeed, this book is all about complexity, mess, or as I would prefer to say, heterogeneity. Pools of order are illusory, but even such illusions are the exception. They do not last for long. They are pretty limited. And they are the product, the outcome, or the effect, of a lot of work – work that may occasionally be more or less successfully hidden behind an appearance of ordered simplicity. So the book is about ordering rather than order. And it's about heterogeneity rather than purity.

A Black Tale of Year Zero

We are drearily familiar with the language of witchcraft-accusation. How many sins have been committed in the name of political purity? How many Year Zeros have we suffered since Marx wrote about the squalor and injustices of capitalism? Did you make the mistake of being an Armenian in the wrong place at the wrong time? Or a Jew? Or a kulak? Or a gypsy? Or a communist? Or a woman? Or a homosexual? Or a Christian? Or a Palestinian? Or a professional? Or a trades unionist? Or a monarchist? Or a student? Or a Hindu? Or a Moslem? Or a Sikh? Or a Serb? Or a liberal? Or a democrat? Or an intellectual? Or a Jesuit? Or an Ethiopian? Or an anarchist? Or a Palestinian? Or a Kurd? Or an epileptic? Or a black? Or a pantheist? Or a native American? Or an Aboriginal? Or a German? Or less than able-bodied?

How many generals have seized power in order to 'clean things up'? How many have come to power hoping or expecting to eradicate corruption and moral laxity? How many juntas have sought to impose 'law and order'? How often have we heard that Communism, or Socialism, or free-market economics, or cost-benefit analysis, or monetarism, would bring the good life (for those who remained) if only they were *systematically* imposed and all the deviant elements were rooted out? This has been the dreary refrain of the world religions and world politics for as long as anyone can remember: the belief in a system that would sort the world out; and the associated language of witchcraft-accusation.

I suppose that there is purity and purity. I guess that most of us like to think that our drinking water is clean. Perhaps there are even forms of political purity that are not morally repugnant. But whenever I think of political purity my mind goes back to a day, in 1975, when I visited Auschwitz. We know, now, about the Holocaust. We have read Primo Levi. We have read the apologies of Albert Speer. We have followed the trials of Adolf Eichmann and Klaus Barbie. And in any case I feel deeply ambivalent about going back to that wet and windy day when I first, and dimly, learned in my soul rather than my mind what political purity might mean. Too many tears have been shed. There have been too many tourists. And there has been too much shocked voyeurism. But let me go back there for just long enough to write the little bit of the story that I want to tell.

For what was almost more monstrous than the crimes committed on that soil was the records that were kept. Thus it turned out that it was not enough that purity should be done. As important was the fact that purity should be *seen* to be done. Documents named names, origins, crimes, movements and fates. Passport photos stared back at us from a different world.

The ordering had all been recorded, step by step, by the bureaucratic iron cage so feared by Max Weber.

I share Zygmunt Bauman's view. It seems to me that we have spawned a monster: the hope or the expectation that everything might be pure; the expectation that if everything were pure then it would be better than it actually is; and we have concealed the reality

Caron v
v

that what is better for some is almost certainly worse for others; that what is better, simpler, purer, for a few rests precariously and uncertainly upon the work and, very often, the pain and misery of others.

To be sure, the vain and brutal search for pure order has been around for a long as human history. But this search has become sharpened, more systematic, and more methodical, as time has passed. There are many ways of telling this story. Karl Marx talked of the rise of capitalist social relations, the discipline of the wage relationship, and the systematic pursuit of surplus value – a denunciation which was to spawn an ordering terror at least as great as that which it was intended to replace. Max Weber told of the rationalization of economic and other forms of life and the growth of the bureaucratic iron cage. More recently, Fernand Braudel traced the development of markets and the rise of speculative capital, a capital which circulates down the networks of trade looking ruthlessly for profitable opportunities. Norbert Elias talked of the 'civilising process' – a secular change involving the simultaneous extension of chains of economic and political interdependence, of predictability, and the development of strategies of personal and control. Michel Foucault described the rise of disciplinary techniques – strategies for ordering human bodies, human souls, and the social and spatial relations in which we are all inserted. Bruno Latour spoke of the development of intermediaries, part social, part technical, and the simultaneous denial of such 'hybrids' in favour of a purist distinction between nature and culture. And Zygmunt Bauman has identified the search for root order with the basic project of modernity itself.[3]

The stories differ, but they have this in common: that somewhere and somehow, between the years 1400 and 1800 a *series* of changes took place in Europe. When taken together, these added up to a thoroughgoing reorganization of the *methods of ordering*. These techniques, and the project that they carry, lie at the heart of the kind of world we know today. They help to generate our commitment to the pools of order to which we would like to cleave. When these are joined to the authority of two much more ancient traditions – a monotheistic commitment to a single source of knowledge, and the hegemonic commitment to spread the good news – we mix the cocktail that has generated the black tales of year zero with which we are so familiar in the twentieth century, tales which seek to hide the heterogeneous but systematic infrastructural work of ordering and dismiss other orderings as noise, as distraction, as technical failure or as deviance.

So what is to be done? The question is ethical, political and spiritual. But it is also sociological. For we, the sociologists, are in an

ambivalent position. Like many other intellectuals, we have our
dreams of purity too. We like to think that our theories are better
than those of our rivals, that we can see further, that we can discern
underlying patterns, the deep structures in the social that drive
appearances. What should we be doing about ourselves?

Theoretical Hegemony

Marx died in 1883, Durkheim in 1917 and Weber in 1920. Between
them (and in the debates that followed), they defined a series of crucial issues, questions, markers, divides, differences and intellectual
resources. But what also impresses me is their *confidence*. A symptomatic
reading of Marx and Durkheim suggests that they really thought that
history was, as it were, going their way (the gloomy Weber is different).
But they were also secure in the knowledge that social analysis was
going their way too. In particular, they reveal a characteristically
Enlightenment commitment to the triumph of reason. And a similar
Victorian faith in the progress of science. Science was the method,
the means, to both social and economic progress, and more specifically,
to social analysis. Science was the key to hidden truths. For Marx,
bourgeois ideology masked social reality, and the science of dialectical
materialism was available to push that mask aside. Durkheim's commitment to science was more empiricist. He tells us that we should build
up from carefully observed social facts to social explanations — and,
as is well known, ignored this advice in his own writing. Only Weber
was less confident, distinguishing between natural science (about which
he was similarly uncritical) and adequate sociological knowledge which
differed from natural science both because it was hermeneutic and
because it was better seen as a tool, an instrument or a simplificatory
representation rather than as an incremental body of knowledge that
increasingly corresponded with reality.

Many of us follow Marx and Durkheim at one remove. We tend to
social monotheism in one form or another, and combine this with more
or less well-developed hegemonic pretensions and a series of techniques
and processes that claim to generate pools of intellectual order. We
cleave to the modern project.

It would be foolish for us to imagine that we're anything other
than creatures of our discipline, and creatures of our time. We're
a *part* of the modern project. On the other hand, perhaps the fact
that we can actually *say* this is some kind of step forward: a reflection of the self-referentiality of high modernity. At any rate,
perhaps it is a step forward so long as we are sufficiently modest
about it: so long, that is, as we are seriously committed to trying
to avoid the creation of yet another form of hegemonic monotheism.
So it seems to me that we're balancing on a knife-edge. We *want*
to order. In particular, we hope to tell stories about social ordering.
But we don't want to do violence in our own ordering. And in
particular, we don't want to pretend that our ordering is complete,

or conceal the work, the pain and the blindnesses that went into it. It is an uncomfortable knife-edge. It violates most of the inclinations and dispositions that we have acquired in generations of commitment to 'the scientific method' and its social, political and personal analogues. Nevertheless, this is the path that I want to recommend, a path of sociological modesty.

3 SOCIOLOGICAL RESOURCES

Sociology tells stories about the social world. Some of these, perhaps most, are stories of order. They claim to tell what 'the social order' or some close analogue thereof really is. And they explain away their limits by telling of deviance, or inadequate socialization, or false consciousness. This is the sociological equivalent of the hideous purity of Year Zero: a hegemonic order, and distractions from that order. It is a sociological form of classical modernity.

But sociology has sometimes managed to do better. And when it has done better, this has often been because it has concerned itself with the description of social processes. Such descriptions simplify, for to tell a story about anything is already to simplify it. But they are less prone to heroic reductionisms than some, for they also tell, or at any rate they assume, that they are incomplete. And they tell that they are incomplete not because they haven't quite finished the business of sorting out the order of things, but rather because they know that it is *necessarily* that way: they will *always* be incomplete.[4] Such sociologies are relatively modest, relatively aware of the context of their own production, and the claims that they make tend to be relatively limited in scope. In addition, they are non-reductionist, concerned with social interaction, empirically grounded, and tend to be symmetrical in their mode of sociological investigation. Finally, they make a serious attempt to avoid starting off with strong assumptions about whatever it is they are trying to analyse.

Note that the different modest sociologies don't add up to a whole: to expect that this would happen would be to misunderstand both their character, and the uncertain nature of social ordering.

Let me talk about some of these assumptions.

Symmetry

To insist on symmetry is to assert that *everything* deserves explanation and, more particularly, that everything that you seek to explain or describe should be approached in the same way. Why is this important? The answer is simple: it is that you don't want to start any investigation by privileging anything or anyone. And, in particular, you don't want to start by assuming that there are certain classes of phenomena that don't need to be explained at all.

In its recent sociological form, the notion of symmetry started out in the sociology of science.[5] David Bloor was unhappy with the idea (common amongst those studying science) that only *false* scientific knowledge needs sociological explanation. For instance, Robert K. Merton (1957) held that true scientific knowledge did not need sociological explanation precisely because it *was* true – the product of proper scientific procedures. On the other hand, it was said that false scientific knowledge did need explanation because, if it was false, then this was because of distorting social factors. David Bloor argued against this and said, by contrast, that *both* true *and* false knowledge deserve sociological analysis. And – this is equally important – they deserve analysis *in the same terms*.

Why is this? The answer is that *both* are social products, at least in part. And both are generated by the same kinds of factors. But there's a more subtle argument too. It is that *judgements* about truth and falsity are also socially shaped, and indeed that they change both over time and between groups. So this is an argument similar to that of the labelling theorists: like deviance, truth does not inhere in knowledge; rather, it is attributed. But – here is the major problem if you don't adopt a symmetrical approach – if you start off *assuming* that some knowledge is true and some false, then you never get to analyse how the distinction is constructed and used.

There are parts of David Bloor's important work that are less consistent with sociological modesty. But the principle of symmetry is surely important to such a project. This is partly because it chips away at the monotheistic and hegemonic claims made for natural science. Even more important, however, is the way in which it may be applied to other divisions and dualisms: distinctions that are said to reside in the nature of things. For instance, Michel Callon (1986: 200) asks why we explore the creation of social, natural and technical phenomena using different kinds of vocabularies and explanatory principles. Why do we distinguish, a priori, between human actors on the one hand, and technical or natural objects on the other?

Perhaps this sounds ridiculous. Perhaps these distinctions are self-evident. But the very fact that it sounds ridiculous should give us pause for thought. *Why* are we so convinced that these distinctions are given in the nature of things? What happens if we treat them, instead, as an effect, a product of ordering? If we do this then we can start to explore *how* it is that machines come to be machines;[6] and what it means to label something as a machine rather than as a person. And it turns out that, when you start to ask questions like this, the distinction between the two is variable. Indeed, quite often it is simply unclear (Haraway 1990; Law 1991a).

Note that to ask about the distinction between people and machines is, in part, an inquiry into the character of agency: what it is, or what it takes, to be a human being. This is a core issue for much contemporary social theory, an issue that is also likely to be central to a modest sociology. For again, the issue is one of symmetry. The argument, as for instance in the writing of Michel Foucault,[7] is that agency is a product or an effect. Thus, since agents are not given by nature, we should be investigating how they got to be the way they are. And, it is worth noting, we might also investigate how it is that genius – intellectual, artistic, military – gets to be so labelled: where or how the notion of the special character of genius is generated.

There is another application of the principle of symmetry. This has to do with the character of the distinction between the macro-social and the micro-social. That some phenomena, actors, institutions or organizations, end up being larger than others is something that we might take on trust, even in a modest and critical sociology. The question, rather, is what we should *make* of this distinction. The principle of symmetry suggests that we might treat size as a product or an effect, rather than something given in the nature of things (see Callon and Latour 1981). I believe that this is a crucial move. For the alternative is to distinguish, on grounds of *principle*, between the large and the small and to assume that these are different in kind. It is to prevent us from asking how it is that the macro-social *got* to be macro-social. And it is to demote the micro-social: to allow that while it might be interesting, it is ultimately of subsidiary importance.

Note that this is often what has happened in sociology. Macro-sociologists such as normative functionalists or economistic Marxists have sought to seize the intellectual high ground by assuming that it is appropriate to distinguish in principle between what is big and what is small. And those sociologies that sought to make sense of social interaction – I am thinking particularly of symbolic interactionism – have been accorded under-labourer status (see Law 1984). Indeed it is only in the last ten or fifteen years that the analytical status of the macro/micro distinction has been eroded. Finally, we are starting to see a series of symmetrical sociologies by writers such as Elias, Giddens and Bourdieu, which treat size as a product or an effect, a process worth studying in its own right rather than something which is given in the order of things.

To summarize, the principle of symmetry suggests that there is no privilege – that everything can be analysed, and that it can (or should) be analysed in the same terms. So it erodes distinctions that are said to be given in the nature of things, and instead asks how it is that they got to be that way. Indeed, looked at in one way, the principle of symmetry is simply a methodological restatement of the relationship between order and ordering. It says, in effect, that we shouldn't take orders at face value. Rather we should treat them as the outcome of ordering.

Non-reduction

Non-reduction is the second candidate component in a modest sociology. Reductionism is common in sociology, and, to be sure, in natural science and in common sense. Lying at the core of the modern project, it is the notion that there is a small class of phenomena, objects or events that drives everything else – a suggestion often linked to a belief by the analyst that he or she has understood these root phenomena. Unsurprisingly, reductionism has many enthusiasts. The usual argument in its favour is that of explanatory parsimony – the capacity to explain a great deal on the basis of a few principles. And, indeed, reductionist modes of reasoning are often practically effective. They tell economical stories that serve. They are the dominant mode of Western rationalist story-telling. And they convert the stories that they tell into principles (see Rorty 1989).

But note what is entailed in reductionism. First, you need to draw a line between two classes of phenomena by distinguishing those that drive from those that are driven. And second you claim that the behaviour of the latter is explained – often you say caused – by the actions of the former. So the danger is this: that you violate the principle of symmetry by driving a wedge between those that are doing the driving and the rest. And (this is the real problem) the former get described differently, or not at all. So reductionism often, perhaps usually, makes distinctions that may come to look strangely like dualisms.

In sociology reductionism is standard practice. After all, the discipline is a child of its western, control-oriented times. But what happens when the purity of explanatory reductionism discovers its limits? We could illustrate this in endless different ways. Consider, for instance, what happened in Marxist social theory. In its classic form, at least when talking of the superstructure, the latter is reductionist. It says that most of society – politics, the law, ideology – is epiphenomenal. That is, it is driven by the social relations of production. Perhaps we should be sympathetic to this claim since in principle it is clear, simple, and indeed testable (see Popper 1962). But therein lies the problem, for it turns out (this is hardly news, of course) that the theory isn't tenable in its economistic versions. So what is to be done? In the 1960s authors such as Louis Althusser (1971a) who were trying to explore the relations between infrastructure and superstructure more carefully, found that they needed to tone down the message. The relations of production, Althusser claimed, determined the character of ideology, but only 'in the last instance'.

I think that there's an interesting tension in Althusser's stance. On the one hand, he was trying to save something from the reductionist wreckage of classical Marxism. (He was also, of course, trying to save a space for political intervention too.) Thus classical Marxism took a fairly straightfoward explanatory form, explaining *why* it is that superstructures take the form that they do. This is a form of reductionism. But Althusser's rescue attempt – an attempt to come to terms with the complexities demanded by a consciousness of ordering – made use of the relational but synchronic explanatory apparatus developed in structuralism. For structuralism is all about *relations*. It is a way of describing *how* it is that effects – originally signs – are generated as a function of their location in a set of relations. So in structuralism there are 'hows', but there are none of the 'whys' preferred by reductionist Marxism. Structuralism describes: it does not explain: it isn't much good at telling stories with beginnings, middles and ends.[8] It lives in the present. Or better, it is out of time altogether. And this is why terms such as 'in the last instance' which attempt to tell 'why' stories in a 'how' vocabulary, don't really add up to much. It is not possible to describe synchronic effects in a language of process. The only way to do this is to step outside the structuralist network altogether.[9]

This, then, is the difficulty. But it also suggests a project for a modest sociology. This will be relational, with no privileged places, no dualisms and no a priori reductions. It will not distinguish, before it starts, between those that drive and those that are driven. But, and this is where it is relational, but not structuralist, it will allow that effects, a relative distinction between the drivers and the driven, may *emerge* and be sustained. Note that this is a conditional and uncertain process, not something that necessarily happens, not something that is achieved for ever. So this is another knife-edge: a modest sociology is one which tries to occupy the precarious place where time has not been turned into cause or reduction, and where relations have not been frozen into the snapshot of synchronicity.

And what do we find in that precarious place? Or better, how do we make and remake that precarious place? One answer is that we tell stories, offer metaphorical redescriptions, ethnographies, fairy tales, histories – so called 'thick descriptions'. And we do not take them too seriously, we do not puff them up with hegemonic pretensions. Another answer is that we may tell stories which suggest that some effects are generated in a more rather than a less stable manner, stories which explore how it is that divisions that look like dualisms come to look that way. These, then, would be stories that tell of the effects that strain towards the differences in quality which we all recognize. For I take it that the job of a modest sociology is also to talk about patterns in the generative relationships, regularities which might be imputed, places where the patterns seem to reproduce themselves. But I take it, also, that we should not get dogmatic about what we turn up, about the stories that we tell.

Perhaps this is a counsel of perfection. Perhaps it is impossible. So let me say, instead, that we should try not to treat the regularities that we discern as if they were different in kind from the contingencies. For they, too, are effects, like everything else, and they, too, may be undone. And so, too, may our own accounts (see Latour 1988b).

Recursive Process

The third part of a modest sociology is closely connected with the first two. It is that the social is better seen as a recursive process, rather than a thing.

Take, first, the issue of process. Perhaps it is obvious that the social is a process? Perhaps it is something that we knew already? It *sounds* obvious, but I'm not certain about this, for large parts of sociology have found it difficult to handle processes. Perhaps this is a symptom of the desire to cleave to the purity of order and avoid the uncertainties of ordering. For one way of putting the point is to note that sociologists, like many others, tend to prefer to deal in nouns rather than verbs. They slip into assuming that social structure is an object, like the scaffolding round a building, that will stay in place once it has been erected.

I say 'sociologists' but I need to qualify this. For there has always been tension in sociology between those who want to explore how things got to be the way that they are, and those who prefer to talk about structures: those, in other words, who would like to cleave to an order and assume that the maintenance of that order is a second-rank, qualitatively different, technical problem. Karl Marx was on the order*ing* side of this divide, committed to a sociology of verbs, for he saw capital as a process, a movement, a set of time drawn-out relations, rather than something that could be locked up in a bank vault. But the insight that society is a process is even more deeply embedded in the interpretive sociologies. For instance, symbolic interactionism treats both the pattern of social relations and the self as an interactive product or outcome – an outcome which reproduces itself (or not) in further performance and interaction (see Blumer 1969a). Nothing is necessarily stable, and consistency is a product.[10]

So a modest sociology will seek to turn itself into a sociology of verbs rather than becoming a sociology of nouns. It will slip up from time to time, for it is difficult to tug away from the dualism of nouns. However, it will seek to avoid taking order for granted. Thus if there appear to be pools of order it will treat these as ordering accomplishments and illusions. It will try to think of them as effects that have for a moment concealed the processes through which they were generated. And – the commitment to symmetry suggests this – it will try not to take their pretensions at face value. Organisations, captains of industry – it will try to see these as more or less precarious recursive outcomes. So it will burrow into them, taking them apart, seeing how they were achieved, and exploring the hurts that were done along the way.

That is the simpler part of the message about process. The more complex part has to do with *recursion*. Here the issue is: what is it that *drives* social processes? I've already talked about symmetry and non-reduction. So I've already tried to argue that there is nothing outside – no 'last instance' – that drives the processes of the social. So we're left with this awkward conclusion: somehow or other, they are driving themselves. They are *self-generating* processes. This is the message of recursion: that, to adapt Anthony Giddens' phrase, the social is both a medium and an outcome.

Look at it this way: the social is a set of processes, of transformations. These are moving, acting, interacting. They are generating themselves. Perhaps we can impute patterns in these movements. But here's the trick, the crucial and most difficult move that we need to make. We need to say that *the patterns, the channels down which they flow, are not different in kind from whatever it is that is channelled by them*. So the image that we have to discard is that of a social oil refinery. Society is *not* a lot of social products moving round in structural pipes and containers that were put in place beforehand. Instead, the social world is this remarkable emergent phenomenon: in its processes it shapes its own flows. Movement and the organization of movement are not different.

This is terribly difficult. At least, I find it so. It is difficult because it is like a *Gestalt* shift. Suddenly you see it — you see the faces instead of the vase. And then you lose it again — you are back to the vase. And it seems to me that the reason it is so difficult is because it is so radical: for when you start to work it through, explore it for yourself, all the apparatus of structural sociology, the habits of thought built up in the course of generations of commitment to the project of modernity, all the nouns and the nice secure dualisms, all these start to dissolve. It's no longer a question of saying that you don't believe in (say) a Marxist, or a functionalist, model of society. Rather, it is a question of saying that you're going to try to do without any nouns, without qualitatively different descriptions of the social. It was (I think) Mary Douglas who once likened the discovery by anthropologists of societies without explicit political systems to the invention of the chassisless motor car. But the metaphor works for a recursive sociology too. At best, when we reach this place where there is nothing beyond what goes on, we feel uncomfortable and insecure. And at worst, we feel we are giving up most of the explanatory resources of sociology. But this fear is right: this is *exactly* what we are doing. It is what we need to do if we are to avoid reproducing the games of classical modernism, and put the experience of hideous purity behind us.

So recursion is the place where a sociology of process usually comes unstuck. It tends to want to say, sure, there are processes. But then it slips away from symmetry to make non-recursive suggestions about how those flows are shaped. It assumes that flows that are already in place are different in kind. So we have to work hard on recursion: though it is central to the project of a modest sociology it is a difficult lesson to take on board.

Reflexivity

Act unto others as you would have them act unto you. Or better, act unto yourself as you would unto others. This is a version of the principle of reflexivity — a fourth part of a modest sociology. Used in this way, the term comes from the writing of David Bloor. Though the term has many related connotations,[11] reflexivity may be seen as an extension of the principle of symmetry: in effect it says, there is no reason to suppose that we are different from those whom we study. We too are products. If we make pools of sense or order, then these too are local and recursive effects, and have nothing to do with immaculate conception, or any other form of privilege.

So this is where modesty really comes home to roost. For the principle reminds us that ordering, our own ordering, is a verb. It reminds us that it is precarious too. It reminds us that it is incomplete, that much escapes us. And it suggests that if we are engaged in the study of ordering, then we should, if we are to be consistent, be asking how it is that we came to (try to) order in the way that we did. In short, together with whatever it is that we write, we are effects as well.

This, then, is what Anthony Giddens means when he suggests that reflexivity is the latest – the final? – triumph of the modern project (see Giddens 1990, 1991). Perhaps he's right. But, as is obvious, it's a pretty corrosive triumph. For modernism seeks to monitor, legislate and control. As it drives towards hideous purity it says how order could and should be. But at the same time it lacks any vehicle for enforcing its ordering pretensions.[12] So what should we do about this? Should we cleave, notwithstanding, to the legislative project of modernity? Or should we, rather, turn ourselves into interpreters? For to lay down principles about reflexivity is surely self-defeating: it is to try to legislate about what might emerge.[13] But not to lay down principles, not to say how things are, is to abandon the traditional warrant for doing sociology – that of telling stories about the world. A nice dilemma.

Provisionally, very provisionally, I tend towards the camp of the modest legislators rather than the interpreters. Thus all that I can do now is to say, as I said at the outset, that I'm clear that ethnography is a product, an interactive outcome, and nothing to do with observation by neutral or disembodied intellects.[14] But you shouldn't, if you're sceptical, seize on this as an admission of inadequacy, of the particular failings of ethnography. This is because the same is the case for any other project, empirical or theoretical. So the way I treat the problem (I don't *solve* it, it cannot be *solved*) in this version of a modest sociology is to expose some of the contingencies and uncertainties – ethnographic, theoretical, personal and political – with which I have wrestled along the way. So, unlike the reflexive sociologists, I'm not attempting a systematic deconstruction of my writing. Instead, I'm saying, defeasibly to be sure, that given my concerns I think that the Laboratory *was* this rather than some other way. So I think that I'm telling stories not *only* of myself, but also of something beyond myself. Accordingly, I'm partially (only partially) persuaded by Richard Rorty's argument that poetry is a private, not a public matter. Thus when I make several voices speak, as I sometimes do, I do this because I want to expose and explore some of the places where I feel vulnerable or uncertain, the places that I experience as sociologically or politically (as well as personally) risky. For a modest sociology, whatever else it may be, is surely one that accepts uncertainty, one that tries to open itself to the mystery of other orderings.

4 THE STRUCTURE OF THE BOOK: NETWORK, MODE OF ORDERING AND MATERIAL

To return to the beginning, this book is an attempt to make sense of what is usually called 'the problem of the social order'. My hope is that it is consistent with the sketch that I've outlined above: that it is symmetrical, non-reductionist, recursive, process oriented and reflexive.

I start by considering the ordering character of ethnography. I try to show that sometimes this process is disorienting, sometimes it is exciting, and sometimes it is nerve-racking and painful. Indeed, sometimes the process of trying to order is so unsuccessful that it is simply miserable. So there are moments when the reflexive project of sensemaking seems to fail, and the experience is one of fragmentation. The point of chapter 2, therefore, is to explore and reflect on this precarious process of ethnography. It is also, however, to introduce the first of three metaphors that I use to shape the argument of the book − that of *network*.

In the way I'm using it, the notion of network doesn't have much to do with the standard sociological usages − for instance as found in the tradition of kinship studies. Instead, it draws on three different traditions. The first is the network philosophy of science developed by Mary Hesse (see Hesse 1974; and Law and Lodge 1984), and the second that of structuralism and post-structuralism. Though there are important dissimilarities between these, most notably to do with questions of process and reference, both are concerned with the way in which meanings (and other effects including agency) are generated within and by a network of relations. The third tradition is the theory of the actor-network.[15] The provenance of actor-network theory lies in part in post-structuralism: the vision is of many semiotic systems, many orderings, jostling together to generate the social. On the other hand, actor-network theory is more concerned with changing recursive *processes* than is usual in writing influenced by structuralism. It tends to tell *stories*, stories that have to do with the processes of ordering that generate effects such as technologies, stories about how actor-networks elaborate themselves, and stories which erode the analytical status of the distinction between the macro and micro-social.[16]

Accordingly, chapter 2 is a network exploration of the process of fieldwork. I consider some of the ways in which both what I learned in the course of fieldwork, and what I have written about it, may be seen as an effect, an outcome, or a product of interaction – an interaction that shaped and formed not only the account itself, but also its author and (who knows?) possibly even the Laboratory too. My object is to show that ethnographers – and social theorists too – are not distant all-seeing gods. They do not stand outside their subject-matter, but are better seen as a part of it. This is my attempt to put one of the lessons of reflexivity into practice: to reflect on the shape, the successes and the failures in the process of studying and writing.

I move on to explore aspects of social and organizational ordering. I start in chapter 3 by telling stories about the history of the Laboratory. The stories that I tell are not 'objective'. Indeed, the very notion of objectivity is problematic[17] for history is the product of interaction between story-teller and subject-matter, an interaction in which we wrestle with the double hermeneutic.[18] Perhaps this sounds cute, but I don't intend it to be so. Thus people in the Laboratory formulate and they tell stories of themselves and one another – layer upon layer of stories. Then *I* formulate and *I* tell stories of them: my stories, too, are just a further moment in the process of productive but parasitic story-telling.

So what is the justification of my story-telling? The answer has to do with patterns, for one of the points of the story that *I* tell is that *how* Laboratory members tell stories, *how* they formulate their past, is an important clue to a much more general issue: how it is that they would like to order the organization in a much wider range of circumstances; and how it is the organization is being performed and embodied in a wide range of circumstances. For this is the point: *stories are often more than stories*; they are clues to patterns that may be imputed to the recursive sociotechnical networks.

It was at the point in the ethnography when I attended seriously to the histories that I started to tease out what was to become the second major leitmotiv of the study: the idea that though matters are contingent, there are patterns in that contingency. Look upon it this way: the search for pattern is an attempt to tell stories about ordering that connect together local outcomes. And in practice, for me, it's an attempt to find some kind of common space or area of overlap, between: first, symbolic interactionism (whose patterns tend to be rather local); second, post-structuralist discourse analysis, whose patterns in some cases seem to be strangely hegemonic; and a third theoretical tradition, that of the actor-network analysis that

I mentioned above. I explore the character of this three-cornered space in chapters 4 and 5.

Start with post-structuralism. I thought that it didn't make much sense to suppose that there was a *single* putative mode of ordering within and recursively performed by the organization. Rather, and this is the empirical conclusion that I spell out at the beginning of chapter 4, I concluded, leaving aside others in the organization, that there were at least four such modes of ordering amongst the managers alone. I came, that is, to believe that if the organization might be treated as a recursive, self-performing, network, then it and its components might be understood as an effect generated in the telling, partial performance, and concrete embodiment of at least four modes of ordering. And, they might, in particular, be treated as effects generated by the *interaction* between these (and other) modes of ordering.

What then *are* these ordering modes? What claims am I making about them? What is their status? Here I am cautious. In some ways they are like Lyotard's 'little narratives'.[19] But I prefer to speak of modes of ordering because I wish to avoid the impression that they are simply ways of telling about the world. Sometimes they come in the form of simple stories or accounts. They tell of what used to be, or what ought to happen. Here they are ordering concerns, procedures, methods or logics, *dreams* of order perhaps, but nothing more. Certainly, they are not pools of total order.

On the other hand, they are also much more than narratives, if by these we mean stories that order nothing beyond their telling. This is because they are also, in some measure, performed or embodied in a concrete, non-verbal, manner in the network of relations. So in the way I think of them, these modes of ordering *tell* of the character of agency, the nature of organizational relations, how it is that interorganizational relations should properly be ordered, and how machines should be. Indeed, it is perhaps in the telling that they first become visible to the sociologist: such, at any rate, was my experience. But they are also, to a greater or lesser extent, *acted out and embodied* in all these materials too. I'm saying, then, that they are imputable ordering arrangements, expressions, suggestions, possibilities or resources.

Perhaps we could say of these modes of ordering that they are strategies, self-reflexive strategies for patterning the networks of the social: that they are, in other words, expressions of the project of high modernism. Indeed, I'm largely persuaded that this is the case. But if we say this, we have to be careful. This is because I'm not simply concerned with explicit strategies formulated or enacted by participants. There are, of course, many such explicit strategies, and they may indeed embody, perform and reproduce modes of ordering. But the latter are much broader. Or better, they are also less explicit. Thus, to repeat a phrase that I have already used, they are better seen as recursive logics, so long as we don't intend anything too rigid by using this term. In short, as I have hinted, in many ways they are like Michel Foucault's discourses: they are *forms of strategic arranging that are intentional but do not necessarily have a subject* (see Foucault 1981: 95). And they are, as I've just suggested, modes of self-reflexivity too.

To say this raises a series of questions. For instance, how wide can a 'strategy' be? Is it not stretching the notion of strategy beyond all reasonable limits to impute strategies in the absence of knowing subjects? And is the notion of strategy appropriate at all?[20] The problem is one of imputation, of interaction with data – for data is another network effect, not something given off by nature. So I'm *imputing* ordering modes to the bits and pieces that make up the networks of the social. In effect I'm saying that I *think* I see certain patterns in the ordering work of managers, and its effects. I *think* that if I conceive of these patterns in this way, then I can say that these are being partially performed by, embodied in, and helping to constitute, the networks of the social. They are, as Anthony Giddens might put it, recursively embodied in their instantiations. And I *think* that it isn't so wide of the mark to assume that these modes of ordering have strategic (though possibly non-subjective) effects. But the imputation is uncertain and defeasible. There are other ways of treating the material. And even if one sticks with recursive embodiment and performance, there are other things going on.

This brings us back to the space between symbolic interaction, post-structuralism, and actor-network theory. I said that the modes of ordering with which I am concerned are related to Michel Foucault's notion of discourse. I'm happy to acknowledge the inspiration of his writing: I have worked in and wrestled with its promise for a decade. However, there is at least one major difference between what I am attempting and the larger part of Foucault's own project. As I indicated earlier, I'm particularly keen to avoid being trapped in a synchronic version of structuralism. But much of Foucault's writing is synchronic. I accept that it is not all that way. Indeed, this is one of the main reasons why his writing is so attractive: for Foucault, discourse is ubiquitously and distributively generative – it performs itself everywhere. So his notion of discourse is recursive. On the other hand, that recursion is often synchronic: the same non-subjective strategies instantiate themselves again and again. So there's a caveat, a difficulty. It is that typically, in his writing, the discourses are already in place. They generate instances, and as they do so they reproduce themselves. But Foucault doesn't tell stories about how they might come to perform themselves differently – how they might come to *reshape* themselves in new embodiments or instantiations. And neither do we learn much about how they might interact together when they are performed or embodied.

This, then, is where I part company with Foucault. For I've been arguing that a mode of ordering is always limited. It sometimes generates precarious pools of apparent order. Certainly it doesn't hold the world in the iron grip of a totalizing hegemony. But if this is right, then there are questions that Foucault tends to refuse. Though there are exceptions in his work – as for instance in the opening chapters of *The Order of Things*[21] – most often he avoids exploring the ways in which discourses or modes of ordering *interact* as they are recursively told, performed and embodied in the networks of the social. But my argument is that questions of changes in the modes of ordering on the one hand, and their interaction on the other, are closely related. Agents, decisions, machines, organizations, interactions between organizations and their environments, speech, actions, texts – I want to say that all of these change because they are recursive *interordering or interdiscursive effects*. They all, that is, tell, embody or perform a network of multiply-ordering relations.

> This is how I try to create space: the precarious place where time has not yet been turned into cause or reduction, and yet where relations have not been frozen into the snapshot of synchronicity. It is the productive place where post-structuralism meets symbolic interaction.

What can we say about the relationship between modes of ordering, or the character of the effects that they generate and perform? In all honesty the answer is, not very much in general. And this is the revenge of symbolic interaction and pragmatism on discourse analysis! A priori accounts of how well or otherwise the modes of ordering might fit together are best avoided. To offer such accounts is to risk the slide into the rigidity of synchronicity: both the supposition that certain relations have intrinsic effects, and the hegemonic belief that we have specified the character of ordering so comprehensively that contigency has been vanquished. We can't be very sure about what will happen when ordering modes butt up together, until we see how they perform themselves in practice. So there's an interesting place here for us to tell stories about how agents or other effects dodge between and combine ordering modes, being both multiply con-stituted and multiply resourced.[22]

Next I turn to the third apex of this theoretical triangle, that of actor-network analysis, and consider the question of materials. For an organization is composed of a wide range of heterogeneous materials. Amongst these, we may count people, devices, texts, 'decisions', organizations, and interorganizational relations. These materials are all important. Thus I find that I can make little or no sense of any particular mode of ordering or its interaction with others unless I also tell stories about these materials. I take it, then, that ordering is told, performed, embodied and represented – for the verb will vary – in materials that are partly but only partly social in the narrow, usual, sociological sense of the term. Or, to put it another way, I assume that the social world is *materially heterogeneous*.

This is a restatement, or a partial operationalization, of the principle of symmetry discussed above. It also, however, amounts to a pretty far-reaching and critical comment on contemporary social theory. Let me be blunt. I believe that much of the latter is strangely reluctant to take 'non-social' materials such as machines, animals or architectures seriously. Indeed, often it seems to me that it is *only* human agents and their knowledge, certain kinds of social interactions, and texts that are taken seriously. Doubtless my feeling is exaggerated. For instance, there are traditions – I am thinking in particular of labour-process theory, and some parts of feminism – which are deeply concerned with the relationships between technologies and social relations. Typically, the argument here is that particular patterns of social relations, often exploitative in character, are embodied in technologies.[23] Then the argument is often made that the technologies in turn act back upon social relations. For instance, they operate to freeze class or gender inequalities. Again, there is a body of work on post-modernity which is concerned with material modes of communication and ordering.[24]

Obviously such writing is important. However, what it has not yet done is to consider the possibility that the *differences* between materials may themselves be a series of (more or less precarious) effects. Machines (or more generally technologies) on the one hand, social relations on the other: it is assumed that the two are different in kind, albeit that they interact with one another. Indeed, it is really only in certain parts of the sociology of technology, in the writing of certain feminists, actor-network theorists, and reflexivists, and in Michel Foucault's writing, that one finds the kind of *relational materialism* that I am pressing for here.[25]

A commitment to relational materialism: this is one of the major leitmotivs of the book. I believe that it is centrally important to social theory for two main reasons. The first has to do with social

ordering itself, and is easily stated: there *would* be no social ordering
if the materials which generate these were not heterogeneous. In
other words, the somatic – the resources of the body – though these
are already heterogeneous, are altogether inadequate to generate the
kinds of social effects that we witness round about us. For orderings
spread, or (sometimes) seek to spread, across time and space. But,
and this is the problem, left to their own devices *human actions
and words do not spread very far at all*. For me the conclusion is
inescapable. Other materials, such as texts and technologies, surely
form a crucial part of any ordering.

So ordering has to do with both humans *and* non-humans.[26] They
go together. So it doesn't make much sense to ignore materials. And
(though it is not quite such a disastrous option) it doesn't make too
much sense to treat them separately, as if they were different in kind.
For the characterization of materials, I want to say, is just another
relational effect. But it is an important relational effect, because
certain material, or combinations of material, effects are more durable,
or more easily transported, than naked human bodies or their voices
alone. This, then, is the first reason I am pressing for relational
materialism: I believe we need to include *all* materials in sociological
analysis if we want to make sense of social ordering, but, symmetrically, I also take it that materials are better treated as products or
effects rather than as having properties that are given in the order
of things.[27]

The second reason for adopting relational materialism is a specification of the first, and it has to do with agency. A concern with the
latter has been central to sociological theory for at least two decades.
Indeed, the 'decentring of the subject' is surely one of the major
triumphs of the symmetry of structuralism and post-structuralism.
For if an agent or a subject is an effect, then how that effect is
generated becomes an important topic in its own right. But in a
relationally materialist sociology, an agent is an effect generated in a
network of *heterogeneous* materials. Or, to put it yet more radically, an
agent (like a machine) *is* a network of different materials, a process
of ordering that we happen to label a 'person'. So the issue becomes
one of setting boundaries, of labelling. It becomes one of deciding
how it is that we distinguish, for instance, between people (or 'types'
of people) on the one hand, and organizations or machines such as
computers on the other (see Turkle 1984; Woolgar 1991).

Though I touch on these boundary effects, I do not explore them
very deeply in the present study. Instead, I explore three other implications of the way in which modes of ordering perform materials.
First, in chapter 6 I consider the question of hierarchy. Sometimes

it is said that 'discourse analysis' is so concerned with language and representation that it cannot make sense of hierarchy and inequality. If this complaint is about a writer such as Michel Foucault, then I think that it is wrong. This is because Foucault's discourse analysis is concerned not exclusively with language, but with a wide range of different materials. Indeed, it is *precisely* about how those materials (people, architectures, etc.) perform themselves to generate a series of effects, including those of hierarchy. Accordingly, I take it that the complaint is not *really* about the insensitivity of discourse analysis to hierarchy and distribution. Rather it is about the refusal of discourse analysts to rest their case on a metaphysical and reductionist commitment to a *particular* theory of hierarchy. This, then, is the issue that I tackle in chapter 6. My object is not to defend Michel Foucault's writing in particular. Rather it is to show that a series of different ordering modes – which might indeed in some circumstances actually be in conflict with one another – may interact to perform a series of materials and material arrangements that have hierarchical and distributional effects. These effects perform themselves through agents, through interactions between agents, and through devices, texts and architectures.

In chapter 7 I turn to the material character of representation. Thus ordering, or at any rate self-reflexive ordering, *depends* on representation. It depends, that is, on how it is that agents represent both themselves, and their context, *to* themselves. The argument, then, is that representations shape, influence and participate in ordering practices: that ordering is not possible without representation. This, then, is one expression, a reflexive expression, of the recursion that we witness everywhere in the social.

To be sure, the idea that representation participates in social ordering is an old empirical and theoretical argument. For instance, it lies at the heart of the various Marxist analyses of ideology, and it can be easily extracted from the writing of Weber. The picture offered by the latter is of bureaucracy as a social technology, one that generates representations in the context of an interest in prediction and control. In his sociology representation is, in other words, an essential adjunct to the process of rationalisation. And similar arguments are also found, though in a somewhat different idiom, in business history, in the social history of technology and in parts of sociological theory.[28] The argument, then, is that strategic management *requires* workable representations – a form of words which hints at why this mode of writing sometimes lapses into functionalism.

These traditions of work are suggestive: they tell, in effect, of the modes of representation that carry and perform the modern project,

and they chart secular changes in the latter. The pull towards cy-
bernetic functionalism sometimes means that they sound Whiggish
– the business-history equivalent of celebratory accounts of scientific
progress. And along with this Whiggishness they sometimes treat
representation as a *technical* problem. But this is too limited. For
representation is far more than a technical problem. It is far more
than a more or less adequate infrastructural support to social ordering. To treat it as such is inconsistent with both the principle of
symmetry and relational materialism. Instead, I believe that we need
to treat representations in the same way as other stories. Representations are not just a necessary part of ordering. Rather, they are
ordering processes in their own right.

The issue here is well recognized in much contemporary sociology
– and also in philosophy of science. Indeed, the analysis of modes
of representation lies at the core of much that is best about social
inquiry in the last twenty years.[29] For issues to do with the character
of representation become important once a correspondence theory
of representation is abandoned: once concern with the *workability*
or *legitimacy* of a representation replaces concern with whether it
corresponds to reality.

Seen in this way, the study of representation, and in particular
how it is that representations are generated, is an important part of
the study of ordering *tout court*. And it is an important part of the
study of the greatest division of them all – the Cartesian distinction
between mind and body. For, viewed in this way, self-representation
– the monitoring, reassessment, imputation and correction – that lies
at the heart of the mind–body dualism and its analogues becomes
another feature of ordering, another relationally materialist effect. So
the processes of ordering which generate and gather representations
(including the representations of centres) together into a single place
– which have the effect of generating a 'centre of representation'
or a 'centre of translation'[30] – are crucial to the modern project
and its strain towards dualism and the celebration of self-reflexivity.
And this is the issue that I explore in chapter 7. Specifically, I
consider the way in which heterogeneous materials combine to tell,
embody and perform a series of ordering modes and, as such, operate
to generate reflexive and ordering places, those that cloistered and
are set aside. I'm concerned, then, with the material gradients and
arrangements that strain towards the western ideal of pure consciousness, of perfect decisionmaking. Or, to put it slightly differently, I'm
concerned with the way in which material efforts generate the illusion
of mind–body dualism – a dualism in which the mind masters the
body.

In chapter 8 I explore some aspects of the political economy of enterprise. I'm particularly interested in this mode of ordering for two reasons. One, perhaps the less important, is that in the United Kingdom the myth of enterprise is now performed and embodied in places from which it was substantially absent at the start of the 1980s. In the National Health Service, in the schools, in science and in the universities – under the impact of the 'Thatcher revolution' this mode of organizing has re-ordered much about these institutions. And, speaking personally, since I embody (embodied?) a series of quite different ordering modes, for instance to do with vocation, I find much about that re-ordering both damaging and painful.

The second reason for my interest in enterprise has, once again, to do with representation. Thus, to cut a long story short, I tend to the view that the political economy of representation in enterprise has certain peculiarities: in particular, it generates a deep division – a particular expression of dualism – between backstage and front. Enterprise, I suggest, is a strategy that turns around a concern with results, with what appears on stage. In the first instance it isn't too concerned with how that performance is produced. But – there is a but – since agents are said to be opportunistic, performances may dissimulate. Which means, in turn, that it tends to become important to look backstage to see what is 'really' going on. So it is that in enterprise a deep moral (and epistemological) division grows up between backstage and front. And so it is that mistrust tends to fuel that division.

How is such mistrust overcome? How is trust restored? At the end of chapter 8 I briefly consider this question. More public performances (or their equivalent, performance indicators) cannot solve the problem. Quite to the contrary, in fact. They merely fuel it. Instead, my guess is this: enterprise tends to create contexts and a web of personal relations where artifice does not pay, and where it would, in any case, be detectable. The argument, then, is that one of the materials of sociation, face-to-face interaction (together with agency), is constituted in a particular, quite specific way, by the political economy of enterprise.

I conclude the book with a short Postscript which reflects on the reactions to the manuscript both by its 'subjects' and by professional colleagues and friends. Its purpose is analytical, and it reflects not so much on what people thought of the book (though this is considered in passing) but rather on the literary and political character of a modest sociology. In particular, it is concerned with the role of text and authorship as a part of such a project. Accordingly, in these concluding pages I touch again on questions of professional power.

And, in particular, I start to try to disentangle humanist and non-humanist versions of pessimistic liberalism. Is non-humanist liberalism a self-contradiction? Possibly this is the case. I'm not certain. Thus the end of the book poses questions rather than offering answers. Questions to do with the links between liberalism, irony and power. And about what liberalism, or its successors, might look like in a world where the human subject has been decentred but we are still being constituted in so many syntaxes of hideous purity.

NOTES

1 See her remarkable study about computers as cultural and psychological categories: Turkle (1984).
2 Sharon's major book is Traweek (1988a); but this quotation is drawn from Traweek (1988b: 250).
3 See Marx (1889); Weber (1930, 1978); Braudel (1985); Elias (1978a); Foucault (1976, 1979); Latour (1991a); and Bauman (1992).
4 I'm thinking of symbolic interactionism (Blumer 1969b; Becker 1982; Strauss 1977) and other interpretive sociologies such as cognitive sociology (Cicourel 1974) and ethnomethodology (Garfinkel 1967), the figurational sociology of Norbert Elias (1978a, 1983), the discourse analysis of Michel Foucault (1976, 1979) and some of the other post-structuralist writers, e.g. Baudrillard (1988a), parts of the sociology of knowledge and especially the sociology of scientific knowledge (Collins 1985; Lynch and Woolgar 1990), the theory of the actor-network (Callon 1991; Latour 1987, 1988a, 1992b), the field and relational sociology of Pierre Bourdieu (1986), and parts of the feminist analysis of gendering and forms of knowing (Harding 1986; Haraway 1990; Mol 1991; Star 1991). But there are many others too.
5 The term is David Bloor's (1976).
6 As do such authors as Sherry Turkle (1984), Bruno Latour (1991b, 1992a, 1992b), Madeleine Akrich (1992) and Steve Woolgar (1991).
7 See Foucault (1979), but note that a similar argument lies at the heart of symbolic interaction – see, for instance, Strauss (1977).
8 Though there are counter-arguments, the same point may also be made of Foucault's discursive analysis of history. I explore this point in some detail in chapter 5.
9 This is the move made by structuralists whenever they have felt the need to offer explanations. Often, as with Lévi-Strauss, Piaget or Chomsky, there is recourse to imagined mental capacities. It is interesting to note that ethnomethodology, which is not usually seen as being structuralist, seems to adopt the same explanatory stance in its conversational analysis.
10 See Becker (1971a). Norbert Elias' (1978a, 1983) sociology similarly erodes the distinction between structure and agency, again treating both as emergent products – generative and productive outcomes – of the performance of a set of relations. And, more recently, Anthony Giddens' (1984) structuration theory has attempted a similar trick: like figuration, structuration refers to the generative principles – rules – that people carry which lead, via resources, to action.

11 In addition to David Bloor's (1976) usage, there are several other more epistemologically radical traditions which use the term to highlight the self-organizing, recursive, character of the social project. I consider some of these below. But it is important to mention ethnomethodology which, abolishing referents, uses the term to explore the retrospective/prospective character of sensemaking (see Garfinkel 1967; Wieder 1974). And also 'reflexive sociology' which explores the grounds of its own narrative, the local methods used to develop and organize sense (Woolgar 1988).

12 This pithy observation comes from Zygmunt Bauman (1992: 21).

13 Rorty (1989) explores this most attractively in his discussion of 'final voca-bularies'.

14 The point is a standard one in recent anthropology. See Clifford (1986).

15 On actor-network theory see Callon (1991) and Law (1992a) for summaries.

16 Its concern with story-telling is in part under the influence of the history of technology (Hughes 1983), Hesse's network theory, and the Annales school of materialist history (Braudel 1975). On the macro/micro difference see Callon and Latour (1981).

17 This does not mean that what ethnographers or social theorists write is necessarily subjective either. Subjectivity and objectivity is another of the dualisms that it seems better to refuse. And there are traditions in the philosophy (and sociology) of science, and indeed in social theory, which do just this by treating knowledge as a contexted product whose status depends upon its workability (Kuhn 1970; Bloor 1976; Barnes 1977; Rorty 1991). These differ from recent post-modern writing (Baudrillard 1988a; Lyotard 1984) in their commitment to a pragmatic theory of truth.

18 Or maybe it is the post-modernist hall of mirrors, for we are here concerned with ordering accounts which go to work upon ordering accounts which work upon yet more accounts.

19 See Lyotard (1984). I'm grateful to Bob Cooper for making this point.

20 There are those who argue that the notion of strategy is a relatively modern discursive invention with (possibly inappropriate) hierarchical effects (Knights and Morgan 1990). I think that this is probably right. Indeed, the argument may be further pressed to say that strategy implies a network topography that it may not be appropriate to impute to all sociotechnical materials (Law and Mol forthcoming).

21 See Foucault (1974), and in particular his discussion of Las Meninas.

22 This space was first, I think, explored in the symbolic interactionist and liberal tradition by Hugh Dalziel Duncan (1962, 1965, 1968). For assessment and commentary see Law (1984).

23 For an introduction to this style of work, see the collections brought to-gether by MacKenzie and Wajcman (1985) and Bijker, Hughes and Pinch (1987).

24 See, for instance, the writing of Anthony Giddens (1990, 1991) David Harvey (1990), and Forty's magnificent book on design (1986).

25 See, for instance, writing by Donna Haraway (1990), Leigh Star (1990, 1991), Madeleine Akrich (1992), Michel Callon (1986a, 1987, and Callon and Latour 1981), Bruno Latour (1991b, 1992a, 1992b), John Law (1991a; Law and Bijker 1992; Law and Mol forthcoming) and Steve Woolgar (1991).

26 I draw the phrase from Latour (1992a).

27 For an empirical exploration of this point, see Law (1986a); for the point originally developed in the actor-network idiom, see Callon and Latour (1981).

28 See, respectively Chandler (1977) and Beniger (1986); Hughes (1983); and Giddens (1990).

29 For theoretical discussion of various post-structuralist positions see Poster (1990); on developments in the sociology of science and art, see Lynch and Woolgar (1990); and Fyfe and Law (1988). For a summary of the important work on the sociology of culture see Featherstone (1991). For a development of the notion of organization as a mode of representation, see the seminal work of Cooper (1987, 1992, 1993); and Malavé (1992).

30 I draw the term from Latour (1990).

2

Networks and Places

1 NETWORKS OF WRITING

Writing is work, ordering work. It is another part of the process of ordering. It grows out of a context. It is an *effect* of that context. But then it tends to go on to hide that context. When we write, we may conceal in various ways. Sometimes we make nature (or society) speak instead of us. Under these ordering conventions the author may disappear from the narrative altogether. Sometimes we allow ourselves a passive voice, and appear in the text as rapporteur, or commentator. But the more we appear in our own narratives, the more we move away from such attempts at empiricist ordering. The less nature seems to speak for itself. And the more the writer becomes visible as composer, crafts-person, or even creative genius. So it is that the work of reading (not of writing) becomes more personal: the balance between the author and whereof the writing tells is changed.[1]

But what happens if the author moves from a single voice (whether that of empiricist, crafts-person or genius) to several voices? What happens if we start to explore the processes of our own ordering? One answer is that some of the certainties of our sociology start to dissolve. We start to reflect openly on the character of our own study, and on the interactive character of our own ethnography.

In this book I sometimes choose to break the narrative up and tell different and somewhat incompatible stories. I know from experience that this can be irritating for the reader: it may look narcissistic, exclusive or indecisive. As Rorty indicates (1989: 90), it can also be humiliating. So I do it here uncertainly. But I do it not because I wish to be clever and try to anticipate objections by covering all possible bases. Neither is it because I want to deconstruct myself, though it is obvious this could be done. Rather it is because I want to try to represent something about the ordering process of research, and some of the ethnographic and authorial struggles that have led to this book. And, in particular, it is because I think that in a modest sociology readers are entitled to know what authors take to be the weak spots, the places where things don't really hang together. Perhaps this is an up-dated version of Popperianism (see Popper 1959). Perhaps it is a matter of offering conjectures and then seeking to explore their limits, rather than concealing the places where they appear to be going wrong. Or perhaps it is – this is Richard Rorty's (1989) suggestion – that the places where the cracks are most visible are the growing places in research.

At any rate this is the conclusion on multivocality, the pragmatic solution that I adopt in this book. There are many voices in the Laboratory, and there are many voices in social theory. And I, the author, do not always want to act like God and seek to reconcile them. Indeed, I *cannot* do this. And neither do I want to pretend that I am reporting about nature, or speaking from a position of great superiority. So my position is this: I spent time in the Laboratory. I have experience of the Laboratory. I have some stories to tell about the character of that experience. But the stories that I tell are not naive. And the way in which I try to tell them is guided by at least three concerns: first, an interest in the work of *ordering*; second, and to a lesser extent, a concern with the work of *distributing*; and, third, a concern with the *materials and representations* of those processes of ordering. So if you read this text you will learn something about the interaction between the Laboratory, social theory and a process of research. And you will also, to be sure, learn something about the contingencies that have generated an ethnographer and an author.

Sometimes, when post-modern writers talk in these terms, they recommend the 'playfulness' of multivocality. The term is intended to point to the possibility of creating places where there is some degree of freedom, some elbow-room, some degree of play. So it is intended as a gesture towards creativity and autonomy, a necessary move away from metaphysical foundations. That is the intention. On the other hand, it is easy to see it as a blithe attempt to talk away real pain and suffering.[2] The issue is this: what right do the powerful have to lecture the oppressed about being 'playful'? Not much, I think. So let me say that the study grows out of privilege: a senior and tenured position in a university, and the chance to do an extended ethnography – these are rare commodities afforded only to a few. I'll return to this privilege in the Postscript – for it cannot be wished away. On the other hand it would, I think, be foolish, indeed unhelpful, to feel guilty about that privilege.

At the same time, however, trying to find out about ordering without reducing the penumbra to distraction is also to find out about pain. So this is another reason why I sometimes write in a number of different voices. Despite the fact that (indeed precisely because) it takes privilege to do this I want to try to move from the security and destruction of a single order. The object, then, is to explore ways of moving towards a locally rigorous sense of the ordering of overlaps, a place where bits and pieces, whatever comes to hand, may be woven together. I want to find ways of talking about what Leigh Star calls 'boundary objects' (see Star and Griesemer 1989). I want to engage in a form of modest legislation (see Bauman 1992). And I want to find ways of empowering rather than disempowering both 'subjects' and readers.

2 NETWORKS OF AGENCY

People are networks. We are *all* artful arrangements of bits and pieces. If we count as organisms at all, this is because we are networks of skin, bones, enzymes, cells – a lot of bits and pieces that we don't have much direct control over and we don't know much about at all. (Though if they go wrong then we are in dire trouble.) And if we count as people rather than as organisms this is because of a lot of other bits and pieces – spectacles, clothes, motor cars and a history of social relations – which we *may* have some control over. But we are equally dependent on these. Indeed, to put it this way is to put it too weakly. We are composed of, or *constituted* by our props, visible and invisible, present and past. This is one of the things that we may learn from reading the symbolic interactionists and Erving Goffman (see, for instance, Goffman 1968). Each one of us is an *arrangement*. That arrangement is more or less fragile. There are ordering processes which keep (or fail to keep) that arrangement on the road. And some of those processes, though precious few, are partially under our control some of the time.

This is a theory of agency, one about which I shall talk more in subsequent chapters. It says that a person is an effect, a fragile process of networking associated elements. It is an unusual theory of agency only to the extent that I want to fold the props – and the interactions with the props – into the person. And I want to do this because without our props we would not be people-agents, but only bodies. So this is a theory of agency, but it is more than a theory of agency. Or, to put it another way, it is a theory that is not simply about people. And here's where I part company from some kinds of social theory. Unlike many, I don't think that actors or agents necessarily have to be *people*.[3] I'm uncertain, but perhaps any network of bits and pieces tends to count as an agent if it embodies a set of ordering processes which allows it (or others) to say 'It is an agent, an actor.'

> Do you sometimes speak of the Government? Or the Internal Revenue? Or your car? Or your employer? Or the Russian Federation? Or your computer? These are putative actors too, networks of more or less successful orderings. For certain purposes you speak of them as agents. Sherry Turkle shows very attractively what kinds of agency children impute to computers and computer games. Adults don't usually think these are 'alive' whereas children often do. But this is a negotiation about what counts as 'life' too.

So this is a theory of agency. And the theory turns around issues of ordering. Can you say of something that it *acts*, or does it just relay messages and act as an *intermediary*?[4] Can you characterize the orderings that lie 'inside' it? Can it say of itself that it acts? Or that it more or less embodies certain orderings inside? Or (a crucial question) that it is reflexive or self-reflexive? These are empirical questions, matters for investigation. Agency and organization is a matter of degree, of quantities, of gradients, as well as qualities.

This is why I fight shy from defining 'the formal organization'. Gareth Morgan is right when he says 'Organisations are many different things at once!' (Morgan 1986: 339). All I can say is that there are organiz*ings* and order*ings* of which we say (which 'we'?) 'they act like organizations'. Just as some human bodies — for instance those with irreversible brain death — may be (said to be) less than 'people'. And some research projects are allegedly 'more successful' than others. If the whole is greater than the sum of its bits and pieces, then there has been some ordering.

3   NETWORKS OF RESEARCH

> So here I am. I am standing at the gatehouse, looking at Daresbury Laboratory. And I can't keep the grin off my face. First, I have actually made it — I'm here! After weeks of nail-biting I have been invited to meet informally with members of the Laboratory Management Com-mittee to discuss the study that I want to do — to discuss whether they will give me freedom to wander round the Laboratory. I am nervous about this, but I am also pleased.
>
> But the real reason that I can't keep the grin off my face is that what I can see is fantastic. Close to me, across some lawns and car parks,

there are several undistinguished brick buildings. Some are obviously
laboratories or offices, while others look more like warehouses. These,
I will learn, house the Synchrotron Radiation Source, together with
various administrative and support divisions. But what is really making
me grin is the building away to the left, up the hill.

Here there is a huge tower which dominates the site and can be
seen for miles around. Indeed, as some of the locals testily note, it
can be seen from the door of Daresbury parish church. It is narrow,
almost spindly, except at the top, where it broadens out like a huge
cylindrical mushroom. I am shortly to learn that this is the Nuclear
Structure Facility. But right now, getting out of my car at the gate, it
looks like a massive statement about the importance of science.

To stand at the gates of the Laboratory felt like an achievement.
Indeed, it *was* an achievement. But how did I get to the gates of
the Laboratory? And how did I get the funding? The story is one
of ordering bits and pieces to create the possibility for a project.
And that process is important if we want to understand the context
of the project.

In the autumn of 1988 I started to draft a grant application for
submission to the ESRC.[5] This was in the context of a particular
research initiative on the 'changing culture of science'. The 'bottom
line' of the initiative wasn't very hard to discern. It had to do with
the relationship between the fashionable culture of 'enterprise' on the
one hand, and the organization, management and market success of
science on the other.

I didn't find it particularly difficult to write a sociological, or indeed
a policy case for a grant – the words seemed to order themselves
fairly well. Briefly, what I said was that I was interested in the effects of
performance indicators on the actual conduct of science. Performance
indicators are measures of (scientific) productivity such as the number
of papers published, the number of times those papers are cited,
or the number of patents filed. They are supposed to measure the
quantity, the quality and the efficiency of scientific work.

Rare in UK science in 1975 but ubiquitous by 1988, I argued that
their rapid introduction must have affected the *conduct* of science.
Indeed, there was plenty of anecdotal evidence to suggest that this
was the case – everyone who knows anything about them has their
own favourite story, usually to show that they don't really work in
the way that they should. For instance, many said that scientists
were reluctant to write book reviews any more, because these didn't
necessarily 'count' as proper publications. But no one had actually
checked out these anecdotes in laboratories, and that was what
I wanted to do: I would look at the way in which scientists and
science managers used such indicators; and, to put this in a useful

context, I would look at the way in which a large laboratory was managed.[6]

> I didn't understand as much about ordering and organizing as (I think) I do now. But the connection between my interest in management use of indicators and processes of ordering is clear enough in retrospect. Indicators embody, and form part of, a range of possible ordering principles.

I have said that writing the grant application took effort, though I didn't find it particularly difficult. What I found much more nerve-racking was the business of negotiating access into a laboratory: I found the thought of having to meet dozens of new people fairly overwhelming. At such times I remembered what Leigh Star told about – I think – Everett Hughes: that he used to find it almost impossible to start ethnography and would find himself walking round the block several times trying to screw his courage up enough to stop at his fieldwork site.

But there were other issues that had more to do with the politics of fieldwork. For a sociologist who turns up at a laboratory is studying people who in many cases already have some knowledge of academic life. In particular, they may have equal or higher status. Thus in the academic pecking order sociology usually comes below any branch of natural science. Often it is simply a joke, and even those who claim to see its virtues (or are simply more polite) may harbour fundamental doubts about its value: there is always the suspicion that sociology is simply common sense; or that it is common sense dressed up as gobbledygook.[7]

So this was my problem: how should I attempt to overcome what I took to be a natural scepticism of a high-status laboratory management about sociology? How should I try to overcome the (reasonable) fear that I would get in the way, make trouble, take up valuable time, or discover potentially discreditable facts about the Laboratory?

A Story about 'Access'

> I work at Keele University and knew a member of the University who was friendly with the Director of Daresbury Laboratory, Professor Andrew Goldthorpe.[8] So I asked him if he thought there was any chance whether Andrew would let me into Daresbury. He said that he didn't see why not, and asked me to write half a page which he could pass on to Andrew. In due course the two of them spoke, and my contact reported back that Andrew was willing to let me make a formal approach to the laboratory management team.
>
> At this point I started to deal with Dr John White, the Laboratory Secretary. After some to-ing and fro-ing John suggested that I should

come to meet members of the Laboratory Management Committee informally to get to know them a little bit and tell them about my study. Once I had done this he thought I should write a brief paper to be presented to the top group of managers, the Daresbury Management Board. Then the Board would approve the study, or not, as the case might be.

And this is why I was standing at the Laboratory gates. I was laughing at the sight of the extravagent Nuclear Structure Facility tower, but I was also extremely nervous. I was about to have a buffet lunch with the fifteen most senior managers on site.

What, then, of that first encounter? I remember a room with perhaps eighteen or twenty people. I remember being aware that they were all men. I remember being introduced to several people by John White. I remember wondering how to hold a glass of orange, a paper plate of salad, a napkin, a knife and fork, a chicken drumstick, a sheet of note-paper and a pen all at the same time. I remember being pleased that the head of the Nuclear Structure Facility, a quiet Scot with a huge beard called Dr Adrian Smith, was friendly, positive about the study, and happy to meet me again to discuss details. I also remember being less happy about my conversation with Dr Jim Haslehurst, the Deputy Director of the Laboratory, and the head of the Synchrotron Radiation Accelerator Division. Jim was helpful and explained that he was responsible, *inter alia*, for the electron accelerator and the storage ring. However he baulked when I exposed my ignorance by suggesting that his role in life was to look after the plumbing!

Apparently I passed this trial by buffet. I met individually with a number of the managers in the weeks that followed, wrote a short paper, and submitted it via John White to the Daresbury Management Board. The response that came back was favourable. I could go where I wanted to in the Laboratory, sit in on meetings, and talk with anyone I wanted to. These were the conditions attached to the study: I had already said that I wouldn't leak information between different parts of the Laboratory, or disclose anything of a personal nature; and I'd said that I'd let the management team (and relevant individuals) see anything that I was hoping to publish; I was told that I should not tape-record committee meetings (though I could take notes); and I was also told that I should leave the room if I found that grant applications from Keele, my home university, were being discussed.

When they say 'It's not what you know, but whom you know' they are wrong. It's what you have, what you know, *and* whom you know. But to say this is to risk being misunderstood for I am not implying impropriety. My Keele contact and Andrew Goldthorpe acted with perfect propriety. And indeed, so did I. Proper procedures were followed. The management team considered the proposal carefully. And I *wrote* the proposal carefully (this was part of 'what you know'). Indeed, I thought (and still think) that it was a good proposal. In effect the 'whom you know' amounted to this: a request to take the proposal seriously when it arrived at the Laboratory. It was another part of the business of trying to order a research project — to assemble a network of bits and pieces. And it should be seen alongside the proposal 'itself', my informal discussions with senior managers, the prejudices and proclivities of those managers, and all the rest.

4　Networks of Integrity

I am grateful to the people at Daresbury for letting me work among them for a year. I liked most of those whom I met, and I found many of them very interesting. I also tended to sympathize with them in their struggles, and to want to take their side in arguments. On the other hand, there were a number of compromises built into the project. For instance, I approached the Laboratory from the top-down, rather than the bottom-up: I don't know whether I was viewed as a management stooge in some quarters. I've no evidence that I was, but it wouldn't be surprising if this happened.

Again and more generally, I now find that I cannot easily write an account that would hurt the Laboratory, or its employees. As I've mentioned, I agreed to let relevant managers look at anything I wrote about the Laboratory before it was published. On the other hand I wouldn't *want* to write an account that hurt the Laboratory either. (But who *decides* what hurts, and what does not?) For instance, there was a horrible moment early on in the study when I was reporting some preliminary findings to a small closed meeting of other sociologists and science-policy analysts. After I finished talking, someone in the room turned to me and said: 'I went and looked at Daresbury Laboratory in 1979, and my recommendation was that it should be closed. What do you think now? Should it be closed?'

I was horrified. How could I recommend (or even think about recommending) the closure of *my* Laboratory? The question had not even posed itself in my mind, let alone been answered. In the end I found myself saying 'Would you close *your* tribe?' And this is, indeed, how I felt. How, I wondered, would the anthropologist Evans Pritchard have responded to a question about whether or not the Nuer should be 'closed down'.

It was only when my anthropologist colleague Sharon Macdonald read an earlier version of this manuscript that I learned that this was indeed more or less the question posed to Evans Pritchard: what, the colonial administrators wanted to know, should be done with this turbulent tribe?

So the requirement that managers should look at what I wrote didn't (and still doesn't) seem like too much of an imposition. This is because I am not a detached observer. And facts and values join together. You could argue – as might perhaps the man who posed the question about closing the Laboratory – that I have gone native. And I would respond: we *all* go native; we *all* interact with what we study. The question is: which tribe or tribes do we choose to join? And here (if it is a choice) I have chosen to join the Daresbury tribe as opposed to that of the science-policy establishment. On the other hand, to agree not to hurt the Laboratory is not necessarily to be uncritical.

I remember a member of the Communist Party talking about 'workerism'. Workerism is the uncritical acceptance of what a party member says because he has a correct class background. I paraphrase: 'You've got this room full of Cambridge Professors. And then there is this Postman. And every time the Postman opens his mouth all the Professors start nodding and agreeing with everything he says, even though it's a load of nonsense, because he's the only one who's a proper member of the working class.'

In the present context, the equivalent of workerism is managerialism. The fact that managerialism is generally thought to be more respectable than workerism makes it far more dangerous. Do I uncritically order my stories around a managerial perspective? Is what I write simply an extension of a managerial view?

Well, you can make your own judgement. Sometimes, to be sure, I will be uncritical. But I also develop some kind of critical purchase on issues to do with class (though I fail on gender). My views here don't mesh in very much with those of the managers. That is the obvious point. But there are two less obvious points. The first is that what I'm after, though it's illustrated by talking about events in the Laboratory, is not very often about the Laboratory as such at all. In other words, I'm chasing after issues in social theory, not matters to do with Daresbury. The second is really a specification of the first. I'm also trying to describe the organization in a way that doesn't involve commitment to any form of pure order. Thus on the one hand, the managers have their dreams of order. And these dreams define distractions and destructions. And, on the other hand, there is order*ing*. I will say that even when the managers dream of order they are involved in order*ing*. But so too are others in the organization. And it is this ordering that concerns me most – ordering that is never complete, and runs at cross purposes in a hundred different locations, and never adds up to the hideous purity of an order – even though it generates a set of processes that we can call 'the Lab'. So I see different stories, and – this is the critical distance – I try not to buy into any of them by turning the others into distractions.

5 PLACES

Is Daresbury Laboratory a set of different and conflicting ideas or
dreams of purity? Is it a row of figures? Is it a set of scientific results?
Is it a site? Is it a lot of people? Is it a set of plans? I really don't
know what it would mean to offer a definition of what it *is*. To
define it would be to breach the principle of symmetry. For there are
many places in the Laboratory, and many different forms of ordering.
Sometimes managerialism, like workerism, speaks in a single voice.
At those moments it speaks of order, and of distraction/destruction.

> If [the shop-floor workers are] only going to put an idea in
> [about how to improve efficiency] if they're going to get an award,
> then the sooner they leave the better!

Here the organization speaks as if it has a right to both the body
and the soul of its employees. But in practice this is unusual. At
least, I didn't come across it very much. There are times when
managers might like to enter into totalitarian contracts with their
subordinates, but most of the time, and more realistically, they aspire
to something much more modest. And in practice the Laboratory is
full of places and orderings, so hideous statements of purity like this
are rare. People know, usually without saying, that things are complicated. Indeed, this was one of the reasons I came to respect the
managers at Daresbury. They reflected, and reflected on, the hetereo-
geneity of ordering, and the many places where it went on. For the
Laboratory is a network of different places. Or, perhaps better, it is
a pastiche. Here are some of the places.

The Machine Area

A fairly nightmarish scene; a large, fairly clear area, dominated by
the first-floor circle of the source, and its surrounding catwalks, by a
monstrous crane, and the new klystron and its failed cousin. There
are large pools of water around the klystron caused by leaks as the
fitters attempt to replumb the new klystron. The klystron is only 40
per cent efficient — as well as pumping out microwaves it also pumps
out a huge amount of heat. The water is demineralized and deoxidized.
It would be fatal ... if bubbles were to form. There would be hot spots.
Suddenly, as we stand watching it, there is a geyser of water from the
base of the klystron as one of the hoses breaks loose — water gushes
all over the floor as one of the fitters rushes to turn off an isolation valve.

I wrote these notes in the middle of a really difficult period for the
Synchrotron Radiation Division. Here's the background: the Synchrotron Radiation Source creates intense beams of photons — of visible

and invisible light – which are used for all sorts of scientific experiments. It generates this light by deflecting electrons in a magnetic field. And in practice it does this by injecting, accelerating and deflecting electrons round a large pipe. The photons – X-rays, ultraviolet, visible and infra-red radiation – are piped simultaneously to about 25 different experimental sites. Since deflecting the electrons absorbs energy, new energy is pumped into the source in the form of RF radiation. This is produced by the klystron – a piece of equipment that lies at the heart of every television transmitter. But when the source breaks down – for instance because of a defective klystron – all 25 experiments come to an immediate halt. And this is what had happened on the day I made these notes. Something – a surge in the cooling water supply, or even a recent minor earthquake – had distorted the klystron and rendered it unserviceable.

Driven by urgency, people were working a 12- or 14-hour day. They were tired to their bones. They were quite depressed. And they were very anxious. I noticed, in particular, the way in which those involved were a mix: managers, scientists, engineers, technicians, fitters and riggers – all kinds of people clustered around the machine as they tried to diagnose its ailments and fix up cures. They talked with one another, they cooperated, they argued, and they complained. And for a few weeks at least they formed a world of their own with its own processes of networking and ordering, a world that seemed to have little to do with the other worlds or places beyond the SR (Synchrotron Radation) Source. Everything else was a distraction. One of the technicians put it like this.

> You can't get away from it. I mean, I go home and I sit with my wife in front of the television, and I'm watching 'Coronation Street'. But my mind's not really on 'Coronation Street' at all. What I'm really thinking about is the Source. And I'm sitting there thinking about it and suddenly I have an idea: 'I know. We haven't thought of trying that. That's what we should try next.'

The Office Area

Here is another somewhat disguised extract from my field notes. The result is a very odd scientific problem, but for the present purposes this does not matter.

> 'I have a problem' says Giovanni. It is about a Dutchman called de Laan. 'He has written to me to ask about the prospects of collaboration.' The Dutch have, he says, found a way of crystallizing cell nuclei. They are huge, absolutely huge. They have a molecular weight of millions, hundreds of million. The size of the unit cell is vast. It is exciting. But it is a tough problem, a *very* tough problem.

Giovanni is doubtful. Why? 'Because I do not believe that we have the critical mass to collaborate properly.'

The problem, as in all X-ray crystallography, is the phase information. I don't understand everything he says, but he notes that they couldn't get the phase information from derivatives. The only way would be by cloning. But for this they would need clean facilities, space suits and the rest .... We are talking here of a major, major project.

This conversation takes place about 100 yards from the world of the machine, but it might as well be on another planet. Six senior managers are gathered together in an office. It is warm and carpeted. There is coffee, made by the secretary, and a plate of biscuits on the table. But as the scientist/managers fiddle with their papers they are talking about the future, the far future, a scientific vision at the end of the rainbow. A dream of order. And the practicalities of ordering.

This – part of the world of management – is the part of the Laboratory I was most familiar with. In these rooms the managers sit and talk: they talk of reproducing the Laboratory; of drumming up customers; of efficiency; of SERC[9] politics in Head Office in Swindon; of the day-to-day conduct of experiments; of attempts to track down illicit phone calls.

The Experimental Area

Almost all of the managers are also working scientists. I don't want to give the impression that they simply sit in their offices and issue orders. I also saw them on the scientific shop floor. So here is another place in the Laboratory. Again I draw on my field notes:

Seen from the scientists' point of view the world looks quite different. The building is huge, with the roof 50 feet above. The control site is a rather inhospitable niche along the side of the radiation hutch. It is rather cold and draughty, it is noisy, there are constant comings and goings – beyond the end of the desk there is a passageway.

The team clearly has strong *élan*. The postdoc is very little older than the D.Phil. students; they tease one another, laugh, they sing to keep themselves awake in the middle of the night. They appreciate the efforts of the laboratory staff. They say that everyone is friendly, if a little straitlaced.

But the Laboratory is a very restricted world for them; they are in and out of the hutch every five minutes, swinging the heavy door open and closed, changing the sample, setting the search procedure, scanning and down-loading the data. Twenty-four hours a day, sometimes they stay up. And then they take their data, and go back to their university. It will keep them busy for months analysing it. So, as I sit with them, they look frustrated that there are no X-rays, that the machine has been down. They have lost a shift, a sixth of their time!

The experimental area is the place occupied by the user scientists (they are universally called 'the users') who come to the Laboratory from outside to make use of its facilities. They tend to know little about the machine, little about management. Instead, they live around and for the ordering of experimental work. They deal with one or two in-house scientists, one or two members of the crew who operate the machine when it is running well, and they trudge between the hostel, the canteen and the experimental site. Sometimes, just sometimes, they go off site — to the pub, or to a local restaurant. But they are serious about their work. You have to be serious about your work to open and close a heavy radiation-proof door once every five minutes right round the clock. For a pittance.

I could talk about other places: there is, for instance a place for the crew which drives the machine; there are places for technicians; there are places for scientists, engineers, computer programmers, draftsmen, administrators, accountants, machinists, riggers, security guards, cooks, cleaners and messengers. There are endless different locations in the laboratory. And endless different modes of organizing. And this is why managerial definitions of what the organization 'really' is do not help. For it is, amongst other things, a network of different worlds.

6 ANXIETIES

Like an organization, an ethnography is an exercise in ordering. And that ordering involves interacting before, during and after the process of fieldwork. I've mentioned that for me the ordering before-hand was stabilized in part by a series of agreements: an agreement by the ESRC to fund the study and an agreement by the management team to let me wander round the Laboratory. Those agreements might be revoked, but they stood at least for the time being. But what of the process of wandering round the Laboratory?

Ethnographer's Anxieties

What does an ethnographer *do*? I worried about this a lot. Partly it was a matter of measuring myself against an ordering idea — that of the ideal ethnographer. Such a creature would have been more energetic, made more phone calls, been more sociable, and have had a better memory. He or she would also have needed less 'time-out' from the Laboratory and its people. All in all, he or she would have been less prone to distractions of all kinds.

> I did not understand that to be professional and try to do a job well
> is one thing, and to have an ordering vision of hideous purity is
> another. And I confused the two.

Partly, however, it was a question of the roles for the ethnographer:
I mean, what are the *roles* that an ethnographer is supposed to play?
I know that there are textbooks that seek to answer this question.
But, for me, it was partly a question of finding ways of feeling
comfortable.

Interviewing was a possibility. It was okay to fix up an appointment
and go and ask someone questions. And I had been told that I
could sit in on meetings. That was also okay. At least it seemed as
if it was okay. But I could only attend meetings if I knew when and
where they were taking place. And this was not so easy. 'You can't
ask about something if you don't know it exists': the old adage
about official secrets held true for the Laboratory too. I'm not implying that anyone deliberately tried to stop me learning about meetings. So far as I know, that did not happen. It was more that they
tended to think that I wouldn't be interested. For it turns out
(shades of the 'two cultures' for this has happened to me before)
that people think that sociologists will not be very interested in
'technical details'. But at Daresbury a lot of the meetings were
precisely about 'technical details'. And what of the discussions and
conversations that didn't take place in meetings? I had no way of
plugging into these at all.

Here's what happened. By virtue of its size, the Synchrotron
Radiation Division had more formal meetings than the others. So
a larger part of the iceberg of 'decisionmaking' was above the informal waterline, which made it easier to track what was going on.
But then I was lucky too.

Heather Mott and Carol Richmond are the secretaries to the two
top managers of the Division. And Heather and Carol turned out
to be sympathetic and helpful. So I found out about the meetings by
asking them to look through the diaries of these managers for forthcoming meetings. Which explains why this ethnography is primarily
an ethnography of the Synchrotron Radiation Division. And also
explains why ethnographers make so much of 'gatekeepers' and 'key
informants'.

> When we use terms like these we disembody and reify people that are
> real to the ethnographer, and we make ourselves sound 'scientific' too!

Going to meetings and conducting interviews – I felt that these
were recognizable research roles: no one would question my legitimacy
if I did these. But what about hanging around? And being with

people as they worked? Or bumping into people? Or being somewhere where people might bump into me? To hang around, at least in a space that is not warrantably 'public', you have to know people: they have in some measure to trust you, to feel comfortable in your presence. Obviously, at the beginning no one knew me. And trust would come later, if it came at all.

Over the first few weeks of the study I came to believe that all of these were more easily managed in the larger SR Division. I think there were three reasons for this. First, I discovered the library. This was a blessed relief. Anyone, even a visiting sociologist, is presumed to have the right to sit in a library. (And it is less shaming to sit in a library by oneself than it is to sit in a coffee room – solitariness in the latter, or so I felt, is a sign of social and ethnographic failure.) So I took to hanging around in the library. And this was good for my mental health too. It meant that I could find my own solitary space – my own time-out – without having to retreat to my car in the car park. For being with people, and on my best behaviour the whole time, was very tiring.

Second, the SR Division was very large anyway, and so much of it was on an open plan, that I could walk round the buildings more or less indefinitely. Here was the trick: to appear to others as if I was purposively striding from A to B; whereas I was really walking in a circle, from A to A, via corridors, control room, coffee machine, workshop, half-a-dozen different experimental areas, and a series of offices. They say that it is better to travel hopefully than to arrive. I travelled hopefully round the SR buildings many times, and sometimes I arrived.

Third, since I sat in meetings, and interviewed people, I started to get to know some of them. And as I knew them a little, so, as I bumped into them, I got to know some of them better. Or they tolerated me. Or they explained what was going on to me. (Some people have a gift for explaining complexity in simple terms.) And it became easier to hang around – to find out who didn't seem to mind if I was there, asking questions, and taking notes.

Where the Ethnographer is, the Action is Not

That is a part of the story. It's an important part. It has to do with ordering the person of an ethnographer and the conduct of an ethnography. It has to do with using corridors, library desks, engagement diaries, official permissions and personal friendships to conduct a study. But it is only a part of the story. For here's the crux: I had a terrible anxiety about being in the right place at the right time. Wherever I happened to be, the action was not.

Sometimes people would say: 'Did you hear what happened at such-and-such a meeting?' Or 'Did you hear that this bit of equipment crashed over the weekend?' Or as I hung around I'd overhear people talking to one another: 'Did you hear what happened to so-and-so?' Always, it seemed to me, that the *real* action was going on somewhere else.

Yet there was an oddity about this. For instance, for a year I attended almost all the meetings of the two most senior management meetings at Daresbury, the Daresbury Management Board, and the Laboratory Management Committee. I also attended most of the meetings of the subcommittee that guided SERC Synchrotron Radiation policy and handed out most of the large grants. Other people, those excluded from these meetings, sometimes assumed that where I was, *there* was the action, and they'd ask me questions — questions that I'd have to deflect — about what had happened at 'important' meetings.

I puzzled about this oddity, and suffered from attacks of panic. But now that I have, as they say, 'withdrawn' from the field, I think that I can see what was going on: I was, implicitly, committed to a perfect version of representational ethnography. I thought that I could describe everything. Or, at any rate, I thought that I could describe everything that was of any importance. I was committed to a version of pure order — that I could order my account to mirror what was 'really going on' in the Laboratory. But at the time I didn't see this. And I didn't see that it was impossible. So I panicked at what I took to be the shoddiness of my fieldwork.

Much of the time in the modern world we pass the time by formulating, reformulating and representing what has gone on elsewhere. Anthony Giddens, I think rightly, sees self-reflexivity as central to the modern project. This process of formulating goes under a variety of names: we call it gossip, or reporting, or describing, or accounting. It may be verbal, or visual, or textual — or any combination of the three. But in the version of representation to which I remain committed, what is happening elsewhere usually remains as some kind of constraint, a set of resources, a somewhat intractable geography of context.[10] And ordering extends only so far into that geography. The very powerful learn this quickly. When they arrive at the seat of power, they suddenly find that what they can know, and what they can do, is limited. Dreams of purity are pure dreams for rulers and ethnographers alike. And for others they are hideous nightmares.

Recently I talked about this sense of panic with Steve Woolgar, an experienced and sensitive laboratory ethnographer. I was encouraged to discover that he also wrestled with a version of the same problem. We know, in our heads, that we cannot describe everything. Indeed, the notion of describing everything is an empiricist nonsense which presupposes an all-seeing ethnographic and theoretical eye. (For to see it all, I have to blaspheme and turn myself into God by claiming omniscience.) But to know that this is the case in our heads, and to know it in our hearts, these are two quite different things. Still, despite everything, we cling to our blasphemies. For we may think that we have given up our commitment to a unified science, but it is much more difficult to abandon our commitment to the unity of the self.

Obviously, I missed out on many important events during my fieldwork. Sometimes I did not know about them. Sometimes I could not be there (as was true, for instance, for the closed sessions of the SERC Science Board, the most senior committee with an interest in Daresbury Laboratory). Sometimes its just seemed inappropriate – I never asked to attend personal appraisal interviews, appointment boards or other important personal rites of passage. Sometimes I just happened to be in the wrong place at the wrong time. And certainly, I did not collect materials that might have attracted other ethnographers with different interests. But, though I know, even by my own increasingly modest standards, that the study is incomplete, I now see things differently: since there are discontinuities in place, and discontinuities in ordering, it follows that the largest part of the action is always being generated elsewhere.

7 NETWORK AND PROCESS

After I'd been in Daresbury Laboratory a few months and I'd got to know some of the people who work there a bit, some of them started to ask me: 'Well, what have you discovered?' Or: 'How does the Laboratory *really* work then?'[11] I found questions such as these disconcerting. Partly this was born out of the knowledge that since they worked there, they *already* knew a great deal about Laboratory ordering. Partly it was because of the ethnographic anxiety that I've described above – the sense (with which I had not begun to come to terms) that I never really seemed to be where the action was. Partly it was because I knew that what would count as 'really' going on from one point of view would almost certainly be thought of as of minor importance from another: that I would probably never arrive at a single description of Laboratory organization that would make sense or sound right to everyone. And finally, it was because the notion of 'discovery' did not make very much sense to me in the first place.

There is a large literature on discovery in the sociology of scientific knowledge (see, for instance, Brannigan 1981). The gist of this is that if you want to understand how facts are generated in science the notion of discovery isn't very helpful. This is because talk of discovery makes it sound as if there are facts, out there, waiting for the scientist to come along and pick them up. It trades, that is, on an empiricist notion of what should count as facts. As a part of this, it also makes it sound as if the process of picking them up doesn't take very long: discoveries, so to speak, happen to those who happen upon the facts which are already lying around. In addition (again this is, I think, an expression of empiricism), it also makes it appear that everyone can agree what should count as a discovery once one has been made.

The counter-argument from the recent philosophy and sociology of science says that all of this is pretty misleading. Scientific observations and scientific discoveries are almost always *processes*. In particular, they almost always involve something much more active on the part of the discoverer – a lot of work, discussion, and agonizing[12] – in which there is *interaction* between scientists and what they are studying. And, since there is interaction, and that interaction takes place in a social context, discoveries are almost always controversial too: the business of labelling a discovery as a discovery takes time, effort and negotiation. And if all these processes don't *seem* to be processes then this is because of a surrounding network of assumptions – the fact that 'everyone' who is relevant takes (for instance) certain theories, methodologies and forms of instrumentation for granted.[13] Or perhaps more often, it is because the uncertainty of these processes is concealed from all except insiders.[14]

If discovery is an uncertain process in natural science, then it is equally uncertain in ethnography. And it is, most emphatically, a process. For instance, I did not know, at least not in a strong sense, what I would 'discover' in the Laboratory once I started fieldwork. And the 'discoveries' that I actually made – the arguments that I develop in the chapters that follow – only emerged slowly and painfully. It is useful, I think, to note that what we call 'data' and 'interpretations of the data' (I'll drop the notion of 'discovery' because it seems to me to be so misleading) are the product of a process in which both simplification and translation play heroic roles.

That there is simplification is easily seen: almost everything that went on in the Laboratory doesn't get to count as data in my story at all. There are many reasons for this: I was not present to record it; it did not seem important; I failed to note it down and then forgot about it; I did not understand its significance; I was unable to record it; and so on. But, in addition to simplification, there is also translation. As they become data, events out there, in the Laboratory, are *translated*. That is, they are converted into representations in other media − for instance into field notes, memories and working drafts. But since translation is a form of conversion it may, or may not, be warrantable. *Traduction*, *trahison*, translation, betrayal − though the pun works best in the Romance languages it is important to understand that data *may* stand for what it claims to represent, but that that claim is always open to contest. Data are not only simplifications, but imputations too. There is, in short, no empiricist way out, no bedrock of hard fact.

In my room, here, as I write, I have several feet of paperwork that derives from the Daresbury study: field notes, offprints, agendas, minutes, letters. These are the documents that I created or collected over a period of more than a year. How did I simplify the Laboratory down to a few feet of papers? How did I translate an unimaginably complex set of processes and events into something that stands, in a docile manner, on the shelf of my study? I've already hinted at a part of the answer. I didn't start out with a strong sense of what I would 'discover'. Instead, these inscriptions are a moment in − and a document about − a difficult, protracted, and painful process that in part took the form of a fishing trip.

The ethnomethodologists sometimes talk about the 'documentary method'.[15] For instance, Harold Garfinkel writes:

> the investigator frequently must elect among alternative courses of interpretation and inquiry to the end of deciding matters of fact, hypothesis, conjecture, fancy, and the rest, despite the fact that in the calculable sense of the term 'know,' he does not and cannot 'know' what he is doing *prior to or while he is doing it*. Field workers, most particularly those doing ethnographic and linguistic studies in settings where they cannot presuppose a knowledge of social structures, are perhaps best acquainted with such situations, but other types of professional sociological inquiry are not exempt.
>
>   Nevertheless, a body of knowledge of social structures is somehow assembled. (Garfinkel 1967: 77−78)

Garfinkel is right: the ethnographer lives through the problem, and she resolves it in the only way in which she can: in a kind of bootstrap operation, in which she weaves between the data on the one hand, and imputations about the patterns that may be expressed in those data, on the other. So it is that something, a sense of pattern, emerges at the end of the process that was not foreseen at the beginning. So it is that the ethnographer interacts with her data, and with her assumptions or theories about the character of the social world. She is, as it were, the contingent place in the network where conceptions about the world, theoretical and otherwise, meet up with the particular bits and pieces that fall within the class of putative data.

This was how it was for me at Daresbury. I had a set of orienting assumptions and interests. I've mentioned some of these above: I thought that the social world was a network; I thought that that network was materially heterogeneous; I thought that it was self-ordering and self-shaping; that is, I thought the network was a process, organizing itself through time; and (this is more specific than my other assumptions) I thought that particular places in the network – for instance management meetings – might be especially important in the process of ordering.

So I didn't arrive at Daresbury innocent, like some kind of clean slate. The set of ordering assumptions made it possible for me to collect material, putative data. On the other hand, I had little sense, within these presuppositions, about how the study might work out in practice. Nevertheless, as I scribbled and I collected away, I moved from my initial concern with the cloistered spaces of elite management meetings to a different sense of pattern, one which led me to gather different *kinds* of material.

The next section is the story of this process, and I'll postpone discussion of the specifics. But I think that Garfinkel's point about the documentary method is well-made. It points to the way in which research (and not just research) is a process, a reflexive process of uncertain and provisional imputation. It points to the ordering process in which we weave to and fro between traces and imputations. It speaks of the process which generates a sense of pattern, and with that, as series of 'decisions' about what will count as warrantable simplifications and translations – what, in other words, will count as 'data'. And it admirably points to the iterative or emergent character of the process of ethnographic ordering.

For this, it seems to me, is what ethnography – and I think, any form of learning – is about. It is about seeing, hearing, noticing, sensing, smelling, and then raking over what has been noticed, and trying to make some sense out of it. And, to be sure, also recognizing the 'non-sense' in it too. And then it is about the process of seeing, sensing and the rest, and going over it all again. And so on. And so on. So, like any other mode of ordering, data – and the imputations which have to do with data – are relational effects. But they are *changing* relational effects, for they are the product of dynamic networkings rather than synchronic structures. So if they stand still for a moment then this is because they have achieved some kind of pragmatic, temporary stability, an ordering pattern, encountered resistances, which momentarily domesticate both the material and its audiences. Or perhaps it is because time, energy, enthusiasm or life itself have run out.

NOTES

1 Latour and Woolgar (1979) speak of 'modalities' when they describe this effect. For recent exploration of forms of narrative in ethnography, see Clifford (1986).
2 This is a point made by radical critics of such authors as Lyotard. See, for instance, Benhabib (1990).
3 My position isn't novel. It's shared, for instance, by Hindess (1982), Callon and Latour (1981) and Barnes (1988).
4 See Barnes (1986, 1988); and Callon (1991).
5 ESRC, the Economic and Social Research Council, is the British Social Science Funding Body.
6 In the present book I don't explore the indicators used by the managers in these terms. Rather, I treat with the role of representation as an aspect of ordering, in a much more general sense.
7 It was ever thus: this is the problem of the double hermeneutic – that sociology is so far, but only so far, from common sense. But now I take it that this is not really a problem but a part of the ironic, liberatory, potential of social redescription.
8 Though Daresbury is the real name of of the Laboratory, the names of all those who work in the Laboratory and appear in this text are disguised. The reasons for this are discussed in the Postscript.
9 SERC is the acronym for the Science and Engineering Research Council, the major source of government funding for academic research in physics and chemistry. Daresbury Laboratory is one of several facilities owned, and largely financed, by the SERC.
10 Though I recognize its force I feel, for instance, somewhat uncomfortable with Jean Baudrillard's (1988b) analysis of simulacra and his notion of the 'hyperreal'. Note, however, Bob Cooper's (1992) attractive Derridaean analysis of organizational representation.
11 Hammersley and Atkinson (1983: 78) note that this is a common hazard for ethnographers.
12 The process is described in ethnomethodological language in Garfinkel, Lynch and Livingston (1981).
13 They are, for instance, located within a Kuhnian paradigm (Kuhn 1970).
14 MacKenzie, Rudig and Spinardi (1988), talking of technological innovation, call this phenomenon the 'certainty trough'.
15 See Garfinkel (1967: 76ff). The term derives from Mannheim.

3

Histories, Agents and Structures

1 INTRODUCTION

Stories are part of ordering, for we create them to make sense of our circumstances, to re-weave the human fabric. And as we create and recreate our stories we make and remake both the facts of which they tell, and ourselves. So it is that we seek to order, and re-order, our surroundings. So it is that we formulate, we try to sum up.[1]

This means that histories may be treated as modes of telling and ordering. They mix and match from the available collection of cultural bits and pieces. And as they circulate they tell us at least as much about day-to-day ordering struggles as they do about 'real' history. For what we find is that there are accounts and accounts. And there are histories and histories. We can talk about the kings and queens of England. Or we can talk about the history of the common people. Neither, not withstanding the myths of Conservative heroism or the Marxists, counts as the 'real' history of England. And if we come to believe that they are, then we have forgotten what it is to know our limits, to be an ironist. We have fallen victim to a hideously pure order. And we have lost sight of the way in which history is an effect just as much as a set of antecedents.

In this chapter I'm going to tell historical stories about Daresbury SERC Laboratory. I'm going to do this not because I want to tell about the 'real' history of the Laboratory. I say this not because I do not care about the past. On the contrary: I hope that I have said enough already to indicate that I am committed to the people of Daresbury Laboratory. Rather it is because I think these histories tell us much more about current ordering than they do about the past. For, one way or another, the past is related to the present: it *justifies* the present. Or it *explains* the present. Historians have considered both possibilities. There is no final solution, for it depends on what we feel about the present. Are we active agents? Or are we carriers of historical forces? This is a political and an ethical question, a matter for endless discussion and negotiation.

2   EVOLUTION AND HEROISM

The facts or stories that I gathered varied. This chapter is about that variation, and specifically about the histories of the Synchrotron Radiation Division of the Laboratory. But (this tugs me back towards the comfortable empiricist feeling that there is a 'real history') certain themes and events regularly surfaced. For instance, when I asked Dr Freddy Saxon, a middle-level manager and senior scientist, about the history of the SR Division he commented:

> The background is that the [machine] has been running for ten years. It was funded as a machine, with stations to be added year by year. These have been quite well funded, and have been added at the rate of two to three per year. Now there are thirty odd, and the running costs as a percentage [of our costs] has increased. In keeping going what we already have, upgrading and maintenance have become more and more difficult.

Here we have a framework: there are dates, there are events and there is a trend. What is important about this is that these are dates, events, and trends running through most of the histories of the SR Division: the Source was completed in 1981; but (Freddy does not say this though others often do) there were large-scale teething troubles and it broke down regularly in the first year; indeed, those troubles were so severe that the whole future of the machine was in jeopardy at one point. But in 1983 the problems were overcome, and the machine has run well since. Furthermore, it has been enhanced in a substantial programme of work, to increase the focus of the electron beam and so improve its brightness. Freddy mentions a further change − an increase in the number of experimental stations. But this has not been all good, for another problem that he touches upon is that of funding. This, then, is another leitmotiv in Laboratory histories: the shortage of money.

I'm going to treat these as historical 'facts'. What turns them into 'facts' is that it appears that they are 'shared'. That is, they are facts to the extent that the histories that I found circulating in the Laboratory do one of three things. Either they cite these facts as facts and build them into their stories. Or they make use of them as an implicit organizing framework even if they don't mention them. Or, more loosely they tell stories that don't actually contradict them.

I'm being pretty cautious here. For instance, I'm not saying that these facts have the same significance for all members of the Laboratory. Indeed, I'll argue that they don't. Neither am I saying that they are incontrovertible. I can certainly imagine that they might be challenged or reinterpreted. Indeed, it is possible that there are places in the Laboratory where they are regularly questioned, though I don't know of such places. Again, I've avoided saying that they are important or central to all versions of Laboratory history: not everyone refers to them when they tell you about the past.

These, then, are the reasons why I have placed inverted commas round the word 'shared' above. Though I may be wrong, I *don't* believe that there is a shared empirical or normative bedrock which holds the Laboratory together. And I certainly wouldn't want to build a reductionist assumption of that kind into any account of social ordering. However, having stressed this, the other side of the coin is that for certain purposes people don't actively contest certain stories, or at least they don't actively contest elements in those stories. And the *effect* of this is that these stories, or at any rate some of their elements, come to look like a bedrock of fact. Accordingly, my argument is that empiricism, the assumption that there *is* a reality about which we can all agree, is an effect rather than a cause.[2] But it *is* an effect. And, since it is an effect, it is one to which I will not only contribute (as I have above) but also seek to take advantage. And I'll do this because it is a useful effect if, as I want to, the object is to talk about the *differences* rather than the similarities between different histories.

So what of the differences? How do the histories vary? After about three months in the Laboratory I started to think to myself that that the histories I was hearing tended to fall into two groups: there were stories that seemed to tell of *evolution*; and there were stories that told of *crisis and radical change*.

Now there is no alternative: I will have to make use of two imputed ideal types, as I attempt to order a mass of detail in what appear to me to be two kinds of organizing principles, two ways of structuring the histories/stories that are told of Daresbury Laboratory, two ways of talking about order and disorder. The methodological hazards are self-evident. There is the problem of imputation, of translation. And there is also a somewhat separate problem to do with selection. For instance, do labour-history tales of the Laboratory circulate through its workshops? The truth of the matter is that I do not know. I will gloss over these difficulties for the moment.

Evolutionary histories tell of the history of the Laboratory in precisely those terms — as a reasonable and unfolding *evolution* of scientific and technical concerns moderated more or less seriously by financial constraints and the need to maintain the Laboratory on an even keel in a difficult world. Sometimes — indeed not infrequently — it is told that progress has suffered setbacks and it has been forced to bend in the face of technical or economic contingencies. Nevertheless, underneath all the superficial pyrotechnics, such evolutionary stories talk of a deeper albeit somewhat thwarted history of rational, orderly and systematic change.

What were the sources of this unfolding order? Story-tellers tended to identify three possibilities. Sometimes it grew from investment in machines and instruments. Sometimes it grew from the character of scientific progress. And sometimes it grew out of a commitment to administration. Very often two or indeed all three of these were run together. Stories of this kind were all, however, incremental in character — they stressed accretion and quantitative change. Correspondingly, they tended to play down the significance of discontinuities. And individual personalities were absorbed into the (more or less) smooth running of a structure.

Ponder the character of political speech: 'Downing Street is said to be relaxed about .....' Or the impersonality of scientific style. Isn't the key to this style of writing to do with seamless monovocality?

Evolutionary accounts tended to sound measured and bureaucratic. Certainly they did not have the narrative flair of the alternative mode of history-telling, that of *heroism*. For many heroic ordering stories about Laboratory history also circulated at Daresbury. In the latter the leitmotiv was one of struggle — of the way in which the Laboratory had struggled to attract resources in the face of adversity.

Heroic accounts are monovocal too. But they pretend otherwise, by establishing a loyal opposition, an opposition that will submit to the genius or the courage or the wisdom of the hero. That, at any rate, is the non-tragic version of heroism. In tragedy it is different. The opposition is no longer loyal, except to the author. Maybe what we need, in the modest writing of post-purity, is to embrace tragedy?

Heroism told of the way the Laboratory had gone through good periods and bad. And, most of all, it talked of revolutionary change and the role in such revolutionary change of crucial individuals. The importance of creative and managerial genius was emphasized by insisting that its absence at times had had allegedly catastrophic consequences.

The distinction between the qualitative and the quantitative has intrigued many. For instance Mannheim (1953b) distinguishes between 'natural law' styles of thought with a reductionist commitment to atomism and quantification, and 'conservative' styles of thought with their commitment to holism and the importance of the qualitative, and discontinuity. Gilbert and Mulkay (1984) point to the same kind of distinction when they write of the 'David and Goliath' theme in history. And now I am doing the same. Of course, such distinctions are always problematic, but so is any ordering attempt to tell stories.

Here are some further factual effects generated by the various Laboratory histories circulating in the Laboratory. Most scientists and managers, like Freddy, seemed to think that the Laboratory was (or at any rate had been) doing too much, and doing it insufficiently well. But why was this? The answer in part had to do with resources. There were cuts in government funding; and there was a political ideology – the Thatcherite idea that publicly-funded facilities such as Daresbury should go out and seek paying customers. But these were treated as facts of political and economic life. Most storytellers – though they might deplore them – assumed, or told of how, such facts were negotiable only around the edges. Accordingly, they *created* an effect of scale, a distinction between the macro-social and the micro-social. And the operating distinction had to do with malleability. You could, it was assumed, *perhaps* influence local events. By constrast, the possibility of affecting large-scale events was remote in the extreme.

That much was common ground, a way of talking that generated the effect of a macro-social background. But laboratory histories tended to diverge when it came to the diagnosis of local responses (and proper local responses) to such facts of life. But this, the point where I have to start talking about individuals, is the moment where I confront a methodological problem. For evolutionary stories are self-effacing, whereas heroic accounts tend to be self-advertising.

Evolutionary stories appear in places like the Daresbury Annual Report: 'he departed after seven years as Director, leaving the laboratory in a very healthy state.' Or they appear in the quiet moments during interviews when thoughtful and administratively-minded managers or scientists start musing about the changes that have taken place during the course of their careers. On the other hand, heroic stories, like the Norse sagas, are oral histories, peopled with heroes, discontinuities and qualitative leaps. They are exciting. And they tend to verge on the unprintable, not because they are obscene, but because they are hurtful.[3]

So here, then, is the methodological problem: to tell histories of heroism is interesting but risky, whereas to tell evolutionary offical histories is safe but mundane. Like other ethnographers, I will turn uncomfortably on the horns of this dilemma, for there is certainly no way of solving it!

3 AGENCY LOST

Heroic story-tellers often say: 'It is a question of personalities.' At Daresbury they tell of good managers, and of bad managers. They say that a good manager is active, resourceful, and creative – a mover and a shaker rather than a passive paper-pusher. Accordingly, though heroic story-tellers are sometimes circumspect, I learned quickly that the management that had presided over the (alleged) decline of the Laboratory in the face of economic and political adversity was not highly regarded by all.

> But this is controversial. There are those who speak warmly of this period. And it could be argued to the contrary, that the Laboratory ran well during a period of unprecedented and successful growth. The NSF [Nuclear Structure Facility] was commissioned, a highly reliable SR Source was built, and much first-class science was the result.

The denunciations of heroic historians tend to lay two charges at the door of the former management. First, they say that it did not sufficiently stand up for the Laboratory in the face of outside pressures. It was allegedly insufficiently 'go-getting' in the entrepreneurial climate of the 1980s. Second, they suggest that within the Laboratory it did not 'bite on the bullet' and impose priorities – the priorities that were needed if the Laboratory was to escape from the trap of doing too much and doing it all badly.

> In its heroism, this story is in danger of getting out of hand, and causing offence. But how can I handle this? Should I pretend that these complaints were not made? I think that the best I can do is to remind us all again that the evolutionary story records the way in which the last management steered the Laboratory quite successfully through a

difficult period in its history. And I might add that it also made some important and difficult decisions about the Nuclear Structure Facility – an observation that starts to redraw it in a more heroic shape.

These complaints shaded off into another. This was that outside committees were allowed to dictate Laboratory policy: that both the right *and* the duty of managers to make decisions had been ceded to a committee of outsiders. One senior manager told me:

> Our problem is that ... we had a managing director who was strongly influenced by the big players. This is no longer true. And Giovanni [Alberti, our Director of Science] is a big player in his own right![4]

In heroic stories – and even in some versions of evolutionary history – committees are said to be a doubtful asset. They meet infrequently. They are paralysed by inadequate information and an avalanche of paperwork. Usually, or so it is said, only the chairperson really understands what is going on. Furthermore, they are hamstrung by the need to strike political bargains. All of which means that, on this account, strategic decisionmaking is difficult, and conservative incrementalism predominates. Freddy Saxon echoes the views of many:

> [Our committees] I see as being a microcosm of the SERC. They are always trying to do one project too many for the money available. They have always found it difficult to take the hard decision, and decide which three out of four they will do. ... Any new *good* proposal is supported.

And they are cautious too. Dr Jim Haslehurst, Deputy Director of the Laboratory and Head of the SR Accelerator Division feelingly observed: 'Our committees won't fund *anything* risky.'

So the heroic diagnosis is this: rule by committee combined with limits to resources is a recipe for disaster. In the middle 1980s the Laboratory was doing too much and it was doing it badly. But neither was it playing the commercial games demanded by the new Conservative science policy properly.

Perhaps everyone who has ever sat on a committee feels this way. I know that I do. So I'm tempted to say that committees are *not* all bad. And I think this is true, in part because I don't want to accept heroic ordering in its awful purity. But let me take a different tack and say instead that *these accounts trade on an opposition between agency and structure*. Here's the opposition as I see it. On the one hand there are agents. That is to say, there are good agents – people – who move, and shake, and get things done. And then, to be sure, there are also inferior agents. These are passive − 'supine' was a word I sometimes heard used. Such are people who have ceded their agency to the structures around them. Perhaps they react 'automatically' to signals coming from that structure.[5]

This is an opposition that pervades western thought: the myth of creativity and autonomy set up against the myth of structure. Are criminals, or animals, or companies 'responsible' for their actions? May they be taken to court? It is the same opposition. And we find it in philosophy and in science (heroic Einsteins) as well as social thought: are social classes, or computers, or viruses active agents in their own right? Or are they acted upon?

We tend to want sharp divisions. And we tend to want the security of knowing that they are set in concrete. Supine committees, or inert machines, are opposed to creative, language-using people! But the divisions are neither so sharp, nor so stable. That is my hope: that we start to recognize, ironically, that there is ordering rather than order.

The story is that *proper* managers pit themselves against the inertia of committees, and in the 1980s they failed to do this. But the inertia of structure also comes in other guises too − for instance in technological form. Dr Philip Smith, a younger scientist in the SR Division, told me that the Laboratory had been: 'not sufficiently [science driven] in the past'; and he added 'we've been driven by expensive pieces of equipment in the past'. This view − that technology has stifled creative science − was widespread. Here's a committee exchange between Patrick Snowden, Head of Engineering, Dr Steven Nicholson, Head of Electronics and Computing, and Giovanni Alberti:

Patrick Snowden: In astronomy there are these things called tombstones. The idea is that people give money for something like a telescope which is the focal point. The problem is that it is the *machine* which drives the organization.

Giovanni Alberti: That is the problem. We are *not* a science driven organization.

Steven Nicholson: That is the nature of Big Science.

Patrick Snowden: The machine is also seen as a security.

So in the heroic stories it isn't denied that scientists *need* technology. It is a vital tool in the hands of creative agents. But it should not be allowed to slip into the driving seat. This is Giovanni Alberti again:

As you know, I think there are two ways of doing science. The first is to build instruments to show in many different ways the truth of Bragg's Law. [Laughter] The other way is to do work on scientific problems. At the Laboratory we have always made the mistake of regarding instruments as a black box. If you do this then you are doing instrumentology. And if you do science without understanding instruments, then you are doing scientology.

Freddy Saxon sums up the contrast, and with it the heroic account of Daresbury's problems in the 1980s:

> We talk about the science, but so much is *actually* driven by technology. Head Office has [invested] in its labs by building machines. This is an accelerator lab for most of the people who work here. The biggest division in the lab is engineering, and the second is computing .... There has not been much *scientific* vision, and I don't know whether there is now. Vision implies a vision of the future. Where we go .... [But] the biggest things are totally dominated by machines.

Thus in the heroic view the machine and its expensive experimental stations, necessary though they are as scientific tools, are said to be a mixed blessing. They tend to introduce a stodgy inertia – a weight that holds back the imaginative and open pursuit of science.

> Here again the histories of Daresbury, its local ordering stories, resonate with those that circulate in other places. Are we passive tools of technology? Have we let technology master us? Are technics, as they say, out of control? Or is it the other way round? Are the machines the tools? Are we, the humans, really the masters? So many of the debates about the character of technology turn around this polarity – a negotiation of the division between structure and agency.[6]
>
> But perhaps the terms of the debate are wrong? Note what is happening. A structure–agency division, this time articulated as a machine–agency dualism, is the *effect* of such talk. Like the distinction between the macro-social and the micro-social, talk of this kind serves to generate a qualitative difference, rather than some sort of gradient. Perhaps sociologists should be refusing both the asymmetry,[7] and the tussle between the two forms of reductionism.

The heroic stories tell that Daresbury had come to a pretty pass: passive instead of active, buffeted by outside forces rather than shaping its own scientific destiny. Of course, no management could hope to solve *all* these problems. But here is the diagnosis: if the Laboratory was to emerge from its supposed decline, management needed both to seize the scientific mettle and to play the games of science-politics with verve and gusto. It needed, that is, to regain its lost agency.

Again it seems to me that in my account it is the heroic story that has gained the upper hand. This is not fair for I doubt very much whether management could have successfully operated for nearly a decade simply by pushing paper around. I repeat: the stories tell that the Laboratory chalked up some notable successes during the early and middle 1980s, that good science was done, many SR experimental points were built, and the SR Source achieved an enviable reputation for reliability.

That is the substantive point. But I also want to repeat the methodological point: heroism makes for good copy; gradualism or evolutionism do not. It's like trying to compare the headlines of the tabloid press with the details of appointments tucked away in the *London Gazette*. It seems to be easier to get a grasp of the personalized doings of heroes and villains than it is to poke through endlessly ramifying complexity. Simplicity is valued. And *personally* reductionist causes, origins and explanations are comforting. Order is appreciated. Other orders are interpretable as disorder, or as stodge. Furthermore, many agents (male agents?) *like* agents: they like to think that they too are autonomous and creative.

4 AGENCY REGAINED: THE STORY OF COWBOY-HEROISM

Heroism tends to dualism, to the contrast of mutually exclusive but mutually dependent opposites. In the Laboratory heroic stories tell of periods of (structural) dark which were followed by periods of (creative) light. The most important of these speak of a revolutionary changing of the guard: the appointment of a new Laboratory Director and a new Director of Science for Synchrotron Radiation.

Here my data change. I heard people talk about the new management just as I heard them talk about the old. But I also *watched* the new management at work.

Professor Andrew Goldthorpe, the Laboratory Director is widely seen as personable, energetic, lively, well organized, persuasive and politically astute. Certainly, this is the way I learned to see him. At the same time I was told that he was tough. One or two people told me that, like Mikhael Gorbachev, his nice smile concealed teeth made out of steel.

Yes. I found him frightening too.

On the other hand I also heard stories from people down the hierarchy (for instance from technicians) which told of how he was a decent bloke, someone with whom you could have a pint in the pub, someone who had no side to him.

I intend no offence to Andrew Goldthorpe if I write that we're dealing
with a heroic myth here, the great leader who also has a human touch.
Have we not all seen pictures of dictators patting childen on the head?

But senior managers told rather different stories about him – stories
about his political and organizational skills. And now we get to a key,
perhaps *the* key, *leitmotiv* in my own story-telling. One day when I
was talking to Professor Stuart Fraser, a senior manager in the SR
Division, he said in passing that: Andrew looks like a cowboy, but
he's really a civil servant!' Perhaps this book ought to be dedicated
to Stuart, for the more that I thought about this, and the more I looked
back through my notes, the more it seemed to index something significant about the Lab. Did it make sense to distinguish between
'cowboys' and 'civil servants' as personality types? I think this is
what Stuart was suggesting, and, as I looked round the Laboratory
and thought of the people whom I had met, I could see his point.

But this was not quite right. In practice, heroes, or villains, were
not quite so clear cut. People sometimes talked (or acted) like *both*,
but they did so under different circumstances: their plotting drew
more from the subtleties of a Shakespeare than it did from the
simplicities of the spaghetti western. So this led me to the argument
that I'll make in the next chapter: that a good way of treating the
data, of writing the history of management ordering at Daresbury, is
to say that there are a number of discourses, a number of modes of
ordering, for thinking of, talking about, and acting out agency –
and, of course, structure.

But it also led me to the simpler narrative contrast that I'm working
on now: the notion that there are evolutionary and structural stories
about Laboratory history on the one hand, and romantic and heroic
stories on the other; as well as to the belief that, under many circumstances at least, such stories depend upon one another. Heroism
implies stodge and fudge as well as villainy: these are, as it were, its
Others. Perhaps we could say that it generates these. And, if less
obviously, I also think that evolution similarly requires if not heroism,
then at least creative agency.[8]

But I see now the wisdom of Stuart's remark in another way. For
in the iconography of heroic story-telling there is a problem: how
is the hero, the active and creative agent, to resolve the problem
of the mundane? He is surrounded by stodge and bogged down by
inertia. But he is supposed to be a hero. How is he to cut through
this? Better, how is he to *mobilize* the mundane? The answer is that
a hybrid, the cowboy/civil servant, is one possible model, one way of
connecting agency with structure, of resolving the dualism in favour
of agency.[9]

Here, then, are some stories about Andrew. First, he often used a language of bureaucratic politics.[10] This is an example. He is talking to his senior managers about an intrinsically unimportant matter:

> I would prefer to stay where we are and fight the office, but you have to know when you are beaten.

In this kind of story-telling the manager-hero knows when he is beaten, but he also, by the same token, knows when he might stand a chance of winning. And, for someone in a job like Andrew's, this means that he knows about the bureaucracy not, primarily, as a set of offices, but as a set of *political possibilites*. For instance, stories were told of the way in which he moved outside the Laboratory, visiting SERC Head Office in Swindon, talking to influential players in the game of science-politics, lobbying, preparing the ground for possible initiatives, and trying to work out what might be made to run, and what could not:

> *Freddy Saxon:* Andrew is spending a lot of time away from the lab .... He's an ambassador, visiting Head Office and [other laboratories]. He's making sure he's there when a decision is made that affects the Lab .... Andrew is personable and outgoing. Its in his nature to wave the flag.

Flag-waving is of the essence in this form of story-telling:

> *Andrew Goldthorpe:* There is no gain in giving negative messages. If [the Prime Minister[11]] asks [about problems during her visit to the Laboratory], okay. But if we complain she will say that is Head Office's problem. We have to give the message about how good and positive we are, what good work we are doing. *And*, though the work is good, we are going out energetically and getting resources and customers. The message must be *good*.

So managers do not whinge. To complain, even if a complaint is justified, is unproductive. In fact Andrew is both approachable and likeable − he would be far less effective if he were not. But on the other hand he is not too sympathetic to those who complain about problems which they should be able to cope with themselves. This is signalled in the language, for certain phrases tend to recur in management story-telling. For instance, 'crying on my shoulder' is out. But so too is 'arm-waving' or 'hand-waving' (making grand but ineffectual gestures). And 'motherhood' (making grandiose but empty commitments to shared values) is out too, not because it is bad, but because we all *know* that it is desirable.[12]

The argument, then, is that heroes are active and creative. And they are effective. Indeed, if they are not effective, then they are not really heroes at all. So here's the rhetorical tension of the heroic theory of agency again: activity is required, but activity of the kind demanded by cowboy stories is only possible if (a) there is surrounding structural stodge; and (b) this is mastered and mobilized. So the cloying embrace of structural inertia, of delegating agency to others, is necessary to the plot, but it has constantly to be resisted.

Now here's another theme from the story of the heroic manager. He is also an *opportunist and a matchmaker*. Indeed, the two go together. For instance, during my period at Daresbury there was much discussion about the possibility of acquiring a new SR Accelerator. This was known as DAPS – the Daresbury Advanced Photon Source. Andrew's general approach to this was to try to match (a) what might be done by the Laboratory if it had the resources, with (b) what might be financed by Head Office if a sufficiently persuasive case for it were put together. The object, then, was to create, discover, define and exploit opportunities for this new machine, DAPS.

Chasing after DAPS was an iterative process of ordering. Here is Dr Harold Watson, a middle-level SR manager and scientist talking with Andrew Goldthorpe:

Harold Watson: Who will this stuff go to? What more should I do?

Andrew Goldthorpe: I just don't know yet. We're pulling ourselves up by our own bootstraps. The idea of £300k [for these support facilities] does not fill me with horror .... We need these sorts of things in a lab like ours, even without the [new machine].

. . .

Andrew Goldthorpe: We have to build this up into a paper, as to why we need [the equipment] for the new machine. But I don't yet know what we will do with the report. It will depend on the response we get from Science Board in the autumn. But I don't want to put you to a lot of work, so I suppose we need a paper which says why we need [the new support facility] whether or not we get the [new machine].

This understanding of the character of managerial agency is (perhaps unsurprisingly) almost indistinguishable from the notion of entrepreneurship. It is a process of match-making. It involves creating, assessing, and (where possible) pairing off possibilities from inside and outside the Laboratory.[13] But here, I think, is one of the keys to the stories of cowboy-heroism: they have to do with *effective decisionmaking* and so with *judgement*. Cowboy-heroes have the power to match-make. And they are effective because they have the knack, the luck or the capacity to make good decisions – decisions that will attract resources and keep the show on the road. By contrast, poor managers are supine paper-pushers, so their organizations suffer. They allow their discretionary powers to be usurped – usurped by a bureaucracy, by a set of committees, or by physical plant and machinery. Such, at any rate, was one of the most consistent *leitmotivs* woven into the heroic version of the history of Daresbury.

Note that agency and organization are being described together: the capacity to make decisions is a *necessary* privilege for the manager. Vital to both the health of the organization and effective managerial agency, discretion is told as being jealously guarded, and jealously parcelled out. Professor Peter Baron is one of the senior managers in the SR Division:

Peter Baron: We've agreed in the past month ... that we would address the priorities.

Andrew Goldthorpe: I am much relieved. You are addressing the priorities. You were *already* doing that.

Peter Baron: Okay, but *you* have to take the decisions.

Andrew Goldthorpe: Fine

And elsewhere:

Stuart Fraser: Will you delegate the *decisions*, Giovanni?

Giovanni Alberti: No! [Laughter]

This is the core: the irreducible power to exercise discretion, and to exercise it successfully by gathering data, by clearing the decks of trivia, and by using the information gathered in a strategic manner to secure resources.[14] And, correspondingly, the notion that if there is no cowboy, no effective manager, then things will drift. This is how it was in the stories told about the Laboratory before the arrival of the new director.

> This is the approved cowboy-hero resolution of the structure—agency problem. It is to use structure to facilitate action.
>   Now here's a nice problem. The hero decides. And he makes his decision by exploring and weighing up the consequences. And he explores and weighs up the consequences by gathering data, and valuing it in one way or another. And the more carefully he does this, the more he depends on his information. And the more he depends on his information, the less autonomous his decisionmaking becomes.

We are caught, here, are we not, in a version of Weber's iron cage? Autonomy is displaced by success. And structure out there is replaced not by creative agency, but by structure in the head.

5 AGENCY REGAINED: VISION AND CHARISMA

I've been talking about a heroic changing of the guard. But that story is not yet complete. Now I need to talk about Giovanni Alberti, the new Director of Synchrotron Radiation Research.

Most often, Giovanni features in the stories that circulate at Daresbury as a visionary, a genius, and a charismatic leader. For here we are dealing with another kind of heroic agency. I want to note that I was always very suspicious of charisma, both as a sociologist, and as a citizen. Indeed, I didn't really believe in it at all. It seemed to me to be some kind of residual term. Following Weber (1978: 215), you started off with tradition, you moved to legality and rationality and then, like a *deus ex machina*, you conjured up charisma. I could see why sociology felt that it did not need charisma. We knew better how things worked. We could depend upon our structures.

I began to change when I saw how much difference one person can make. The context was my own institution, Keele University. It was clobbered by a swingeing cut to its government grant in 1981: suddenly we lost about a third of our core funding. We got by, sort of, but in 1985 we got a new Vice-Chancellor. He was — he is — perky and entrepreneurial. And charismatic. And within about two years Keele was buzzing with activity and initiatives. It was growing. Demoralization was a thing of the past, and we all seemed to be working 60 hours a week to build a better future!

Then I started to ask questions about other charismatics: would Britain have regained the Falkland Islands under a different prime minister? Would the USSR have withdrawn from Afghanistan if Gorbachev had not been President? Would my local Choral Society attract so many of us if Ken Sterling were not musical director?

I did not see, then, what I think I see now: that charisma is another manifestation of agency in the great dualist drama of agency versus structure. And I did not see that it is part of the mobilizing ordering of heroism. But at least I saw that charismatics might make a difference.

The stories tell that Giovanni is very, very smart. One manager told me:

The trouble with Giovanni is that he is so smart that you never know whether to take him seriously. You never know whether what he says is something that he *really* thinks, or whether he just made it up on the spur of the moment, and will say the opposite tomorrow.

Here is *my* perception. Giovanni is very, very smart. He is an out-standing scientist. He is a scientific visionary. He is iconoclastic. He is an inspirational teacher. He is fast on his feet. He is witty – wickedly funny with words in English despite the fact that it is not his native language. He is committed to science. He is a workaholic. And he is attractive too. Is there anything to be said *against* him? Yes: he smokes heavily; he plays havoc with day-to-day adminis-tration; his written English requires 'correction'; and he says that he does not suffer fools gladly.

Now I want to raise another methodological problem. For these are the elements of some of the stories they tell about Giovanni. And they are part of my own story too. For perhaps there are those who find his charm resistable, but I am not among them. Which makes me uneasy. Here is the difficulty. How does an ethnographer deal with someone like Giovanni, a charismatic? Surely it cannot be right to write hagiography? On the other hand, neither can it be right to pretend that charisma and charm do not exist.

This worries me almost more than the fact I did not treat with the trades unions and seek out and record labour-process stories. For I know that those who are committed to class analysis will notice this absence, just as feminists will observe that I'm not treating with gender. So I guess that if I write male managerialist stories, then people will complain. And that is fine. But I am less sure that anyone will notice if I write hagiography, so long as I do so in a suitably cautious manner. As I have said, we sociologists have trouble in coming to terms with charisma. Aside from denying its existence – or at any rate its sociological importance – we don't really know what to do with it.

> I think, now, I see a way through this. It is to treat charisma as an ordering pattern, another mode of story-telling, a form of being. Perhaps it does not matter that I am caught up in it too. For we all live in our own stories and act out our own orderings. Perhaps what really matters is that I do not wish it away.

Giovanni first came to Daresbury as a relatively junior scientist. After a time he left, to go to a similar but better-founded laboratory in Europe. But then he came back to become a more senior scientist-manager – the Director of the Biological Support Laboratory. He headed this laboratory successfully, finding funding from a variety of sources including the Medical Research Council, and energetically built a substantial facility – all the while maintaining his own fundamental research. Thus, though it isn't always what people tell first when they talk about Giovanni, it turns out that he is also depicted as a pretty good bureaucratic politician. In particular, he is said to have wheeled and dealed the Biological Support Laboratory to financial and institutional as well as scientific success. Giovanni shares this with Andrew Goldthorpe: that they both play the role of cowboy-heroes in Laboratory mythology.

At this point the tales about scientific lassitude are woven into the story: SERC decided that the SR Division needed *scientific* leadership.

> Why did they do this? Why on earth would the pudding seek out a hero to devour it? There are other heroic stories to be told, stories about the SERC!

So the post of Director of SR Research was created, and Giovanni was appointed to the job. Again, this was partly to do with managing, with 'biting on the bullet', with extracting the Laboratory from its alleged state of scientific drift. Here he is himself:

> When I started two years ago two facts struck me. First, there was a lack of focus and matching between the research pro-gramme and our resources. And second, the Laboratory was not bothered enough about human and technical investment in the future.

So far I have said little about Giovanni Alberti that would not also, in general terms, apply to Andrew Goldthorpe, or indeed any of the other senior managers in the Laboratory. They are heroes.

> They are heroes because the seek to master the inertia of structure by bending that structure, by acting as entrepreneurs.

But now the story starts to become distinctive. For Giovanni tends to affect indifference to mundane organizational matters. Sometimes this indifference is just that, an affectation. For instance Giovanni sat staring out the the window at one important day-long meeting. At a break I commented to him:

John Law: You look pretty bored, having to listen to all this.

Giovanni Alberti: No. You are quite wrong. I look bored whenever there is something *really* important being discussed, something vital to the future of the Lab. It is a ploy. That way I don't give anything away. But I am listening to every word like a hawk!

If this is the extension of bureaucratic politics by other means, then at other times his indifference is real. For instance, one day he read article proofs right through a meeting, and didn't participate at all.

Then afterwards, as people drank coffee, as if to show what was *really* interesting, he passed round the photographs accompanying the article. Andrew Goldthorpe, who had chaired the meeting, laughed:

Huh! *Now* I know what you were doing during the meeting. Remind me to be reading the proofs of one of my articles the next time you come to cry on my shoulder about the size of your budget! (from memory)

Here is a possible moral: Giovanni is telling that creative science can and should be separated from committees and their mundane wheeling and dealing; but Andrew is telling us that it *depends* upon the mundane. Two modes of scientific heroism are being played off against one another: the hero-scientist as worldly entrepreneur; and the hero-scientist as unwordly visionary. In the first of these stories, the hero defeats the inertia of structure by mobilizing it. In the second, he defeats it by ignoring it.

What potent ordering myths these are! They run like threads through western history. What was the character of a Calling: to withdraw from the world into a life of contemplation, and so give oneself up to God? or to act in and upon the world? This was the difference between monastic Catholicism and ascetic Protestantism. To handle distraction from ordering by ignoring it, by assimilating it, or by using it, by mastering it? That is the question.

In the Laboratory story, Giovanni Alberti plays both these roles. He is a bureaucratic politician, a manager-cowboy; but he is also a visionary, a charismatic. And he acts this part, because he talks of science as something apart, set aside from the world. Something that is special, and sacred. Something which drives those who are graced. Something removed from the profane.

You know my attitude. I think [the proposal] is pathetic. It's not to do with science. It's to do with [science-politics].

Perhaps we can talk of this as an example of Mertonian role-conflict.[15] But it is, I think, more interesting to treat it as a way of talking about another tension, a three-sided tug between structure and agency on the one hand, and two forms of heroic agency on the other.

This is charisma in the old sense: to be touched by God. Do we invest those we find attractive with divine qualites? Do they so invest themselves? And what of evil?

6 SUMMARY

In this chapter I've imputed what I take to be a widely reproduced pattern to the networks of the social at Daresbury Laboratory. I've been arguing that one of the ways in which the Laboratory goes about the process of making sense of itself and of its history is to tell stories, stories about heroes. These stories run as follows. Daresbury fell upon hard times and was buffeted by a cruel environment. But, at the same time, there was rudderless drift. And to accept that drift was to be irresponsible. For to accept that environment determines outcome is, in heroic dualism, to embrace fatalism. It is to embrace a passive view of the character of human and organizational nature. And to do this is – I repeat the term – to be irresponsible.

So, as they talk of hard times, and tell about the difference between the large scale and the local, the stories are also moral tales. They tell of the past absence of effective management. They decry that absence. And then they tell of qualitative change, of the arrival of new and effective leaders. The balance between structure and action shifts. Daresbury once more seeks to master its own fate.

I use Michel Callon's terms: the managers are agents, not passive intermediaries. Or Barry Barnes' similar distinction, between powers and authorities.[16]

But what is the character of the new leadership? What is the character of that agency? I believe that there are two ordering forms. First, there is the hero who works in and upon the world. Andrew Goldthorpe is cast in this typifying role as expert bureaucratic politician or entrepreneur. Second, there is the hero who works outside and beyond the world. This is the role cast for Giovanni Alberti. A charismatic driven by other-worldly dreams, he is drawn as the scientific leader, the scientific visionary.

Now here are some of the qualifications.

These are heroic stylizations, drastic simplifications. The stories themselves are documentary imputations which stabilized, to some extent, as I worked at them, but they could certainly be told otherwise. There are other histories to tell of Daresbury Laboratory. And, more specifically, there are many others in the Laboratory who are told of partaking of both grace and politics. And, in any case, the two managers are not 'really' like that. We could talk about them – they talk about themselves – in all sorts of other ways too. These, then, are simplifications, and the imputations can easily be treated as betrayals.

So I apologise if I cause offence. My object is sociological, not to cause offence. And, in any case, the ordering stories are flawed in their very dualism. Decisionmakers do not exercise their powers in a vacuum. Their decisions are the effect of, perhaps determined by, (structurally shaped) data. And neither, at any rate in science, are visionaries able to subsist on a diet of locusts and wild honey.

Histories and stories are ordering resources for working on and making sense of the networks of the social. I believe that versions of the stories that I have identified have helped, in part, to reshape Daresbury. For they are not idle. They shape (and are embodied in) action too. They have changed the actions of the people at Daresbury. But they have also affected the actions of outsiders, those at Head Office who make fateful decisions about Daresbury.

This is why I said, at the beginning of this chapter, that, though I didn't want to say that these ordering modes were simply fictional, I wasn't really clear about the distinction between the stories told, and 'real' history. For 'real' histories are also modes of ordering. But stories, too, tell of real histories, real actions and real people. They are a part of, a way of talking of, some of the ordering patterns in the recursive features of the social.

NOTES

1 This lesson can be drawn from many traditions – for instance from cultural anthropology (Traweek 1988a). An attractive version of it is to be found in the notion of formulation, as developed in ethnomethodology. See, for instance, Wieder (1974).

2 This argument can be teased into two parts. There is the empiricist effect that generates a *particular* 'bedrock of facts'. And there is the assumption, I think closely related to this particular effect, that there is indeed a reality out there which about which incontrovertible factual stories can be told. On the latter, see Garfinkel (1967) and (in a different tradition) Baudrillard (1988b).

3 The division between orality and heroism on the one hand, and writing and evolution on the other, is not as simple as this suggests, if only because heroic histories may be written, and evolutionary stories told. Nevertheless, without wishing to make a technologically reductionist argument, there are good reasons for arguing that story-telling opens up a set of rhetorical possibilities that differ from those opened up by story-writing. For this argument, see Goody (1977); Ong (1988); and Latour (1990).

4 Professor Giovanni Alberti is Director of Synchrotron Radiation Research.

5 I am using Barry Barnes' language here. See Barnes (1986, 1988). Note that Michel Callon (1991) makes essentially the same point.

6 For sensitive discussion of these distinctions, see Winner (1977, 1986).

7 As some of them are. See Akrich (1992); Callon (1991); Haraway (1990); Latour (1992b); Law (1991a); Star (1991); Woolgar (1991).

 8 Here the argument is Wittgensteinian: that proper rule-following is a creative
   and interpretive activity. See Wittgenstein (1953, pt II, xi, 1967) and Winch
   (1958), and their numerous applications, as, for instance, in Wieder (1974).
 9 I say 'he' here because I agree with Sharon Traweek (1988a): these are myths
   of scientific mastery, versions of male ordering.
10 Though the term 'bureaucratic politics' has wide currency, I draw it in
   particular from the literature of political science. See, for instance, Sapolsky
   (1972).
11 Mrs Thatcher, subsequently Baroness Thatcher, was prime minister at the time
   of this study. She is referred to as Mrs Thatcher throughout the text.
12 Note that the iconography of these phases suggests that neither women nor
   children rank as plausible heroes. The passivity of nurturing motherhood is
   confined to the home.
13 At first I played with the metaphor of marriage – the marriage of possibilities
   within the Laboratory with resources from outside. But I am grateful to
   Wendy Faulkner for her suggestion that the metaphor of a dating agency more
   adequately catches the opportunistic and iterative process of moving from
   one possible coupling to the next. With stories of cowboy-heroism, we find
   ourselves closer to the *zweckrational* than the *wertrational* (Weber 1978: 24–26).
   And we also echo one of the characteristic findings of the recent sociology
   of economics and technology – that markets are the effect of an active
   process of building and inter-relating supply and demand. For a superb
   empirical study see Garcia (1986); and also Callon (1986b, 1991).
14 The notion that power amounts to discretion is one possible definition of
   the term. It is, however, only one of a number of possibilities. See Barnes
   (1988) and in particular, Law (1991b).
15 See Merton (1957); for an interesting recent discussion of similar questions,
   in the functionalist tradition, see Hackett (1990).
16 See Callon (1991: 134) and Barnes (1986: 182).

4

Irony, Contingency and the Mode of Ordering

1 INTRODUCTION

In the last chapter I quoted Stuart Fraser: 'Andrew', he said, 'looks like a cowboy, but he's really a civil servant.' Or did he put it the other way round? Thinking back, I'm no longer quite so sure. But in this case, at least, it doesn't really matter. For, as I mentioned, I went away with the contrast between civil servants and cowboys ringing in my ears. It seemed to make sense: though the detail was complicated, Andrew Goldthorpe often seemed to assume the mythical mantle of the cowboy by finding ways of cutting through red tape.

So in the way which I explored in chapter 2, Stuart's contrast started to shape the way in which I did my fieldwork. As I walked round the Laboratory, and sat in management meetings, I started to look for talk that appeared to embody, tell, or look like a per-formance of one or other of these categories. And, encouragingly, I found it too:

Ruth Sweeting: The concern is, who clears the revised timetable for the DAPS Steering Committee?

Giovanni Alberti: Andrew Goldthorpe has delayed the report because the Chairman [of Science Board] has said that he should.

Ruth Sweeting: Yes, but Science Board approved the original timetable. You can't change it without Science Board agreement.

This kind of exchange seemed to me to say that those whom Stuart was calling cowboys like to bend the rules. And that, by contrast, civil servants like to follow them. I heard versions of this collision time and time again:

Stuart Fraser: The politics dictates which way we will go. The science case has to fit this. And that has meant *delay* because Andrew Goldthorpe thought the case would fall.

Karen Jones: Do you consider that to be good management?

Stuart Fraser: What, ignoring the time scale, the terms of reference, of the original DAPS study?

Karen Jones: Is this management?

Stuart Fraser: [Reluctantly?] No.

So, though the term itself wasn't so widely used I often heard that 'cowboys' or their equivalents tend to bend civil-service rules. And, as the above suggests, I heard that they bend *scientific* arguments too. The conclusion was that there seemed to be a way of speaking and working which defined itself primarily in terms of the art of the possible.

As I write, I realize that I am making the mistake of personalizing. I can practically hear the management consultants rubbing their hands together. So let me insist that I am *not* in the business of postulating a series of personality types. I'm not saying that there *are* cowboys, and that there *are* civil servants. Rather, I am saying that it is possible to impute several *modes of ordering* to the talk and the actions of managers. And I'm saying that people are written into them in varying degree. So this is a sociological and a structuralist argument. I'm saying that agents are effects which are generated by such modes of ordering. The subject has been decentred. Indeed, since there are several ordering modes, I'm going to be able to argue, in good post-structuralist company, that subject is not a unity.[1]

Later I will explore this, and talk about some of the difficulties of imputing such modes of ordering. But before I celebrate those difficulties and try to expose my reasoning, I think that it will help if I first sketch these out as ideal types. So, at the risk of some repetition, I will describe what I'm calling *enterprise* and *administration*. Then I'll talk of *vision*. And finally I'll add a further ordering mode, one which has not yet appeared in this story, which I'm going to call *vocation*.

2 FOUR MODES OF ORDERING

Enterprise

Enterprise generates agents that are sometimes said to be cowboys. But I prefer to speak of 'enterprise', in part because it sounds less like a term of abuse.[2] Indeed, sometimes I've been told that it sounds *too* respectable: shades of Thatcherism and all that. But at least it tugs us away from the psychologism of the personality type.

Enterprise tells stories about agency which celebrate opportunism, pragmatism and performance. Giovanni Alberti: 'I'd sooner take risks and be kicked in the pants and get the job done even if it *is* unorthodox, than not get it done!' So it tells of the way in which agents — heroes *and* organizations — are sensitive to shifting opportunities and demands. It tells of capitalizing on those opportunities. And it tells of deploying resources, of adaptability, and of riding with the punches. So failure is a practical matter — something to be put right by trying again. For there is no such thing as absolute failure. Rather, there are setbacks and strategic withdrawals. So whingeing, as I mentioned earlier, is out. And inquests over things that went wrong are only held in order to learn lessons for the future: recriminations and witch hunts have no place in this syntax.

So the perfect agent is a mini-entrepreneur. She is someone who can take the pieces and pull them together, making pragmatic sense of all its components. She doesn't rejoice in the predicament of post-modern fragmentation and celebrate incoherence. Instead, she is a thoroughgoing modernist. So she takes it that a process of shifting wholeness is both desirable *and* possible so long as she is sufficiently good at seizing her opportunities. As a part of this, she can calculate the possibility and the desirability of different options. She can, for instance, calculate where her interests lie, and then act on the basis of that calculation:[3]

Patrick Snowden: We got into a discussion about scientific politics. David Amery has done very well in building up [his lab]. It was a good idea, and it was timely to go after the money, so he got both the money and a promotion .... Other people said 'What about us?' Giovanni [Alberti's] attitude to that, and I agree with him, is that they've got to get off their backsides and get it for themselves.

So this is an ordering mode about agency, about how people are, or how they should be. But it is necessarily, at the same time, an ordering practice that has to do with structure too. As I've already said, the fragments of structure add up to a set of opportunities, a

set of resources. For if they are not treated as an opportunity, then
the agent is no longer acting responsibly; instead she is in the
process of retreating from the proper performance of agency; she
is undermining her very status *as* an agent. So, like other modes
of ordering, enterprise is a morality tale as well as a description. It
hopes to order, and it distributes blame: distractions tend to become
sites for demolition.

The stories of enterprise tell that people are driven by self-interest.
People are sometimes wrong about what is in their interests. They
may miscalculate. Or, perhaps more seriously, they may make calculations that are correct for them, but incorrect from other points
of view. For instance, it is said that sometimes people, especially
those lodged in large organizations, get too comfortable. Their interests
then lead them to resist changes to the status quo. Preserving their
status and their privileges, they stand in the way of enterprise.
This is the basis of the denunciation of the 'civil servant'.[4] By contrast, good people, proper agents, are active. They marshal resources.
And they get on with the job. So a good scientist, or a good manager
is one who seizes her opportunities and makes the most of these.
And a good organization is one that makes this possible.

> If the mode of ordering sounds like a version of Conservative Party
> politics, or Reaganomics, then this should come as no surprise: classical
> liberal economics draws amply from the reductionist well of calculative
> and unified agents in a competitive world to describe the perfect social
> structure, shaped as it is, by the invisible hand. While civil servants,
> who exist in an imperfect world of rules and red tape are thought to
> be inert.

The enterprise mode of ordering also tells of training. The latter
is a *practical* matter. The issue is, is it *useful*? And it tells of
organization too. A good organization is a set of harnessed opportunities. So the proper mode of organization is one of delegation,
the delegation of responsibility. Lively subordinates are charged with
tasks, given the necessary resources and incentives, and left to get
on with it. And the acid test is performance: a successful organization
is one that performs, performs in the market by selling goods. Or
in terms of some kind of market equivalent, by scoring well on
performance indicators.

> We must take *responsibility* for our actions. We must extract agency
> and initiative from the jaws of the collectivist monster. Enterprise is
> the ordering mode indexed by Burns and Stalker when they talked of
> 'organic' order (see Burns and Stalker 1961). And by Mary Douglas
> when she talked of low-grid/low-group modes of social organization. We
> are in the territory of Big Men. Or of little Big Men (see Douglas 1973).

Administration

Administration looks at first sight as if it is nothing more than a rhetorical foil for heroic versions of agency. For who has a good word to say for the civil servants? Certainly not the cowboy-entrepreneurs. The civil servant is told as the antithesis of the heroic agent. She absorbs like a sponge. She routinizes. She picks over the details. She worries about formalities. She dilutes and diverts. In the stories of the heroes, the bureaucratic wheels grind slow and fine as they wear down the entrepreneur and his works.

But this won't do. Though I found, when I was at Daresbury, that I often wanted to go native in the mode of enterprise, this has to be resisted. 'Civil servants' are not all dead weight. Not at all. So here (and partly, again, because I am trying to avoid psychological typologies) I don't want to talk of 'civil servants'. Instead I'll speak of *administration*. And I'll argue that this a form of story-telling about agents and their relations that is quite other. So my story is that administration is better seen not so much as a whipping boy for heroism, but as a coherent mode of ordering in its own right – one that was explored, at length to be sure, by Max Weber (1978).

Administration tells of and generates the perfectly well-regulated organization. It tells of people, files and (to go beyond Weber) machines which play allotted roles; it tells of hierarchical structures of offices with defined procedures for ordering exchanges between those offices; it tells of organized and rational division of labour; and it tells of management as the art of planning, implementing, maintaining and policing that structure.[5] This is Dr Donald Courtauld, the Safety Officer at Daresbury, telling of the proper relationship between dangerous X-rays and people:

> The Management Team Meeting was saying that a new hardware system was not needed. And Freddy Saxon's people have said what they think is workable. [But] we say that there should be more than one device between them and radiation.

Here there is a contrast between what is taken to be workable (an expression of enterprise?), and what should be done if safety is to be properly achieved. So the story tells of the way in which enterprise[6] may collide with administration.

I have already noted that those who might speak on behalf of administrative ordering are consistently underspoken in their pursuit of undemonstrative excellence. But I've also quoted a couple of instances where administration told of entrepreneurial irregularity. Perhaps administrators are not passive after all.

So people and machines are rule-followers. They subsist in hierarchies, or at any rate in carefully organized and well-regulated networks of roles. Training takes the form of careful induction into duties – though sometimes, of course, the administrators fail. Here's Jim Haslehurst, being jokingly serious about safety regulations: 'I take great exception to things which are built over signs which you can just see, saying "*Do not obstruct*"!'

So good scientists and above all good administrators are careful, meticulous and dutiful. Give or take the machines, this is standard Weberian sociology. Or it is Mary Douglas' category of high grid and high group (see Douglas 1973)? But it is also another mode for defining agency and structure. For the issue is: what does it mean to follow a rule?

Let's not fall into the trap of normative sociology with its automatons and its cultural filling-stations. This is a mad modernist dream of pure order. And by now there are whole industries given over to showing that conformity to rules is indeed creative.[7] So we ought to listen carefully when we hear administrators telling of the innovatory character of proper administration, of the difficult judgments that they have to make – for consistency is a calculative and structurally shaped achievement in its own right (see Becker 1971a).

To be crude about this, in part, the question is: can dull, conforming, people be active agents, or not? Or does creative agency necessarily demand excitement? Heroic stories tell us that civil servants are passive. But a modest sociology is sceptical. Perhaps the issue has to do with the *size* of the dragons that are to be slain, and the extent to which they are visible. Do they have to be large or not? And do they have to be apparent to others? And how, in any case, do you measure them?

Remember Mr Pooter. Didn't he tell of fighting dragons too? And wasn't the mockery possible because his dragons were small and everyday?

So administration tells that we are *all* potential agents. Like the interpretive sociologies, it is not elitist. It does not demand large-scale heroics. It says that no one is a programmable device. It says that learning how to conform is the end product of a long drawn-out process of learning a language, rather than an attribute that can be reduced to an algorithm (see Collins 1975). It tells of generating special agents, agents who will creatively conform.

Does the organization run as it should? Do its parts play their allotted roles? Is everything done according to the book? Have justice and equity been achieved? These are the acid tests in the story-telling of administration: smooth running, legality and rationality. So the good agent is careful and systematic and fair and above suspicion. She is committed to *due process*. Or, perhaps better, is committed to a particular version of due process — for it would not be right to imply that other modes of ordering have no concern with justice or legality. It is rather that they perform these differently.

> To talk of administration is to talk, again, of Weber. And Weber is right. In his characteristically ambivalent manner he depicts administration as a virtue, a virtue that transforms itself into a vice as its superior ordering turns into a widening pool of pure order. I'm not as pessimistic as Weber, or if I'm pessimistic, then this is for different reasons. For I don't think that orderings ever turn into orders though they may commit unspeakable crimes as they try to do so. So I doubt very much whether the iron cage is made of iron. On the other hand, he's right in this: there is a lot to be said for consistency and an overt commitment to the rule of law. So we shouldn't be too negative.

Vision

Administration tells of sustaining due process in the face of the opportunistic irregularity of enterprise. These are two modes of ordering, two ways of drawing the line between agents and structures. But what about charisma? What of the mantle assumed by people like Giovanni Alberti? I want to say that this is a third candidate mode for ordering and being.

Vision tells of charisma and grace, of single-minded necessity, of genius and of transcendence. It tells of separation from the profane, of special and privileged access to ultimate truths. It tells of the way in which visionaries cut themselves off from mundane organizational matters, of the way in which practical matters are either immaterial or actively stand in its way. Both Durkheim *and* Weber have been here, of course. In what I am calling vision, power is drawn *from the other side*, a sacred place that is sacred *because* it is set apart. That is Durkheim.[8] And Weber? 'In its pure form charismatic authority has a character specifically foreign to everyday routine structures.' (Weber 1978: 246). So agency is an effect generated by the *denial* of structure; or better, by the juxtaposition of structure and non-structure.

So where do visionaries come from? In their purest form, the stories tell that they are born, not made. Adolf Hitler, Franklin D. Roosevelt, Mahatma Gandhi, Mother Teresa of Calcutta — these are told as natural charismatics, able to draw on the power of grace just because they are that way, chosen, elect, special:

Giovanni Alberti: [Sceptically] Maybe we can put [these visiting schoolchildren] off science for good, if we do it right!

Jim Haslehurst: [Laughing] Giovanni doesn't believe in training, education, or any of those things. He believes you're *born* a scientist!

But sometimes the stories of vision also told of the way in which visionaries pass through a process of apprenticeship with a series of rites of passage. In this way they are distinguished from the common herd.[9] And they also tell, though haltingly, of the need for support. Locusts and honey are not enough. So in this way of telling, an organization may be spoken and performed as an adjunct to the single-minded pursuit of the vision of the creator. Indeed, until recently the Medical Research Council allocated much of its funds on this principle.

So vision is profoundly elitist. It tells of, it performs, a few – the elect – who are distinguished from the others. They partake of grace. They partake of the agency that can draw on the well of grace. And the rest are deprived of agency. Perhaps it is unsurprising that vision may take the form of racialism. Or other forms of exclusion. Easily perverted into hideous purity, into a *Führerprincip*, it is very dangerous. But it is also very exciting, for it allows the rest to partake of grace too, albeit at one remove. So it is that, as we touch the hem of kings, we are, for a moment, transfigured by the spark of divinity.

Faced with this argument, Leigh Star makes this crucial additional point. She says that we all have visions. The argument is that at times we are *all* touched by grace, and find that the doors of the sacred places are thrown open. I'm mostly persuaded that this is right, for I guess most of us are taken out of ourselves one way or another, by love, or beauty, or fear, or hate. But – this is her point – there is a crucial difference between those of us who are, as it were, routine, and those who are charismatic, those of whom it is said that they are inspired. For mostly *we* don't have the resources of an organization behind us when we seek to draw from wellsprings of grace. So our visions are not public. Rather they are private. Or they are part-time. Or perhaps, if we are particularly unlucky, they are treated as signs of our insanity.

So this is the difference between people like Giovanni Alberti and those who work on the equivalent of the shop floor. The latter are graced only *outside* work, when they go home, on their allotments, in their books, or at their places of worship. But those, like Giovanni Alberti, are graced as visionaries in part because, much more than most, they have harnessed the efforts of others: the taxpayers and followers of this world.

Vocation

Enterprise, administration and vision – under other names these were the three modes of ordering that featured in the histories that I told in the last chapter. But now I want to write about a fourth. For there is also, I think, also an ordering pattern that has to do with that alternative form of (wordly) calling, *vocation*:

James: You learn a lot from the way Ph.D. students tell you things. Having put him on the rails [this student] does not go. You have to bump into him!

Andy: To be a [technician] does not take any initiative. To do *science* does. If a person does research, the research does not get done by having someone [say] 'Measure this, then measure that ....'

James: It is not his job. It is his *vocation*.

The story speaks clearly enough. It is telling of another mode of organizing – it even uses the term 'vocation'. It is telling of the way in which people – here proper scientists – embody expertise and skill. And it is telling of the creative and self-starting way in which expertise is properly linked to practice. So now we are in territory that is not only Weberian but also Kuhnian: the scientific agent is told of, and performed as, a puzzle-solver who seeks solutions that are both creative *and* conservative (see Kuhn 1970; and also Weber 1948).

This mode of ordering tells of science or, more generally, about the proper character of certain kinds of work. It tells of the way in which such work is an expression of embodied skills. Distinctively, it speaks of the importance of the roles that are played in this by the body and the eye, of the tacit knowledge acquired during the course of a professional training which comes to shape both perception and action. And it tells of the need, but also of the difficulty, in incorporating these ways of seeing and doing into the body of the person.[10]

Like the others, this ordering mode defines and performs a version of agency. I think that it shares something with administration, for they both tell of embodied skill. Perhaps the difference lies, in part, in the way in which vocation tells that agency is creative in its capacity to *innovate*, while administration has more to do with the creative character of *consistency*. I'm uncertain. But possibly the *leitmotiv*, here again, is Foucauldian and has to do with the disciplined body and how the disciplined bodies of agents relate to, and yet may be distinguished from, their surroundings. So the story is also of the proper character of the social world and the proper character of training.

Here is Giovanni Alberti telling what I take to be a vocational tale, one which draws a sharp line between itself and administration: 'The standard [training] course is to do with the protocols of the organization ... but it doesn't build beam-lines.' Thus we understand that book-learning is important, but so too is hands-on experience, practice and tacit knowledge. So the story is of the importance of apprenticeship – of working alongside an expert, of watching and of being.[11] In effect, then, it tells of commonality, of social relations, and of the *social* basis of skill. And sometimes, as a part of this, it tells of the importance of the caste-practices of professionalism, while telling that careers are an organizational reflection of the increasingly successful application of ethical expertise.

> Perhaps the vocational mode of ordering works best for independent professionals, but less well in organizations. Mike Savage tells me that this is recognized in class theory where organizational assets are distinguished from credentialled professional assets. But it is also recognized in organizational practice which tends to distinguish between line management and staff functions. And again, it is to be found in the debates of economists and political scientists about the relative ordering merits of markets, hierarchies and networks.[12]

Are we all skilled? Are all of us constituted as vocational agents too? This question is like that posed by Leigh Star about vision. And I think that the answer has in turn to be similar: that we can all tell of ourselves as skilled. We are skilled language users, skilled employees. And somewhere along the line the metaphor of apprenticeship can be made to work for us, even if we do not normally see it in this way. But whether or not we do this – and in particular, whether our claims to skill are recognized by others – these are contingent matters. I'll discuss shop-floor skill in the chapter 6. But here I want to note that the complaint on the shop floor is always that no one recognizes the skills that it takes to do low-status work. So in its organizational and hierarchical manifestations, vocation also tends to perform a class system. Or perhaps better, class systems perform and articulate themselves in part in the stories that tell of vocation.

3 THE STATUS OF THE MODE OF ORDERING

What should we make of these 'modes of ordering'? What is their status? I've made various suggestions above, but now I want to deal with the question formally. So the short and abstract response to these questions is that I think of them as *fairly regular patterns that may be usefully imputed for certain purposes to the recursive networks of the social.* In other words, they are recurring patterns embodied within, witnessed by, generated in and reproduced as part of the ordering of human and non-human relations.

I've deliberately put this very cautiously because I want to head off a number of possible misunderstandings. First, I'm not suggesting that they are imaginary, that they are dreams, or they are misleading ideologies.[13] They are much more than this. On the other hand, neither am I claiming that they represent all the possible patterns to be found in the ordering of the social. There are plenty of other ordering modes, and other forms of patterning – for instance, normal organizational forms. Again, I wouldn't want to claim that these patternings have to divide themselves up in the particular way I'm claiming they did at Daresbury. Divisions between ordering modes could be otherwise.[14] This is an entirely empirical matter. Indeed, since they are embodied and performed, I would *expect* to see both diversity and change. Again, I certainly don't see them as necessary responses to the problem of social ordering. I haven't dreamed them up by axiomatic means,[15] and I don't see them as fulfilling supposed functionalist prerequisites. Indeed, though contexts pattern problems (and problem solutions) the *construction* of those problems and problem solutions is part of what these ordering modes are about. So I take it that the search for functional prerequisites is parochialism dressed up in imperialist clothing.[16] Accordingly, my only assumption is that recursive ordering patterns may indeed be discerned in social networks. I know nothing, in principle, about the nature of those patterns. Instead, I believe them to be contingent.

Again the *representation* of ordering modes (as, for instance, in my story) is not exhaustive. This is because no verbal expression defines the uses to which it is put[17] – a point I have chosen to make by talking of the non-reductive and recursive character of the networks of the social. But there is a connected but more general point. For reasons I have already noted, I want to avoid the reductionism of saying that modes of ordering stand outside their performances. So in my way of speaking, they are patterns or regularities that may be imputed to the particulars that make up the recursive and generative networks of the social. They are nowhere else. They do not *drive* those networks. They aren't outside them. Rather, they are a way of talking of the patterns into which the latter shape themselves.

In addition, I am very cautious about saying that ordering modes 'exist'. This is why the formal statement above is pragmatic: they may be *usefully* imputed to the patterns of the social for certain purposes. So I'm trying not to say that they are (or for that matter are not) there. This is because I'm trying to avoid a correspondence theory of knowledge (for knowledge, it seems to me, is better thought of as a set of tools). And, at the same time, I'm trying to resist one of the great totalizing myths of western modernism, the master-narrative which seeks to convert the mystery and incompleteness of verbs into the nouns of order. Instead, for both epistemological and political reasons, I'm trying to argue that my ordering modes are tools for sensemaking and, just that, ordering – tools that may usefully do certain jobs for certain purposes.

Note that this commitment to pragmatism does not mean that I have to give up looking for what we might agree are good reasons for my imputations. First, it isn't the case that 'anything goes'. Empirically, it's obvious that this is wrong. We do, as a matter of fact, distinguish between fantasy and knowledge. Sometimes, of course, fantasies become realities, or realities fantasies. There's a *gradient* between the two, a gradient to do with ordering, rather than some kind of absolute rupture. But, most of the time we don't find difficulty in distinguishing between them in practice

> I have written, 'We do, as a matter of fact, distinguish between fantasy and knowledge.' But to write of 'a matter of fact' is to use a phrase that poses questions. What does it mean to say that 'as a matter of fact' 'fantasy' isn't workable in the world. Whereas 'knowledge' is?
>
> Perhaps this is a tautology? Or a covert commitment to realism? Possibly. But possibly not. When she read these words Annemarie Mol noted that fantasies may work wonders. And Bob Cooper observed that if we don't have a problem in distinguishing between fantasy and reality then this is probably because we are unreflective much of the time. So it is possible to stress the gradients, the slopes. The possibilities. And the fecund spaces which lie between that which is performed as real, and that which is not.[18]

The second point is ethical or political. As a pragmatist I can't claim that the distinction between force and reason is given in the nature of things. Indeed, unlike some pragmatists I think that knowledge and power are indissolubly linked. But there is nothing to stop me celebrating the importance of trying to distinguish between them. Which, again, is something that we tend to do in practice.[19] So there's nothing to stop me saying that I prefer the use of discussion rather than physical force: to adapt Leigh Star's memorable phrase, pragmatism does not lead to Nazism (Star 1988: 201). On the one hand, we cannot ever hope to achieve an ideal speech situation. On the other hand, I don't have much difficulty in saying that some speech situations are even less ideal than others. Nazi ones,

for instance. And, though this is difficult in practice, in principle I
don't have any difficulty in struggling to distinguish conviction based
on argument from that based on force – to broaden the basis of
our speech and the character of our argument.

What does this mean in practice? First, story-telling always leaves
a series of analytical loose ends and problems. But in a modest
pragmatism it is right to acknowledge that this is the case. I believe
this because I'd like to encourage a practice where we can affirm our
weaknesses as well as our strengths. And I'd like us to do this, not
because I wish to celebrate the process of deconstruction. This is
uninteresting since we all know that such deconstruction is possible.
Rather it is because this is a good way of creating *intellectual tools
that are locally robust on explicit rather than implicit discursive grounds.*
And, of course, exploring the places where they do not work (rather
than covering these up) is one good way of doing this.

This should be fairly uncontroversial: for instance, a lesson of this
kind can be extracted from the early writing of Karl Popper (1959)
with his commitment to falsificationism. But I want to make another
less standard argument. This is that it is useful for you to know why
my claims make sense to me *given the context in which I am located.*
In sociology (and many other academic disciplines) the conventional
definition of appropriate context treats with theory, data and method
– and, to be sure, with the way in which they interact. However,
I want to recommend a context that is a little broader than this.
I want to include a number of questions to do with the personal
and the political. My reason for this unconventional reflexive or
ironic inclusion is that it helps you to determine the useful limits of
my story-telling.

This is the argument. We know that theoretical, empirical and
methodological story-telling is a function of context. Conventionally,
to expose the local provenance of argument is taken either to under-
mine that argument, or it is treated as irrelevant. My position is that
in the abstract we cannot judge whether local provenance is irrelevant
or otherwise to the robustness of the argument. (And if it *is* relevant,
neither can we know whether it increases or decreases robustness.)
So though there are limits to the exploration of provenance and
I do not know where these should be, I would like us to redraw
the conventional boundaries of relevance and irrelevance to include
some matters that are normally excluded.[20]

This, then, is what I do in the remainder of this chapter. I draw
first from the ethnography to illustrate both what I take to be some
strengths *and* weaknesses in the imputation of modes of ordering.
Second, I offer a more personal account of the relationship between

these and context. I *think* that this strengthens my story – it suggests that the four ordering modes do useful work in other contexts – but you may read this differently. And then, in chapter 5, I recontext the mode of order in the three-cornered theoretical space between the pragmatism, contingency and process of symbolic interaction, the similarly contingent, technologically sensitive Machiavellianism of actor-network theory, and the attractive necessities of discourse analysis.

4   More Stories from Ethnography

I don't believe that imputations *have* to be acknowledged by participants before they can be sociologically useful. This is because sociologists work in a different context and have concerns that don't map on to those about whom they seek to write. But it is usually reassuring if the participants agree that the sociologist has caught *something* about the way in which they live. Such, at any rate, is the position of interpretive sociology, and it is one which I share.

So it was interesting that terms like 'cowboys' and 'civil servants' played regular roles in the stories told by managers. Indeed, as I have noted, this was where the terms came from in the first place: they were, as the ethnomethodologists would put it, 'members' terms'. And if my corresponding sociologisms are not members' terms, they are at least closely connected with the vocabularies of the managers.

But what of vision? One day, a number of months after my first conversation with Stuart Fraser I found myself standing at the end of a lunch queue with him. Stuart was talking about the trials and tribulations of the Laboratory:

Stuart Fraser: You've got to understand, John, that the problem with this Lab is that it's been run by civil servants for too long. And its only now that the cowboys are starting to have any kind of influence.

John Law: No, Stuart, its not as simple as that. You've got civil servants and cowboys. But you've got visionaries as well – people with distant scientific visions.

Stuart Fraser: [After a moment's thought] Okay. Yeah. You're right! There's civil servants, and cowboys. And there's visionaries.

Stuart and I were the last in the queue and we had to sit at different tables. But after lunch Giovanni Alberti joined me as we walked to another building:

Giovanni Alberti: In this Lab. There are cowboys, and there are civil servants, and there are visionaries.

John Law: [In alarm] Huh?

Giovanni Alberti: If you want to understand the Lab, what you need to know is that there are three kinds of people: cowboys, and civil servants, and visionaries.

John Law: You mean, you mean, you'd *already* worked that out?

Giovanni Alberti: Sure. It's obvious. It is very simple!

Only later did I realize that I was the butt of the joke – that Stuart had sat next to Giovanni over lunch, and Giovanni in turn was taking the opportunity to ironize the activities of the sociologist. But despite my discomfiture, exchanges such as these gave me some confidence that the ordering modes that I wanted to impute to the networks of management resonated with those being told by people in the laboratory: that the three-way classification pointed to by enterprise, administration and vision seemed to make sense of parts of their activity to many of the managers.

But was a three-way division of the organization of management ordering enough? For a while I thought it was. But you already know that ultimately I concluded that many of the scientist-managers with whom I talked told stories of *professionalism*. They managed within enterprise, administration and the rest, but they *also* worked at science. And their work seemed to me to look like the Kuhnian puzzle-solving that I have already described. So in the end I found that I wanted to add vocation to my list of ordering modes.

Having pressed the managers to agree that there were three terms, an ordering triangle, it was a bit of a let-down, to have to tiptoe into the Lab one day and say 'Well, actually there are four. Its not a triangle. Its a square!' But, though I don't think the idea of a square grabbed them in the same way as the triangle, they didn't actively dissent from the new diagnosis. Of course it is possible that they were just being kind to the visiting ethnographer. Or that they didn't care what I thought, one way or the other.

This, then, was a loose end that wove itself back into the fabric of the ethnography. But it points to another loose end that does not. For I'd moved from two modes of ordering to three, and then to four. But why should I stop at four? Why not five or six or, for that matter, fifteen? It was Leigh Star who put this point to me. In response I said 'Well, its an empirical matter, really.' And she said something like this: 'No, it isn't empirical. It's theoretical.

You tend to see big blocks of things, whereas I tend to see differences and contingencies.' So why would we see different things? That is at least part of the question – one to which I'll come back shortly.

Now here's a second loose end which is connected to the first. Some of the modes of ordering seemed – they still seem – to hang together more satisfactorily than others. Let's concentrate on vision. For, more so than the others, I think that what I'm calling vision is unstable. I touched on this above, when I mentioned that Leigh Star said: 'But we *all* have visions.' She is right, of course. We do all have visions. We may all tell visionary stories about ourselves.

> What is your vision? What is the form of your grace, your sacred special place? Are you in love with the another person, his limbs, her voice? Do the beech trees of the chalk woods speak to you on a summer's day? Do you cry when Wotan kisses Brünnhilde to sleep, and cloaks her with flames? Do you stand in peace and awe, your palms crossed, to receive the flesh and the blood of the risen Christ? Do you sit quietly on the misty bank at dawn waiting for the first fish to rise? Do you watch the match, hoping for that moment of ecstasy, the goal that will win the game? In what shape and form does the transcendental – or the immanent – come to visit you?

So we *all* have our visions. But I think I know one of the reasons that I didn't see this sooner. For having frequent contact with someone like Giovanni Alberti placed an extra burden on the critical part of the ethnography. Instead, it was easy to embrace the ordering mode within which he was located. So I tended to set him and his organizationally certified visions apart from the rest of us.

But here's another ethnographic loose end to do with vision. Does the latter have to be *scientific*? Along the way I've already answered this question: I don't believe that it does. Other visions are possible too. There are visions of the perfectly ordered administration. And visions of vocational puzzle-solving. And visions of perfect enterprise.

> Did the Masters of the Universe at Salomon Brothers habour dreams of the great entrepreneurial coup? I can't really believe that they were in the business simply to make more money!

So the difficulty is this: I've tried to tie up stories to do with commitment to science with something else – stories about immanence and transcendence. And I have a loose end. I can either treat them as a block, as a single unit, which is what I have so far done. Or I can pull them apart, and say that vision is a mode of being that may inform other ordering arrangements. Again, then, it's the problem of imputation: the question is, how big are the blocks, the ordering patterns that tell and perform themselves in the networks? And the answer is that there is no ultimate answer. It depends on what we are trying to do.

Is it a sign of weakness for me to say that I can see virtue in both large and small blocks? I'd like to say: 'No. It isn't a weakness. Perhaps it is (almost) a sign of strength.' For I'm trying to work myself out of a concern with order into a pragmatic concern with ordering. This is a question of morals, of ethics and of politics: I'd like to leave the hideous purity of distraction/destruction behind. It is also theological: to claim to know it all is a claim to omniscience which is a blasphemy. And it is a matter of authorship and the academy too: I really don't believe that I know it all, and I'd like to stop pretending that I do. So it is that my voice, as an author, will fragment.

And how about your voice? I'd like the same modest liberation to come about for you. I'd like us all to work at the pluralism that is needed to listen out for the voices that do not really fit.

5 PERSONAL STORIES FROM POLITICS

Ethnography is one kind of story, but it intertwines with stories about personal processes of provenance. This is where I want to redraw the boundaries between provenance and argument a little. So let me say that there are moments when the demands of work all seem too much. I grub away at my ethnography, puzzling at the material that I gather. That's hard and its tiring too, but it seems to be okay. And I teach students. This has its ups and downs, but it's okay as well. But then I play, or I'm supposed to play, the perky games of entrepreneurship. So I look, or try to look, bright-eyed and bushy-tailed. And I write grant applications. And I try to look enthusiastic as the student numbers increase, and staff–student ratios decline. And as I attend the committee meetings. And as the paper-work floods across my desk.

Perhaps it is the paperwork that is the *coup de grâce*. Ten, or fifteen, or twenty times a year, I'm asked to describe what I do, 'in three paragraphs or less'. Or to fill in some questionnaire about my research, or my teaching so that someone can appraise it and can determine whether I am up to scratch or not. Or to tick the spaces in a form that will be fed into 'an EC-wide computer data-base'. Or to present the activities of my department or my research centre in an appropriately euphoric mode.

I find this hard, even leaving aside the other parts of my life, and the gendered costs that are borne by my partner as I let, as I want to let, all this activity occupy more and more space. I get tired, and I get bad

tempered. But I'm lucky, for I know of others in a similar position who
are ill, whose marriages have broken down. I speak personally: something
is going wrong.
    This is whingeing. It cannot belong to entrepreneurship. This belongs
to another mode of talking.

I tell stories about paperwork in chapter 7. Let's just mention
some of the presenting symptoms here. The teachers have this thing
called SATs: Standard Attainment Tests. They do tests on all the
children. The first year these tests took *weeks*. I watched as the
teachers wrung their hands: 'How can I do the tests? How can I fill
in the forms, *and* hope to teach the children anything at the same
time?' But they had no choice. They had to report on the children.
And report on themselves too. The paperwork is a symptom of a
lack of trust: the idea that they will not teach responsibly unless
they are also accountable.

They get tired, and they get bad tempered. I know of teachers who
are ill, whose marriages have broken down. When they speak personally
they say that something is going wrong.

I think this is the dynamic of the paperwork: scientists, teachers,
academics, doctors, nurses, we are 'responsible'. We are supposed
to *perform*. But we are not thought to be responsible enough to
perform without performance indicators. So someone looks over our
shoulders to see how well we are performing. And that allows them
to compare us, to see how well we are doing. It allows them to tell
how we rank as agents, on a scale. And it seeks to generate the
hideous purity of the sovereign consumer.

My Head of Department sends round a leaflet which says 'Academic
Audit is Coming!' More reporting. More checking. More comparing.
More ranking. Which is not to say, of course, that we did what we
should have been doing in the 'good old days'. There were never any
'good old days' except in the stories of the privileged. And the ordering
stories were self-serving then too.

So this is why the stories retold by the managers at Daresbury
Laboratory make sense for me personally. Though I didn't go to the
Laboratory *expecting* to find them, the patterns that they form, and
in particular the collisions that they generate, resonate with the
pattern of the demands and the stresses that I experience in my
own life. For the professional part of me – the ethnographer, the
writer, the teacher – is under pressure to create performances and
offer justifications. I feel that what I have learned to call enterprise
is pressing on vocation; that enterprise does not really *understand*
profession; and worse, that it mistrusts it too. But here's the rub:

in our brave new world, profession *depends* on enterprise: if there are no grants, then research is pressed ever thinner.

> 'Why are you crying on my shoulder? Unless *someone* has the guts to get the resources together, to make sure we are competitive, there will be no universities left.'
> This is right. Truly, there is much to be said for enterprise. And, as I write about the Laboratory, I am trying to make that case. We *depend* on our Andrew Goldthorpes. So I am making a political point. (But so, too, are you.)

We can debate whether the brisk Conservatism of Mrs Thatcher should be taken at face value and treated as a revolution.[21] Nevertheless, its commitment to the values of the market, to enterprise, and to performance throughout education and research has run deep in the places that I know best – in the political economy of the universities, science facilities such as Daresbury, and the personal lives of many scientists and academics. So this is the relevance of this personal story: *it isn't only personal*. It indexes a place where, in the words of C. Wright Mills, 'the personal troubles of milieu' join up to 'the public issues of social structure' (Mills 1959). Like the managers at SRR (Synchrotron Radiation Research) Daresbury, I am an effect too, a troubled boundary object generated by the grinding together of a series of structuring patterns.[22]

So this is the importance of provenance. Now you know a little bit about it you have a choice. On the one hand you can say, well, though he may not have *meant* to do this, he simply discovered what he already believed so we're in the presence of self-fulfilling prophecy. Or on the other hand you can say, well, his modes of ordering make sense of his own world for him, but they also make sense of events in a large laboratory. That's interesting. We're learning something. This is a tool that might do work in other contexts too.

NOTES

1 There is a huge literature on agency and the formation of the decentred subject. As examples of contrasting approaches to this, consider Poster (1990) and Rorty (1989).
2 The way in which I wish to use the term is closely related to the way in which it is used by Keat (1991).
3 I am not, to be sure, recommending a reductionist theory of interests. For comment on the imputation of interests see Callon and Law (1982) and Hindess (1982).
4 For discussion of the term 'denunciation' in an analysis similar in some ways to this, see Boltanski and Thévenot (1987).
5 Burns' and Stalker's (1961) notion of 'mechanistic' management structure indexes a similar mode of ordering.

6 Or it may, perhaps, be vocation. See below, pp. 81–82.
7 This industry grows out of the later writing of Wittgenstein (1953). But also out of the pragmatism of symbolic interactionism (Blumer 1969a; Rorty 1989). For a review of the debates in interpretive sociology see Wilson (1971).
8 See Durkheim (1915).
9 Sharon Traweek (1988a) tells of this process and the vision that informs it.
10 There is a substantial literature in the sociology of science which explores the creative character of the acquisition of skills, usually within a Wittgensteinian framework. See, for instance Collins (1985).
11 This is again like Kuhn, but see also Polanyi (1958).
12 For an introduction to these debates see Thompson et al. (1991).
13 So the notion has more in common with Jean-François Lyotard's 'narratives' (1984) and in particular his 'little narratives', than it does with the myths of Claude Lévi-Strauss, or the simplificatory ordering schemes mentioned by such writers as David Harvey (1990).
14 I do, however, believe that these particular modes of ordering are found in other contexts, which is why it is interesting to try to characterize them. In addition, I think that there are theoretical reasons why established patterns tend to reproduce themselves if everything else is equal. This is Laurent Thévenot's (1984) point when he speaks of 'investments in form'. But analogous arguments are to be found in a wide range of other literatures: in writing on organizational isomorphism (reviewed by Clegg (1989) in his discussion of organizational outflanking); in Barnes' (1988) reformulation of the social as a cognitive order; in Callon's (1991) analysis of 'punctualisation'; in Douglas and Isherwood's (1979) approach to the scale and scope of meanings; and in Giddens' (1991) writing on 'lifestyle'.
15 In this respect they differ from the 'cités' of Boltanski and Thévenot (1987)
16 This approach is most associated with the writing of Talcott Parsons (1951).
17 This claim can be seen as a version of the Wittgensteinian notion of the relationship between rules and the way in which they are enacted (Wittgenstein 1953, 1967).
18 This perhaps, is Jean Baudrillard's point when he talks of the 'hyperreal'. See Baudrillard (1988b).
19 Correspondence theorists distinguish between reasons that are good and those that are bad, and assume that force undermines good reasoning and so the relationship between representation and represented. The search for rules of good reason, or for social regulations that will underpin and support those rules, unites such otherwise diverse writers as Robert Merton (1957), Karl Popper (1959), Louis Althusser (1971a) and Jürgen Habermas (1972). For the pragmatist, the distinction between reason and force is not given in the nature of things. Rather, it takes the form of a set of ethical and moral commitments that have to do with practice. Note that this is *not* a way of saying that anything goes, either epistemologically or morally (Star 1988; Rorty 1991; Law 1991a). I *believe* that it is better to live in a society which seeks to distinguish between reason and force. I *believe* that a pluralist society in which orders do not seek hegemony, one in which they seek to avoid totalizing claims, is one in which what I think of as reason and force can most easily be disentangled. So my preferred idea of the search for the truth takes the form of a local, reflexive, instrumentalism – which means that I

actually end up disagreeing with the general character of the stipulations of the above writers. But it is still, of course, incumbent upon me to offer reasons for what I believe.

20 Here my story is differs from those of both Richard Rorty (1989) and Barry Barnes (1977). Both these are pragmatists, who drive a distinction between private and public. Rorty's argument is political. For him the creative irony of poetry (though a good in itself) is politically irrelevant since it does not lead to a pluralist society. He catches this point when he observes, memorably, that: 'Michel Foucault is an ironist who is unwilling to be a liberal, whereas Jürgen Habermas is a liberal who is unwilling to be an ironist' (Rorty 1989: 61). Irony, then, is a private matter, to be distinguished from public argument where we should press the utility of our knowledge in the standard, publicly sanctioned, theoretical, methodological and empirical ways (while, to be sure, accepting its contingency). Barnes (1977) and Bloor (1976) somewhat similarly distinguish between (theoretical, empirical and methodological) 'reasons' for an argument, and private 'causes' for belief, and note that bad causes may lead to reasonable knowledge. Accordingly, the provenance of knowledge has no bearing on its value.

My story is different: I'm suggesting that ironizing provenance may be an important part of the process (it will always be a *process*) of generating least worst speech situations.

21 See, for instance, Keat and Abercrombie (1991).

22 For the notion of boundary object, see Star and Griesemer (1989).

5

Contingency, Materialism and Discourse

1 INTRODUCTION

So we get to theory. The problem that I have is this. If everything about the networks of the social (including our own knowledge of them) is contingent, then what kinds of patterns can we look for? What kinds of strategies for *imputing* patterns should we adopt? And how can we make sure that we do not tip ourselves over the edge into necessity?

In this chapter I explore these issues in four parts. First, I clear some ground by touching briefly on the question of contingency and necessity in social theory. Second, I extend this ground-clearing exercise by characterizing and commenting on symbolic interactionism. I wouldn't call myself a 'symbolic interactionist', in part because I'm drawing on a variety of theoretical resources, and in part because I believe that such declarations of allegiance have the disastrous effect of stereotyping and foreclosing debate. On the other hand, though it isn't very fashionable to say this, I *do* believe that symbolic interactionism has laid out a conceptual space that should be occupied by *any* pragmatic sociology. As a part of this I touch on certain difficulties in the writing of George Herbert Mead – difficulties which grow out of Mead's commitment to an optimistic version of liberalism.[1] So my argument (though here I am simply following a number of recent interactionists) is that the optimism needs to be ditched. Once this is done, symbolic interactionism turns itself into a fruitful inquiry into the inequalities of social ordering: into an inquiry about how work and effort is made invisible and deleted by those who are thereby able to profit from it.

In this respect it is close to another sociology, that of actor-network theory. In the third section I explore and comment on the latter. Like symbolic interactionism, actor-network theory is concerned with the symmetrical analysis of ordering, deletion and profit. Its focus is the methods by which the large and the powerful come to be large and powerful. However, it is particularly concerned with materials. The argument is that the networks of the social come in a variety of material forms: for instance, people, texts, machines, architectures. But (here is the symmetry) these materials are not given in nature, but are more or less precarious ordering effects which express themselves in different ways, including that of durability. The argument is that the large and the powerful are able to delete the work of others in part because they are able, for a time, to freeze the networks of the social.

So a pragmatic sociology concerned with ordering and inequalities will attend to materials: we could say that it will be *relationally materialist*. But what can we say about ordering strategies? I've made it clear that I think these are contingent but not idiosyncratic. The notion of the mode of ordering is an attempt to find a way of imputing quite general patterning strategies to the materially hetero-geneous networks of the social. I address the theoretical context of the mode of order in the fourth section by commenting critically upon and drawing on post-structuralist discourse analysis, and in particular the later writing of Michel Foucault. From the point of view of a modest and contingent sociology Foucault's writing poses a series of problems. He is committed to a powerful and ironic form of non-reductionist ordering recursion. That is what discourse is all about. On the other hand, the legacy of synchronic linguistics means that there is relatively little about *process* in his work. Foucault comes close to refusing history. This is, to be sure, a well-worn observation. But what should we do about it?

My proposal is that we take the notion of discourse and cut it down to size. This means: first, we should treat it as a set of patterns that might be imputed to the networks of the social; second, we should look for discourses in the plural, not discourse in the singular; third, we should treat discourses as order*ing* attempts, not orders; fourth, we should explore how they are performed, embodied and told in different materials; and fifth, we should consider the ways in which they interact, change, or indeed face extinction.

This, then, is a way of handling the notion of discourse within a pragmatic and relationally materialist sociology. But what has such a sociology actually carried over from Foucault? My answer is that it has imported a powerful tool for imputing putative *modes of ordering* to the networks of the social. Thus, bending Foucault, I want to say that *the networks of the social carry and instantiate a series of intentional but non-subjective reflexive strategies of social ordering*. They are, in other words, identifiable *strategies of modernity*. They are variable. They are incomplete. They come and they go. They are certainly not exhaustive. And they are, of course, defeasible imputations. On the other hand, they are contingent but coherent reflexive and self-reflexive patterns that may be imputed to the networks of the social, patterns that generate effects to do with distribution, deletion, perception and accounting.

I may, of course, be wrong. Perhaps contingencies don't work out that way. This is partly an empirical matter. On the other hand, my hunch is that such modes of ordering – which will allow us to move between actors and contexts and obtain a powerful handle on inequality and issues that are normally considered to be macro-social – can, indeed, be successfully imputed to many of the modern networks of the social.

2   CONTINGENCY AND NECESSITY

Let me start this way. Right through modern social theory I see a tug of war between contingency and necessity.[2] The root of the argument is simple. Contingency says that things are the way they are for rather local reasons. The argument is that local arrangements reflect local circumstances. And this means that we can't say anything very ambitious or general about how or why they turned out the way that they did. By contrast, necessity says that things were pre-ordained for general and possibly determinable reasons to work out that way: that they were shaped by large-scale, long-range factors of one kind or another. So necessity suggests that it is our job, the job of social analysts, to sort out as best we can what those forces are.

A modest and pragmatic sociology tends to pull in the direction of contingency. It tends *not* to want to say that God, or the scientific method, or human nature, or the functional needs of society, or the economic relations of production, determine how things turn out in general.[3] And if this pragmatism is linked to a commitment to recursion – to the idea that events are self-organizing in character – then the tug from necessity is even greater. The assumption is that the search for distant causes is, indeed, a lost cause.

In a modest and recursive sociology this is the place to start. It is certainly where I wish to start. But it is not necessarily the place to stop. For, interpreted narrowly, it could be (and indeed *is* sometimes) treated as an invitation to celebrate idiosyncracy. No doubt such a celebration has its place. But as a mode of social inquiry, this doesn't follow at all. For to talk of contingency is not to give up the search for pattern, but to assume that patterns only go so far. It is also, of course, to be aware of their defeasibility. In other words, it is to be committed to an order*ing* inquiry into order*ing*, rather than to an ordered inquiry which uncovers other root orders. But it doesn't stop us trying to impute patterns across a range of circumstances.

The conclusion is that commitment to contingency doesn't stand in the way of a search for powerful ordering patterns. Or, to put it a little differently, *theoretical modesty is not incompatible with theoretical boldness.* The two, modesty and boldness, are different in kind. Which means, to introduce a note from the philosophy of science, that a modest sociology is not committed to some version of the inductive method in which it builds up its patterns from particular cases. It might, following Karl Popper (1959) conjecture patterns and then seek to refute them. Or it might (and I think this is most consistent with a reflexive understanding of the *process* of social inquiry) treat data, theory and method as all going together in some self-testing, self-exploring, but suitably modest form of inquiry.[4]

3 LIBERALISM, OPTIMISM AND DELETION

There are several important sociologies that rest on a commitment to recursive historical contingency.[5] For instance, symbolic interactionism is a process sociology built around a social theory of mind, a thoroughgoing commitment to the contingent character of social (and mental) outcomes, and a pragmatic theory of knowledge. Indeed, its development is very closely associated with that of philosophical pragmatism. Interactionists say that agents or, as they tend to put it, selves, are constituted in social relations. And they go on to say that agents negotiate their way though social relations, constituting and reconstituting these as they go in a process akin to negotiation. So, though it does this without any great theoretical fuss, the approach washes away the agency–structure dualism that has plagued so many sociologies. And, as a part of this, it doesn't look for root orders, either in the head, or in the 'larger' social structure. Instead, (though it does not normally use this language) it hunts for recursive patterns that work indifferently through the media of people and their social relations. So mind is an outcome, or a moment in a process. But so, too, is society.

Symbolic interaction is an old, primarily American, tradition. When you read it you aren't usually treated to theoretical fireworks.[6] But this, as Paul Rock indicates, is no coincidence. This is because it is a modest, pragmatic form of *craft* sociology whose centre of gravity lies in its empirical studies, and in the imputation of patterns to the material generated in those studies.[7] These are patterns which might, for instance, have to do with personal trajectories or careers, with processes of labelling, with bundles of practices that hang together and so form a contingent social world, to the reproduction of institutional 'going concerns', to the character of marginal experience, to the difficulties of managing the intersection between different social worlds, or to the deletion of low-status 'invisible' work.

Symbolic interactionism is a minority sociology: to put it plainly, at least in Europe it is unfashionable. I believe that there are some good reasons for this, but also some bad reasons. One reason is wholly regrettable: the fact that it fell victim to the hegemonic expansion of normative functionalism, the immodest sociology of order that came close to sterilizing American social thought in the 1950s and the 1960s. However, the story of European neglect is rather different. European social thought has wrestled with problems of inequality, and in particular, class inequality. It isn't always obvious to Europeans that symbolic interactionism does this too. This is because it goes about it differently. It doesn't *start* with a metaphysical credo, a set of assumptions about the character of inequality. Instead, symmetrically, it treats the latter as an outcome. I think that it is the absence of a credo that has turned many Europeans off.[8]

This, then, is a part of the reason for European neglect: an unwillingness by interactionism to adopt metaphysical stances on the character of root social order. But in defence of the Europeans, this isn't *quite* right. There is something else: the fact that symbolic interactionism has been seen as the the sociological expression of an optimistic liberalism. Thus there is an assumption, explicit in the writing of George Herbert Mead (1934), and not always denied elsewhere, that if reasonable people sit down and discuss their differences, they will be able to find a solution which suits them all. So the paradigm for interaction is negotiation – negotiation between agents in an approximation to a Habermasian ideal speech situation. And there is an assumption that liberal democracy generates ideal speech situations, or something like them. It may not be a good system but, to paraphrase Richard Rorty, paraphrasing Winston Churchill, it is the least worst political system that we've got. This, then, is an assumption about root order which sticks (in my view rightly) in the European craw.[9]

Mead was a man of his times. What European social theory doesn't notice is that symbolic interactionism has moved on. I mentioned above that interactionists write, *inter alia*, about the way in which low-status work is deleted by those of higher status. I could have added that there is symbolic interactionist work in the sociology of knowledge which points to the way in which we tend to believe those at the top of the heap rather than those at the bottom.[10] And there is also a large body of work, sometimes influenced by radical feminism, which explores the inequalities in the conditions under which negotiations take place – as, for example, in the labelling of agents as deviants, or the awkward places between conflicting demands which may generate pain and powerlessness.

I'm saying, then, that the optimism disappeared from symbolic interactionism some time ago. I don't know whether it has been replaced by pessimism, but the commitment to liberalism has certainly been enlarged. It's important to note that liberalism doesn't have much to do with free-market economics. I'm using it in the American political sense. Thus Richard Rorty, following Judith Shklar, tells that 'liberals are the people who think that cruelty is the worst thing we do' (Rorty 1989: xv). I don't have much problem with that – except, perhaps, that asymmetrically, it limits itself to people. But neither does the symbolic interactionist. For here is the difference between optimism and pessimism. The *optimistic* liberal thinks that though we need to tinker with our political arrangements, we already know pretty well both what it is to be cruel, and who it is that should count as a person. But the *pessimistic* liberal knows that we are always finding out that we have been cruel in ways we never thought about before. And she sees no reason to doubt that the same will happen again.

This isn't news. Indeed, it is central to the radical European critique of social inequality. For instance, it lies behind Karl Marx's inspired critical analysis of the supposed freedom of the proletariat in the capitalist labour market. But it also underpins feminist writing on the character of gendering. Or the arguments of the animal rights activitists. Or the green critique of industrial society. Or, indeed, the arguments between children, philosophers, and sociologists about the character of machines.[11] But it also lies behind symbolic interactionism where much writing is about the endless struggles about whom or what may speak on behalf of whom or what; about when who may say about whom: 'You are being cruel'. So, though she might agree that some social arrangement (possibly even liberal democracy) is the least worst system that we've got, the symbolic interactionist tries to listen out for the mystery of different voices. And she tries to avoid getting too comfortable and smug about the way things happen to be.[12]

I don't want to 'convert' people to symbolic interactionism. Indeed, as I noted above, I don't think the imagery of adherence to a faith is helpful. Such is the road to the hideous purity of the jihad. On the other hand I do believe that symbolic interaction long ago shed much of its comfortable white, male, middle-class commitment to an optimistic version of liberalism. Instead it has looked to the places where there is no particular reason to be optimistic. It has tried to explore why many find themselves in contexts which do not even begin to approximate to an ideal speech situation. And it has sought, modestly but persistently, to ask awkward questions about particular cruelties. This, then, is why I believe that symbolic interactionism has so much to offer: it has helped to create the space for a modest but liberal sociology of contingency.

4 AGENCY, DELETION AND RELATIONAL MATERIALISM

Actor-network theory is another recursive sociology of process. In some ways it is remarkably like symbolic interaction. But it is symbolic interaction with an added dash of Machiavellian political theory, a portion of (suitably diluted) discourse analysis, and a commitment to the project of understanding the *material* character of the networks of the social.[13] So what does actor-network theory say?

First, it says that agents may be treated as relational effects. You can derive this finding from structuralism and post-structuralism, just as you can from symbolic interaction's social theory of self. But actor-network writers tend to fall (though they often say otherwise) on the symbolic interactionist side of the divide. This is because, like the symbolic interactionists, they like to tell *stories* and trace *histories* rather than tending to take synchronic snapshots.

Second, however, it says that agents are not unified effects. There isn't too much Enlightenment optimism here. Instead there is the scepticism of high modernism. Agents are an effect, an effect of more or less unsuccessful ordering struggles. Perhaps the stories told by actor-network writers tend towards the heroic — that, at any rate, is one of my anxieties about the approach (see Law 1991a). But in its interest in fragmentation and the decentring of the subject, actor-network writers draw on post-structuralism. Indeed, many of their stories tell how it is that agents more or less, and for a period only, manage to constitute themselves. Agency, if it is anything, is a precarious achievement.

Third, it treats the social world as a set of more or less related bits and pieces. There is no social order. Rather, there are endless attempts at ordering. Indeed, this is where I have gone to draw my own picture of the social: the recursive but incomplete performance of an unknowable number of intertwined orderings. But actor-network theorists do not, on the whole, talk about *modes* of ordering. (Here, as I argue shortly, I believe that they, together with the symbolic interactionists, are missing out.) Instead, they talk of 'translation'.

This is the process in which putative agents attempt to characterize and pattern the networks of the social: the process in which they attempt to constitute themselves *as* agents.[14] Thus an agent is a spokesperson, a figurehead, or a more or less opaque 'black box' which stands for, conceals, defines, holds in place, mobilizes and draws on, a set of juxtaposed bits and pieces. So, symmetrically, power or size are network effects. There is no a priori difference between people and organizations: both are contingent achievements. And if some things are bigger than others (and to be sure, some are), then this is a contingent matter. 'Macro-social' things don't exist in and of themselves. Neither are they different in kind. It is just that, in their propensity for deletion, they tend to *look* different.[15] And we tend (as in the labelling processes explored by the symbolic interactionists) to *say* that they are different.

This argument draws on structuralism. But it isn't really structuralist because network ordering is an uncertain process, not something achieved once and for all. Big organizations – the Bank of Commerce and Credit International – may come tumbling down if the network which it fronts and for which it speaks is not kept in line. Neither does network ordering take place out of time in the synchronic limbo of semiotics. So here actor-network is close to symbolic interaction. Both are pragmatic, recursive sociologies of process with an interest in the (uncertain) processes of deletion which generate power and size.

But how are things deleted? How are the bits and pieces kept in line? How are the networks of the social stabilized for long enough to achieve any kind of ordering at all? Actor-network writers answer this question in two ways. First, they explore the *tactics of translation*, how it is that potential translators assemble the bits and pieces needed to build a coherent actor. This is the dash of

Machiavellianism that I mentioned above: several authors in this tradition refer, approvingly, to the author of *The Prince*.[16] They consider, for instance, the attempts by potential translators to foresee and forestall the resistance put up by the bits and pieces that make up the networks of the social. Second, and perhaps more originally, they consider the different *materials* of sociation. For the argument is that agents are materially heterogeneous in character, and that translation is always a form of what is sometimes called 'heterogeneous engineering' (see Law 1987).

This is the *relational materialism* to which I referred in the Introduction. At root, the argument is simple. It is that some materials last better than others. And some travel better than others. Voices don't last for long, and they don't travel very far. If social ordering depended on voices alone, it would be a very local affair. Bodies travel better than voices and they tend to last longer. But they can only reach so far – and once they are out of your sight you can't be sure that they will do what you have told them. So social ordering that rests upon the somatic is liable to be small in scope and limited in success.[17] Texts also have their drawbacks. They can be burned, lost or misinterpreted. On the other hand, they tend to travel well and they last well if they are properly looked after. So texts may have ordering effects that spread across time and space. And other materials may have similar effects. The Palais de Versailles has lasted well, and machines, though they vary, may be mobile and last for longer than people.

This, then, is the simple way of putting it. The argument is that large-scale attempts at ordering or distanciation depend on the creation of what Bruno Latour calls 'immutable mobiles', materials that can easily be carried about and tend to retain their shape (see Latour 1987: 227ff.). But to put it in this way is too simple. This is because it isn't symmetrical. It sounds as if I am saying that mobility and durability are properties given by nature. But this is wrong. *Mobility and durability – materiality – are themselves relational effects.* Concrete walls are solid while they are maintained and patrolled. Texts order only if they are not destroyed *en route*, and there is someone at the other end who will read them and order her conduct accordingly. Buildings may be adapted for other uses – for instance as objects of the tourist gaze.[18] So a material is an effect. And it is durable or otherwise as a function of its location in the networks of the social. This is why I speak of *relational* materialism.[19] For actor-network's concern with materials has nothing to do with technological or architectural determinism – with the views of those many writers from left and right who take it that technologies or buildings determine social relations.[20]

So the actor-network argument about ordering is this. Agency and size (together with machines, social entities and every other kind of object to which one can point) are uncertain effects generated by a network and its mode of interaction. They are constituted as objects to the extent, but only to the extent, that the network stays in place. But the components of the network have, as it were, no natural tendency to play the roles to which they have been allocated. They tend to want to make off on their own. Indeed, they act in the way they do only because they, too, are effects generated by a network and its mode of interaction. So agency and other objects, together with the dualisms that infest the modern world, are all relational achievements. And since they may be undone, this is a sociology of contingent ordering, a sociology of verbs rather than of nouns.

Translation, then, is to do with verbs, but one could say that its object is to try to convert verbs into nouns. Of course, this is impossible. Verbs are verbs are verbs. To think otherwise is to cleave to the modernist dream of pure order. Nevertheless, some verbs may end up acting for longer than others. Some may even look like nouns for a while. So translation is a play to achieve relative durability, to make verbs behave as if they were nouns. This is where relational materialism comes into the picture. And it is also, I think, where the actor-network approach to ordering is most innovative. For it is not that some materials are more durable than others. To say this is to fall back on nouns. Rather, it is that some network configurations generate effects which, so long as everything else is equal, last longer than others. So the tactics of ordering have to do, in general, with the construction of network arrangements that might last for a little longer. They have to do with trying to ensure that everything else is equal. And this means forms of association – crudely materials – which most sociologists tend to assume derive from, are independent of, or (most commonly) are simply thought of as differing in kind from, the social.

So what tends to last? What tends to spread? What are the patterns that actor-network theorists discern in the material tactics of translation? Here they are cautious for they are too aware of the risks of technological determinism to abandon the relational part of their materialism. But these writers do make suggestions of two kinds.

First, they point to sociotechnical innovations that generate new forms of immutable mobiles: writing; print; paper; money; a postal system; cartography; navigation; ocean-going vessels; cannons; gunpowder; telephony.[21] Note that I say 'sociotechnical'. This is important, for it isn't simply a matter of technology. Rather it is that

certain heterogeneous sociotechnologies (which are themselves ordering effects) open up the *possibility* of ordering distant events from a
centre. They have, in other words, the potential effect of generating
peripheries and centres. And the translator who acts at a distance
is likely to be one who has embedded some of these possibilities
in her ordering tactics.

The second argument is related to the first. It has to do with
what happens at the centre. For an ordering centre – a *centre of
translation* – strains towards reflexivity and self-reflexivity. That is,
it monitors what is going on, and acts on the basis of this monitoring. So an ordering centre is (probably) constituted by gathering,
simplifying, representing, making calculations about, and acting upon
the flow of immutable mobiles coming in from and departing for
the periphery. But this means that there is a further overlapping
series of heterogeneous effects or procedures recursively embedded in
the ordering tactics of the centre of translation, procedures that have
to do with representation and calculation. Roughly, then, a centre of
ordering is (likely to be) a place which *monitors* a periphery, *represents*
that periphery, and makes *calculations* about what to do next in
part on the basis of those representations – though such monitoring,
representation and calculation are themselves heterogeneous effects.
Examples might include bureaucracy; double-entry book-keeping;
logarithms; statistical methods; cartography; xerography; computing;
accounting procedures; and the distinction between management and
administration.

I have indicated that the actor-network theorists are quite cautious
in their claims about immutable mobiles. They aren't technological
determinists. And neither are they information-theoretic functionalists,
arguing, from necessity, that certain informational problems have to
be solved.[22] Instead the emphasis is modestly empirical. It is to say
that if you look at the sociotechnologies of ordering, it appears that
there has been a series of (potentially reversible) changes since,
say, about the year 1400 to do with interdependence and relational
materials.[23] And it is to say that it is worthwhile going out to look
at the ordering strain towards self-reflexivity that (or so it is suggested)
characterizes the modern world.

5 THE MODE OF ORDERING

The pessimistic version of symbolic interactionism clears the ground
for a pragmatic sociology that is symmetrical and non-reductionist.
It reminds us that orderings are never complete. It tells that society

and mind are recursive processes. And it tells stories about the
in which orderings delete work to generate power and pain. To
simplify a little too much we might say that now it has abandoned its
optimism, symbolic interaction has become a sociology of the under-
dog. It looks at the world from the bottom of the heap, from the
point of view of those who are done to, rather than those who do.
It listens to unfairnesses and deprivations. It hears (or perhaps it
helps to create) silences. And it speaks, eloquently, of the distance
that we have to cover before we can stop being cruel.

Actor-network theory tells matching stories. But it tells them the
other way round, seeking to characterize the self-reflexive tactics of
ordering cruelty. So it is a language for telling of the doers. It decodes
the ordering techniques of those who would be powerful. It shows
how they translate, conceal and profit from the networks which make
them up. And as a part of this it speaks of the relationship between
durability, materials and orderings. So actor-network theory is close
to symbolic interactionism. Both deny that the powerful are powerful
in the nature of things. But actor-network theory tells stories about
the reflexive sociotechnologies of silencing, whereas symbolic interactionism is a language which generates stories from the underworld,
stories which contest those silences.

But there's another place which tells of ordering, speaking and
silencing, another place that speaks of the materials of the social. This
is post-structuralism. So what can a modest sociology learn from this?

Let me start with a paean for the writing of Michel Foucault.
Once every few years I find that I am reading a book that is going
to mark and shape the way I practise sociology. Michel Foucault's
Discipline and Punish was one such book (Foucault 1979). I read it more
than a decade ago. And, though its implications took a long time
to work through for me, its lessons about the continuity of structure
and agency, the formation of agency, the material nature of the
social, and the ubiquitous character of power, have all stayed with me
consistently ever since. So the present book would have been impossible without Foucault's writing. And in particular, it would have been
impossible without his analysis of what I am calling *modes of ordering*.

A few preliminary comments. When I read Foucault I do not usually
take it that he is talking about process. Rather, my sense is that he
is painting us pictures of the past. Pictures, not histories. For he
tends to refuse histories. Instead, he offers us snapshots.

I should note that he does not see it this way himself.[24] And it is,
indeed, possible to mount good counter-arguments. For instance, large
parts of *The Birth of the Clinic* approximate to narrative history. And,
as Bob Cooper points out, there are moments — for instance in his

analysis of Velazquez' *Las Meninas* — which are precisely intended to upset the snapshot, to show that it is incomplete and inconsistent, that it depends, unstably, on things which it does not itself contain.

But if we turn to *Discipline and Punish* we learn, as we might expect, about discipline. We see it performed. We understand its logic. We can see how it generates its effects. But just at the moment when we want to ask him how this led to that, how it was that discipline came to displace punishment (or did it?), he turns the page of the photo-album. And we find, instead, that we are watching brilliant dissection of another discursive logic for generating the subject, another luminous analysis of the generation of effects. Foucault, then, tends to refuse us stories. Or at any rate, narrative histories.

Why is this? What is going on? A part of it has to do with the structuralist method. 'Explore the way in which the terms define one another within the semiotic system. Understand that you can only grasp them altogether, as a whole, synchronically.' This would be a way of characterizing the method of synchronic linguistics that led to structuralism. It's a position that shifts our attention away from reference to sense, from what lies outside discourse to the internal structure of the linguistic system itself.

Or, perhaps, and this is the point of the study of *Las Meninas*, to the incompletenesses that are constituted by a set of structural relations.

It's an attractive position, in part, because it is an argument against reductionism. That is, it makes you take what you are looking at seriously, and asks you to try to think about it in its own terms. It stops you bleaching out specificity. So it stops you thinking of it as an epiphenomenon which may be explained by simple stories about external causes and origins. Or it means that you have to deal with the latter quite separately by looking for them outside (behind?) the semiotic system. This, then, is what you learn. On the other hand it's rather a drastic way of coping with reductionism. This is because at the same time it tends to stop you talking about historical processes and changes too:[25] the baby has been thrown out with the bathwater. This, at any rate, is what appears to have happened to Foucault.[26]

So much of the time Foucault sticks with synchronicity. But he is also the supreme ironist. Discourse is all. There is no escape. Truth only knows and recognizes itself in a context — a context which it creates for itself. There is some similarity here with pragmatism, though the latter doesn't abolish reference in favour of sense. But the similarity reaches further. Foucault's resistance to reduction pushes him in the direction of recursion. Discourses, so to speak, perform and instantiate themselves. There is nowhere else to go. Nothing else animates them. There is no puppeteer. Instead, they animate themselves. And this, this refusal of reduction, is why he doesn't see power as something that a group, a class or an apparatus might 'have'. Power isn't a fluid that slops around, concentrating in particular places, and driving other parts of the system. It isn't something to be stored up. Rather, it is a ubiquitous relational effect. He approaches it symmetrically.

Foucault does not, to be sure, come down on the side of necessity. Discourse is contingent. It *could* be otherwise. It has been otherwise. But from the point of view of a modest and pragmatic sociology it is a very odd form of contingency. For the refusal of process means that any particular discourse is, as it were, hegemonic. Discourse is discourse is discourse. That is the beginning and the end of it. For a discourse is a pattern that performs recursively. This means that we can look for the pattern in its performances and embodiments and ask how these generate the discursive effects of which they are products. We may also try to consider what discourse both presupposes and suppresses. But that is where we have to stop. So if we carefully follow Foucault we don't look to see where discourse tails off. We don't consider how it might interact with other patterns. Indeed, arguably we don't even have anything interesting to say about the particular form taken by its performances. So *in principle* discourse is a contingent pattern. But *in practice* it tends to behave like necessity. And we, of course, are simply further expressions of that necessity – constituted, with Foucault, as non-liberal ironists.

So what is to be done? Here is a possible answer. It rests on the assumption that there is something valuable to be learned from Foucault's writing. This is the intuition that it is *plausible to go out and look for fairly coherent and large scale ordering patterns* in the networks of the social. It is, in other words, plausible to look for orderings which (to the extent they are performed) generate, define, and inter-relate elements in relatively coherent ways. And, in particular, it is plausible to look out for specific strategies of reflexivity and self-reflexivity. This, then, is what I have in mind when I think of *modes of ordering*. And it is the theoretical component of my response to Leigh Star's question about my preference for imputing blocks rather than smaller patterns to the networks of the social.

Why is it so plausible? The answer to this question lies outside discourse analysis itself, and has to with the grounds of action. The argument comes in two stages. The first is general. It is that agency is only possible because it is generated by and located within relatively regular patterns in the networks of the social. A common-sense way of putting it would be to say that unless an agent can anticipate outcomes some of the time, then action will never succeed. And another common-sense way of putting it is to say that unless agents can in some measure manage ordering for a time, and 'front' the networks for which they speak or act, then they won't be identifiable as agents at all. Put more abstractly then, it is because aspects of these networks, so to speak, reproduce themselves that identifiable agents, together with the possibility of action, are brought into being.

I need to be very cautious about this first move. There is no point in throwing out a sociology of order in favour of a sociology of ordering, simply to reintroduce the former by the back door. But I think that I *am* being cautious. Thus I'm still committed to the idea that the patterns in the networks of the social are unknowably complex. I'm still committed to the idea that ordering always experiences its limits. And I'm still committed to the idea that it is an uncertain process, rather than a noun that can be locked up in a box. So I still take it that patternings in the networks of the social change, peter out, break down, and they are, in any case, unknowably complex. This is why agency – and all the other effects such as size – are unending processes and are not given in the order of things. And it's also why agents sometimes unravel. But, though all this is true, some regularity – some patterned translation – is a *sine qua non* of agency.[27] Without it, no verbs would ever struggle any part of the way towards apparent noun-hood: there would be nothing there to unravel.

The first part of the argument says nothing about the *character* of the patterns, about the balance between local and not quite so local contingencies. So the second part of the argument is to say that there are significant reasons for believing that some of the patterns in the networks of the social come in blocks. Look back to the first part of the argument. One way of restating this would be to say that patterns embody, generate, or perform agent-relevant economies of scale. Thus agents do not have to deal with all the intricacies of the networks that they confront and seek to translate. (Some of) those networks come as units, as (so to speak) blocks. They are 'fronted' by much simpler bits and pieces.[28] We deal with shop assistants rather than biographies; or electric current rather than nuclear power stations. That these simplicities may dissolve goes without saying, for things that look like nouns are really verbs. But simplifications, while they last, represent economies of scale.

How large are such economies of scale? How big are the networks which they front? And what is their character? The answer, of course, is that it depends. We may impute simplicity in different ways, and at different levels of scale. But Foucauldian discourse analysis, reinterpreted in the way that I am proposing, tells us to be bold. It says, in effect, that there are large-scale patterns which reach through and are performed in the networks of the social. And it tells us to treat some at least of these patterns as reflexive and self-reflexive *strategies*. Thus Foucault writes that relations (he says power relations) are

> intentional but non-subjective. If in fact they are intelligible, this is not because they are the effect of another 'instance' that explains them, but rather because they are imbued through and through with calculation: there is no power that is exercised without a series of aims and objectives .... The logic is perfectly clear, the aims decipherable, and yet it is also the case that no-one is there to have invented them, and few who can be said to have formulated them.[29]

I'm suggesting, then, that modes of ordering may be seen as intentional, but (often) non-subjective, self-reflexive strategies. And I'm suggesting, following the arguments from economies of scale, that though their scale and character are both contingent, there are good reasons for assuming that such strategies or imputational blocks, tend to get embedded and performed in the networks of the social.[30] In effect, then, I'm suggesting that there is an indefinite number of possible modes of self-reflexivity; but, on the other hand, that only a relatively small number may be instantiated in the networks of the social at a given time and place, in part because if everything else is equal, they may successfully reproduce themselves.

This, then, is what my 'modes of ordering' are about: they represent a way of imputing coherences or self-reflexive 'logics' that are not simply told, performed and embodied in agents, but rather speak through, act and recursively organize the full range of social materials. They offer a way of exploring how these modes of ordering interact to create the complex effects that we witness when we look at histories, agents or organizations. They are intended to speak to, shape, and enhance our imputational sensitivity within the project of a modest sociology. I'm recommending the notion of the mode of ordering as a tool for doing that job, one analogous to that done by concepts such as 'style of thought', 'ideal type', 'ideology' and 'discourse' in other sociologies.[31] Except, perhaps, that unlike some uses of these other terms, it isn't reductionist, but it is relationally materialist.

Now some cautions. First I really don't think that it is possible to sit in an armchair and dream up modes of ordering. Here I part company from those who work from an analysis of functional necessity, or otherwise attempt to derive social logics by axiomatic means.[32] Instead, since I take it that they are embedded in the indefinite complexity of the recursive networks of the social, I assume that they will interact with one another and so reorganize one another. Thus their character is contingent and, in part, a matter to be determined empirically.

Second, it is important to observe that coherence is an outcome too – something that the networks of the social generate for themselves. A consequence of this is that things don't cohere, in and of themselves. And neither, notwithstanding the views of the logicians, do arguments. So the issue of coherence is also empirical, or more specifically, a matter of ordering success. If things *appear* to go together, and nothing says or acts otherwise, then they *do* go together. That is, they fall into a pattern that instantiates a prospective mode of ordering. On the other hand, if they can't be made to go together – why then they simply don't cohere.[33]

6 THE MODE OF ORDERING: A CHECKLIST

I have tried to say that I'm cautious about speaking of modes of ordering in general. Instead the issue is better seen as one of imputational sensitivity, sensitivity to the possibility of extended pattern or coherence. And (equally important), an analogous sensitivity to the possibility of difference, to the possibility that it may be feasible to impute extended boundaries, fault-lines, or non-continuities to the networks of the social.[34] Nevertheless, the particular modes of ordering that I have imputed to Daresbury Laboratory, but also in some measure, to my political and occupational circumstances, suggest a possible checklist, a checklist of the kinds of patterning effects for which we might search if we go out looking for modes of ordering. I conclude this chapter with this – a brief statement of some of the possible attributes of modes of ordering.

(1) Modes of ordering may characterize and generate different *materials* – agents, devices, texts, social relations, architectures and all the rest. That is, they may embody and perform particular patterns of relations between materials, distinguishing in characteristic ways between such objects as people, machines, animals and formal organizations.

(2) They may have effects of *size*. That is, they may characterize, generate, distinguish between, allocate and perform phenomena of different sizes in relatively standard or regular ways.

(3) They may have *dualist* effects. That is, they may tell and strain towards the performance of differences in kind between materials such as mind and body, or agency and structure.

(4) They may embody and perform relatively consistent patterns of *deleti*
They may, that is, generate objects and entities in characteristically patterned
but asymmetrical relations such that some are deprived of the ability to
act in certain ways. And, contrariwise, they may tend to empower certain
kinds of entities or objects with specific and extended rights. This, then, is
an issue to do with patterns of enfranchisement and disenfranchisement.

(5) They may have the effect of generating and embodying characteristic
forms of *representation*. This suggestion is a version of the point about deletion
immediately above. It is that a mode of ordering may define and perform a
characteristic way of speaking or acting for whatever parts of the network
have been deleted. Thus a mode of ordering may perform and embody
what amounts to an epistemology and, as a part of this, a mode of silence.
Accordingly, each mode of ordering defines its own version of an ideal speech
situation, and each tells what would count as interference to that ideal.[35]

(6) They may generate and perform *distributions*, defining or embodying a
characteristic approach to what might, does or should pass from whom to
what, under what circumstances. This is an issue to do with metaphorical
trading relations, and in particular the definition and distribution of what it
is that might count as a surplus.

(7) They may generate and embody a characteristic set of *problems*. Here
the issue concerns patterns in the relationships between what *is* on the one
hand, and what might or should be on the other. It is the gap between these
that defines the problem (and so a need for resources). Note that problems
are ubiquitous, because modes of ordering only ever achieve partial success.

(8) They may be expected to generate and embody a characteristic set of
resources. The argument is that since a mode of ordering is a recursive
pattern embodied and recursively instantiated in the networks of the social,
it *also*, at the same time, tends to define and perform what would be required
in order to reproduce its version of the patterning of the networks of the
social.

(9) They may define and generate a characteristic set of *boundary relations*.
The issue, here, has to do with the relationship *between* modes of ordering.
Remember that they are never fully performed. Neither do they exist in a
vacuum. Accordingly, they interact. Indeed, one way of looking at this is
to say that the networks of the social are *all* interactive boundary effects,[36]
and treat them accordingly – something that I have sought to do with my
empirical material in the present book. But what is the character of these
effects? I think that this is where our imputations of ordering modes experience their limits. Other kind of patterns, other contingencies, intervene.
On the other hand, it is also likely that where they co-exist they develop
protocols for dealing with, profiting from, or resisting one another.[37]

This, then, is a sensitizing checklist for the imputation of contingent
modes of reflexive and self-reflexive ordering to the networks of the

social. It raises *questions* about strategic patterns, questions that represent an attempt to save something important about discourse analysis from the timeless jaws of the synchronic without, at the same time, falling for reductionism. It is an attempt to create a tool for imputing patterns to the recursive networks of the social. It is an attempt to fashion a tool that deals, at one and the same time, with the silences and the hurts explored by symbolic interactionism *and* the modes of silencing described in actor-network theory. And, perhaps most important of all, it is an attempt to create a tool for imputing patterns to the networks of the social that treats with materials in all their heterogeneity as effects rather than as primitive causes.

NOTES

1 George Herbert Mead was a philosopher and social theorist who made important contributions to the development of symbolic interactionism. See Mead (1934).

2 I accept Zygmunt Bauman's (1992) view that contingency is generated by the modern project. That sociology should inhabit the space opened up in this way is, of course, no surprise.

3 Note that there is a difference between contingency and necessity on the one hand, and free will and determinism on the other. Contingency does not imply free will or voluntarism.

4 This would be consistent with the Duhem/Quine position developed by Mary Hesse (1974) in her metaphorical and network-oriented philosophy of science.

5 Consider, for instance, the figurational sociology of Norbert Elias (1978a, 1978b), and particularly his masterpiece, *The Court Society* (1983). For a helpful introduction to figurational sociology see ch. 7 in Rojek 1985. There is also the theory of structuration, as developed by Anthony Giddens (1976, 1984, 1990, 1991).

6 Sometimes it is difficult to find explicit statement of theory at all. But see Blumer (1969a). And for an historical introduction see Rock (1979).

7 See, for instance, Becker (1963) on deviance, Dalton (1959) on organizations, Glaser and Strauss (1965) on medicine, Becker (1982) on art, and Star (1989) on science.

8 Simplifications breed exceptions. That is, they are too simple. For instance, Pierre Bourdieu has generated a subtle, interactionist, theory of stratification. See Bourdieu (1986).

9 Note that if there *is* a root order, then agents are able to work their own individual way towards coherence and unity – another questionable assumption.

10 Consider, for instance, Howard Becker's (1971b) notion of the hierarchy of credibility.

11 Note that this is the ethical parallel to an analytical commitment to symmetry. For a moving discussion, see Star (1992).

12 I take it that in principle this is close to Richard Rorty's position. However, he seems to be more optimistic than I feel.

13 For a somewhat fuller summary of the actor-network approach, see Law (1992a).

14 Writers often talk of 'translation' when they explore these attempts at ordering. Indeed, actor-network sociology is sometimes called the 'sociology of translation'. See, for instance, Latour (1987) and Callon (1986a).

15 For this point see Callon and Latour (1981).

16 See, for instance, Latour (1988c).

17 This argument is developed by Callon and Latour (1981).

18 John Thompson (1990: 24) calls the idea that texts have necessary effects the 'fallacy of internalism'. This is one place where actor-network theory can be distinguished from semiotics.

19 This argument is more fully developed in Law and Mol forthcoming.

20 It is interesting, for instance, to observe that Mark Poster lapses into a form of technological determinism in his discussions of the mode of information. See Poster (1990: 43ff). For comments on technological determinism, see the Introduction to MacKenzie and Wajcman (1985).

21 Sociologists from other traditions are now doing this. See, for instance, writers such as Anthony Giddens (1990) and David Harvey (1990).

22 For this kind of approach, see Beniger 1986.

23 Though the empirical arguments are different, the explanatory attitude of these writers is not so different from that of Norbert Elias in his sociology of figuration.

24 See, for instance, his comments on this in *The Order of Things* (1974: xii). Note, also, that there are sections of his work – for instance considerable parts of *The Birth of the Clinic* (1976) – which tell stories that are akin to those of narrative story-telling.

25 So as I mentioned in the Introduction, when structuralism climbs into bed with causes that lie *within* the semiotic system – as it did for Louis Althusser (1971a) – the effect tends to be oddly indecisive. We learn both that a part of the system is determinant in the last instance and that all parts of the system are effective in some degree.

26 Though, as Derrida's concern with *differance* suggests, it does not have to turn out this way. See Derrida (1976).

27 This argument can be derived from a variety of sources, but it is common in *verstehende* sociology. See, for instance, Barry Barnes' (1988) characterization of society as a (somewhat) shared distribution of knowledge.

28 Michel Callon calls this process 'punctualisation'. See Callon (1991).

29 See Foucault (1981: 94–5). The aim is to avoid starting out with the agent as a knowing subject and thus to treat it as an effect rather than a cause – something I want to take from Foucault. I want to say that modes of ordering express and embody calculations – that they imply patternings, or tend to create and arrange things in one way rather than another.

30 The argument crops up in and underpins a range of different sociologies. For instance, organizational behaviourists talk of institutional isomorphism. For discussion of this literature, see Clegg (1989). Mary Douglas and Baron Isherwood (1979), following a tradition from both *verstehende* sociology and social anthropology, talk of the character of scale and scope in the formation of meaning. And Pierre Bourdieu's (1986) notion of habitus represents an analogous attempt to tackle the issue of (partially implicit) strategy.

31 The notion of 'style of thought' was developed by Karl Mannheim (1953b) and that of 'ideal type' derives, of course, from Max Weber (1930). 'Ideology' is often, though not always, associated with Marxist sociology.

32 For an interesting example of the latter, see Boltanski and Thévenot's (1987) discussion of 'cités'. But also consider Michel Callon's (1991) notion of the 'regime of translation'. It is possible that some of the work on networks, hierarchies and markets is similar. See Thompson et al. (1991).

33 The point derives from the later Wittgenstein (1953). But see also Latour (1988b).

34 This is a point that is of concern to actor-network theory. Roughly the problem is this: once it is said that the networks of the social are heterogeneous, and the common-sense distinctions that we make, for instance between structure and agency, or large and small, are effects rather than having been given in the nature of things, the question is: what follows next? The notion of the mode of ordering is one possible answer to that question – one possible way of obtaining purchase on what Thomas Hughes (1986) calls 'the seamless web' of the sociotechnical.

35 Note that, though I remain a liberal, in this way of thinking ideal speech situations are neither necessarily democratic nor liberal.

36 See this point, well developed, albeit in a different idiom, in Star and Griesemer (1989). See also Star (1991).

37 Though I will not develop the point here, I take it that this is the place where the reflexivist or the ironist can turn back into a liberal.

6

Rankings

1 INTRODUCTION

To tell stories of agency and organization is to tell stories about hierarchy and distribution. This much *all* the managerial modes of ordering have in common: that they are celebrations, performances and embodiments of ranking and reward; and, as I shall argue, of deletion. This commonality is important. For the managers it means that there is sometimes, perhaps often, common ground *between* the stories that are told and the ordering modes that they perform: it means that there is often practical performance of hierarchical and distributional orderings. And for the political philosopher, and perhaps for the sociologist too, it means that all the modes of ordering tell of the *performance of hierarchy as a necessary part of organizational life*. 'There is', as Mrs Thatcher used to tell us, 'no alternative' — except that in the case of organizational hierarchy there is no need to say anything at all.

So this is what they have in common: they *assume* that hierarchy and its distributions of agency, like the poor, are always with us; and (I shall come to this) they ignore most of a hidden iceberg of effort and work concealed behind and within the ordering patterns that makes their performance possible.

> This is another way of saying that no ordering mode tells everything, that it fronts a whole network of bits and pieces. But what is its attitude to that whereof it does not tell? This is the question that I want to explore.

Of course the *differences* are important too. For the modes of ordering also tell different kinds of stories about the proper character of rank and agency. And, when things start to go wrong they offer different diagnoses about the origins of that failure. This chapter is about some of the differences and commonalities. It is about the rankings that they perform in practice. It is about the ways that they intersect with other, non-managerial ordering patterns. And it is an argument against those sociologists who press the necessity of order by trying to drive a distinction between 'discourses' on the one hand, and social structures on the other.

2   RANKING AND THE MODE Of ORDERING

Each ordering mode tells of ranking, and each tells of the (lowly status of?) other modes of ordering. So we start with two hierachical processes. For, when a single ordering mode claims that it is an order, then we contemplate the possibility of hideous purity, of the marginalization of other ways of being. But when *all* the ordering patterns are said to line up it is even worse. There is no quick escape: only the hope that we might listen very carefully to the voices that tell of, are constituted in, other, different, orderings; or to the silences that have no name.[1]

Vision tells elitist stories. In its dualism some people, a very few, are said to be graced. Most of us are not so touched, at least directly. But, as Weber knew, charisma also tells subversive tales, tales in-different to the rankings that embody and perform other orderings. So charisma is hierarchical, but it is also an irritant.

At Daresbury they tell tales of Giovanni Alberti as charismatic irritant, of the way he ignores the ordering practices of administration or enterprise, and of his propensity to stick his nose into anything. One day they were talking about his visit to a construction site – the location of his new beam-line, his 'pride and joy'. It seems that he had wandered on to the site to check on progress, to watch the pouring of concrete for the foundations, or whatever. The point of the story, and the reason they were laughing, was that he had been ordered off the site by the foreman because he was not wearing a hard hat. Ordered off! So the stories tell of hierarchy and its inversion or collapse. Here is another manager:

> We all know that Giovanni has his own management style. He will jump over the project manager and get information from people at the bottom, and interfere as he sees fit, and be biased by it. Whatever one writes down as the management structure will be different from the practice.

The singleminded grace of vision blots out other possibilities or complexities; for instance, it blots out organizational charts. If the most important thing in the world is to talk to the fitter, then that is the most important thing in the world. It doesn't matter that the fitter is told of elsewhere as a lowly form of life. And it doesn't matter that he has his own boss, his own chain of command. So the fitter may feel that he is graced – or he may be angry if the charismatic, who always knows best, tells him how to do his job.

But even so, in the stories performed in vision, hierarchy does not go away: still they talked of Giovanni as the boss.

To be sure, the charismatic is, as they say, interpolated in other forms of ordering too; there are places, many places where they mesh together.

What was it that Louis Althusser said about the instruments of the orchestra playing the same score?[2] The metaphor is attractive, except that if we talk of a score, then we are in the business of imputing a root order. This may be for the best of motives. But I'd prefer to stick to the uncertainty of order*ing*. And explore the arguments, between the sections of the orchestra, about whether the score is indeed the same or not.

Indeed, Giovanni was said to be a dangerous boss, since, uninterested in boundaries, it was told that he was liable to turn up unexpectedly in the underworlds:

Giovanni Alberti: It would help if you were there at one o'clock in the morning. You would know *exactly* what was happening. Unless there is a problem there is no one in the control room [and] ... if the user support scientist is any good he is at a station.

But that's the negative part of the story of charisma. The positive part is that all sorts of more or less lowly people tell of its levelling propensities. Here's an excellent station scientist and junior manager, someone who told me how good it was to work with Giovanni:

He's only ever been mad with me once. He went off absolutely fuming. But he was back within two minutes, carrying two cups of coffee. It was his way of saying sorry. He's really good to work with. He's a great teacher. He's very patient.

Here's a possibility: vision connects with scientific vocation; if you are already caught up in scientific vocation, then you are caught up in vision too. And if not, then not.

Democracy is not the word I want, for these are not stories about egalitarianism. Instead I should be saying that the currency of vision,

its social cement, is that of personal contact.[3] So let's put this
another way. Visionary orderings don't leave much room for delegation: who can be trusted who is not already graced? The answer
is: only those who touch the hem and partake of the state of grace.

> But, believe me, that hem is charged with power. Do not laugh at
> the extravagence of my language, for I have touched the hem too.
> Vision is potent. Do *you* not feel graced when you eat of the body,
> and you drink of the blood? Was it not said of Adolf Hitler that he had
> remarkable eyes?

So here's the moral. The orderings of vision tell that there are
three states, three levels of possible hierarchy. There is the visionary.
There are those who partake indirectly of the vision. And then there
are those who do not.

> Sometimes I have been privileged to touch the hem. But I hope that I al-
> ways choose to touch the right hem.

Vision performs and embodies a difference in *quality*, a difference
between those who are graced, and those who are not. But, as the
stories run, this is a matter beyond our control. For, as the Calvinists
said of their Saints: they are of the Elect. And they said of the others:
they are the Damned.

The other ordering modes also tell of hierarchy, but on the whole
these are less exclusive, more meritocratic. At any rate, in their
stories they say that more of us may hope to qualify as agents. So
more of us may aspire to office. They also tend to say that entry to
the higher places is more within our own control. Effort, diligence,
skill, eagerness – these are some of the currencies that may allow us
through the eye of their particular needles. So predestination plays
a smaller role – though, to be sure, it is also the case that some
are 'naturally' better endowed than others, so ascribed status is still
with us.

'Qualifications for entry': the term is performed in its most literal
sense in the ordering mode of vocational agency where the stories
tell of pieces of paper. Here is one of the managers:

> If I were a research assistant I would choose to go to a uni-
> versity. At a university there is a chance to do a higher degree.
> At Daresbury there would be no problem *if* we had in-house
> research.

So when they talk of vocation they tell of M.Sc.s and Ph.D.s. They
tell of City and Guilds. They distinguish between those who have
the credentials that it takes and those who do not. They tell of

skills, and guarantees of skills.[4] So they say of scientific agents that they are skilled and creative puzzle-solvers. You've heard this story already:

James: Having put him on the rails [this student] does not go. You have to bump into him.

Andy: To be a [technician] does not take any initiative. To do *science* does. If a person does research, the research does not get done by having someone [say] 'Measure this, then measure that ....'

The exchange speaks volumes about the character of vocational agency, about what it takes to be a scientist. To be skilled, self-starting and ingenious, these are the keys.

Giovanni Alberti: I'm *impressed* by that guy. With the machine being broken, he couldn't get to do his experiments. But he's gone to the BSL [Biology Support Laboratory], and got some bits and pieces together from God knows where, and he's been working away all this time. I'm *impressed*. (from memory)

But here's an implication that is also told: of the many hours that are put in. Dr Hugh Roper is a well-respected younger station scientist:

Hugh Roper: I work about 46 hours a week on User Support. And then, outside that, I push the research when I can.

So vocational ordering tells of creativity and competence. And so too, in its own idiom, does enterprise. *Performance* is the watchword here. There is performance of the organization as a whole:

Giovanni Alberti: The Lab will survive or die on the basis of the Second Wiggler [magnet], and the performance of the existing Wiggler. That is why the Second Wiggler is top priority, and the First Wiggler too.[5]

But there is individual performance too: for the ordering of enterprise tells, as I noted in chapter 4, that hierarchy takes the form of delegated responsibility. *All* office holders are responsible. They are all supposed to perform. But the responsibilites carried by those higher up the tree are greater. So agents are promoted – promoted to the point where their responsibilities match their ability to turn in a performance. And those that are less responsible, less able to perform, are not promoted.

But here's something that these ordering modes all have in common: they also tell of workaholism.[6] And this is important because here, in their celebration of work, the stories of vocation, vision and enterprise tend overlap. They *all* tell stories about extra hours. And they *all* tell stories about indifference to time. Here is Dr Emma Twomey, a first-rate station scientist. She has put in a full day's work on a Sunday setting up an experimental station. It's 7.00 p.m., and Giovanni Alberti, who has also put in a full day, is hammering away at a computer keyboard:

Emma Twomey: Well, I've got to go home now, or I won't have a marriage to go home to.

Giovanni Alberti: That's alright!

Emma Twomey: [Jokingly] What's alright? That I've got to go home? Or that I won't have a marriage to go home to?! [General laughter]

The joke speaks volumes about agency and ranking in vocation and in vision. But also of its character in enterprise, with its obsessive concern with performance. For when you perform, clock time loses its sense and significance. You work until you drop − a fact which also had ethnographic implications. Thus it was much easier to talk to people 'out of hours'. It wasn't that they were necessarily busier between nine and five, but inside hours they had no way of telling whether I was simply a 'nine-to-five' sort of person, one of the *Untermenschen*. Or whether, instead, I was in my own way, a member of the vocationally committed, or the entrepreneurially performing elite. How *committed* was I? Those who are committed put themseleves out more for others who are similarly committed.

> Sometimes, as I drove back after a twelve hour day at the Lab, I would feel tired: so tired that I cannot find the words to say it. Forty-five miles at night − that is a long way on a winding road. And to know that I had not seen the children that day. Or my partner. And too tired, too preoccupied, to *want* to see them. Too caught up in the place where charisma and puzzle-solving overlap with the need to perform. Too caught up in the Lab. Too caught up in *my* work. This is modernity, distraction, destruction.

So this is one divide. It is a new version of the old division, built up at the time of the industrial revolution, between work and the world.[7] But the difference is that work is not, so to speak, kept in its place. Let's play with words: in the ordering modes performed by managers and scientists the work of the world is deleted from the world of work. Leisure, family, the efforts of a partner − these things are outside, elsewhere, pressed into a corner. Of course this is a form of ranking. It tells of the importance of work, and in the same breath it tells of what can safely be deleted. And it is all the more potent because of the isomorphism of the different modes of ordering.

So that's one way in which the divide of hierarchy is generated. But it expresses itself in other ways too. Think again, for instance, about the distribution of agency *within* the hierarchies of work – about the proper gap between the workaholics and the rest. For this is a place where the world of non-work comes to be related and performed in the stories of enterprise, vocation and vision. So they don't tell many stories about their children. Or about the varieties of religious experience. Instead the stories elaborate themes around a problem: how to deal with those who march to the sound of a different drum, the drum of the otherwise committed, when they come to work. So they tell of contrariness. Or indifference. Or lack of initiative. Or failure to perform. Or incompetence. In the ordering modes of work this is the limbo of the anti-hero. And her ally, the zombie.

So isn't this the voice of enterprise?

We *have* to put pressure on people; to embarrass them at a meeting [if they fail to deliver what they have promised].

And isn't this the voice of that allied trade, vocation?

Which good scientist will be so stupid to decide that he will spend the next few years working on maintenance? *Financially* its a dead end, and *scientifically* its a dead end! ... Anyone doing that job *becomes* a zombie!

And the heroic stories don't claim that 'civil servants' actually *sleep* on the job. Instead it is said that they are supine. Or, if they are feeling energetic, it is said that they pack their bags and go home at five after an obstructive day in the office:

Paul: Paula likes to be involved in the minutiae.

Pauline: And she is reluctant to take decisions.

And this tells a similar story:

Giovanni Alberti: The standard course is to do with the protocols of the organization. But it doesn't build beam lines.

So this is a second commonality: the celebration of workaholism in the matter of ranking agents *within* the organization. And the complaints about resistance to workaholism.

3 PERFORMING RANKS

For a period I watched the work of the crew in the Nuclear Structure Facility (NSF). The crew are the people – the technicians – who run the huge tandem Van de Graaf generator that stands over 40 metres high, in the tower of the NSF. The 'tandem' hurls atomic nuclei at one another. It is a basic tool for research on the structure of the atomic nucleus. And it is large, impressive, and very costly.

And it has been closed. But that's a ghastly and quite different story.

One day I was in the control room. I knew various members of the crew, but I'd also talked with some of the machine physicists. On the day in question I was tracing some experimental work by the NSF physicists who were in the process of commissioning an additional linear accelerator, or LINAC. This is an excerpt from my notes.

> There is the crew; there are engineers; there are scientists – at one point there are about twelve people milling about. I feel uncomfortable – and I suddenly realize that it is role conflict – that I am, in effect, straddling a boundary. How can I speak to [a senior machine physicist] and [a crew member] at the same time? The answer is – I can't – except for certain very specific reasons they don't interact at all.

Since I'm telling hierarchical stories, I'd like to avoid misunderstanding by being clear that these are *all* good people. I'm not trying to say that they are difficult, or badly motivated. Or arrogant. They are quiet, modest and professional. They do a good job. And I liked them all. But here's another excerpt from a little later on in my field notes:

> Crew members are trying to see what is going on, trying to learn about driving the LINAC; this gives them few rights to speak; but occasionally a question about the beam from the Tandem is raised; then they have rights – no even *duties* – to speak, to act, to put right; also, at times of slack they are allowed to ask technical, informational, questions; they are also called upon to assist the engineers.

And again:

> Here I am, stuck in crew world – low-status end; the three senior people are standing at Bay 7 and 8 – looking at the low-energy buncher. I am beginning to get a sense of the frustration of the crew. They don't get to know what is going on, or why; during machine physics, they have little or no control.

They are, as a crew member puts it, spoken to on a 'need to know' basis. But I am bound up by my identification with crew-world; what can I do?

I want to say that the control room of the NSF, where the crew oversee this monstrous and beautiful machine while the physicists commission new accelerators, is just one of the places where modes of ordering are mobilized and embodied, just one of the places where agency and ranking are played out.

I found that I sympathized with *both* the machine physicists *and* the crew. I'd talked with quite a lot of the physicists. But I'd spent a lot of time with the crew too. This is one of the horrors of ethnography. To experience the fragmentation of orderings rather than the purity of order. But, to be sure, the horror is also an opportunity.

My notes suggest that this interaction *performed hierarchy*; or, perhaps better, hierarch*ies*. Together, the physicists, the crew members, and the equipment and the topography of the control room, embodied and were constantly performing asymmetries in the distribution of agency. But what were the patterns of agency that they performed and *how was this done?*

This is one of the places where different ordering modes butt up against one another: it is a place or a performance that instantiates intermodal arrangements. [8] For instance, the physicists perform a version of vocational stories of hierarchy, stories about the distinction between creative puzzle-solvers on the one hand, and those who are passive, uncreative and unskilled on the other. I need to be cautious. This is why I speak of 'a version'. For in practice I don't think that the physicists would say of a competent crew member that he was a 'zombie'. Or even begin to think it. And, in any case, though I can't tell you what their paper qualifications looked like, the crew are not untrained.

So the physicists are hard at work puzzle-solving; they are designing, building, conditioning and calibrating a new LINAC accelerator. Let's be clear that this is not a routine task. And it's even less routine when you have to do it on a shoe-string, using bits and pieces cannibalized from other machinery up and down the country. So, no, the physicist's work is not routine at all. But what of the crew?

The crew are being performed *by the physicists* into a set of restricted roles. I'd like to say: these are passive roles. But looking at the story again, I don't think that this is right. I need, instead, to say that in the modes of ordering performed by the physicists the room for initiative left for the crew is very small. I mentioned

that one of the crew members says that they learn what is happening on a 'need to know' basis. And that's a fair way of telling
it. So some creativity is called for, some initiative, but (at least
in the eyes of the machine physicists) not a lot. That is in the
'nature of technicians'.[9] And that is what the physicists both expect
and perform. And (this is very important) that expectation and
performance is not radically subverted by the members of the crew.

This is a performance of hierarchy. The crew are being performed
(and, so to speak, performing themselves) as technicians. And, in
the stories of vocation, they are told (and embodied) as agents
that differ in *kind* from scientists. They rank less. But *why* do the
crew perform themselves in this way? Do they *agree* with what is
going on? Are we watching the enactment of some kind of dominant
ideology?[10]

I think the answer here is pretty clear. It is that we're not. The
crew don't like what is happening at all. Indeed, in some ways
they bitterly resent it:

Jerry: The crew is being driven mad – because they have nothing
to do. When the physicists have finished fucking about, then the
crew will be left to clear up the mess.

John Law: There's nothing for you to do?

Jerry: Absolutely zero involvement. When they've got bored, then
we'll be left with it.

So here's the next question: if the crew don't like it, if there *is* no
'dominant ideology', then why do they go along with it? Why do
they perform hierarchy? Why do they embody lower status agency
in this way? What can we say about the networks of the social
that generate distributional effects of this kind?

Michel Foucault advises us against treating power as something
that trickles down from the top. He pictures it, instead, as an *effect*,
a product, that is generated and penetrates right through the social
body.[11] He also advises us against distinguishing between structure
and agency. That is, he warns us against saying that there is a
structure 'in the last instance' which drives agency, or there are
agents 'in the last instance' who direct structure. Surely this is
right. At least it is consistent with a pragmatic sociology of ordering. But the modest version of the Foucauldian insight that I am
pressing in this book suggests that we might explore a further
question. This is that we should consider *in practice* how and how
far ordering modes tell, perform and embody themselves in the
networks of the social. So here are some of the things that I take

it were going on that day in the control room while the machine physicists were trying to tune the new LINAC.

First: the performance told not only of vocational but also of administrative inequality. Let's say this simply. The technicians are, what, executive officers? I'm not certain. But in the language of the bureaucracy they are some way down the tree; well below the physicists. So the administrative ordering was speaking, or straining to speak too; and it said: technicians are office holders who obey commands from certain kinds of superordinate office holders.

But I *do* want to avoid a 'last instance' argument of the kind 'in the last instance, the crew will be sacked if they disobey orders'. This catches a truth, but it catches it in the wrong way. It isn't that the threat of sacking lies *behind* the performance of bureaucratic duties. It is that sometimes, rarely, it is performed, so to speak, in its own right, as an embodiment of bureaucracy. *If* other hierarchical performances don't work out then this is a possibility. But, for the most part, other hierarchical performances *are* successfully completed. Like the one that I've been telling stories about.

One can do everything with a bayonet except sit on it. The symbolic interactionists are right. And Louis Althusser was wrong.

Second: the technicians resented the physicists. But that resentment was part of – how shall I put it? – an economy of desire or seduction.[12] Let's put it simply again. The physicists tell of desires that the technicians do not. They tell of wanting to make the new LINAC work. They tell of wanting the NSF to be a world-class facility. They tell of wanting to excel in their own science and engineering. Of course, it is possible that some of the technicians are frustrated scientists: that their desires would have been scientific in another universe. We all know stories of this kind. But here's the point: in practice the technicians tell of other quite different kinds of desires. Of other kinds of crafts. Of other visions. And the relationship between these and work is less direct.

For instance, one of the crew leaders has a boat, an inshore fishing vessel. When he's on leave he goes down to the sea to repair it, to paint it, to keep it shipshape. He speaks well of the NSF. He is proud of his work. But one of the reasons that he works shifts is to earn more, so that he can retire early. And when he retires, which will be quite soon, he'll skipper the boat, and rent it out. He'll make a living in part by doing what he likes best. So this man is committed to his boat in much the same way that a machine physicist is committed to the LINAC. Commissioning a boat, commissioning an accelerator – perhaps they aren't so far apart. They're both possible forms of being. They're both part of a network of loves and hates, and commitments and preferences and habits and anathemas – except that the boat does not embody or perform a major commitment to work. Quite otherwise, in fact. It's separate from work. It's part of a non-organizational vision. And an enterprising vocation too! But the skipper of the boat *needs* work, at least for a time, to sustain this project. So he sits at the controls of the NSF, he listens in to the physicists, and performs a kind of hierarchy.

> Of course there are libraries full of books on working-class instrumentalism! But again, I'm trying to tug away from a 'last instance' argument to do with a special form of class conflict. Sometimes, in the economy of desire, there is a last, reductionist instance. We do something for a single reason. This is an empirical possibility. But usually desires are more complicated than this. There are *mixtures* of orderings embodied in us, performed by us. And by our surroundings too. Some of these are class-relevant. But some are not. And the technicians, as I'll tell in the next section, are not simple instrumental workers. They *care* about the Tandem. They listen to the whispering of the great machine under their control. And they drive it, test it and repair it. In ways that are required of them, to be sure. But also in ways that are not.

Third, there is the question of skill. The performances of agency and hierarchy also have to do with economies of embodied skill. Or, to put it more straightforwardly, all the stories tell that some people have skills which others don't. For instance, when I walked into the control room of the NSF, for all that I could make sense of the endless VDUs, chart recorders, dials and meters, it could have been an air-traffic control centre. Of course (here is a first sign of skill) I *knew* that it wasn't because I also knew that Daresbury's business had nothing to do with air-traffic control. And because I was told things like 'This is the NSF control room'.[13]

Gradually, as I spent time with the crews, I watched, and I asked questions: I learned, for instance, that one of the consoles had to do with safety, another with the operation of the Tandem, and a third – the one of most interest to the machine physicists – with the new LINAC. But though I could look over the shoulders of the crew, and sometimes make some sense of what they were doing, there was no way that I could actually have 'flown' the Tandem. Their skills were way, way beyond mine:

> Working on the machine is like a black art. It is easy to run the Tandem well when it is working well. But it is a bitch to drive when it is running badly.

Well, easy for him, perhaps.

Here's the point of the story. The LINAC was brand new. Indeed, I was in the control room when the machine physicists first managed to tune it up sufficiently well to thread a beam of ions through its oscillating magnetic fields. For me this was a 'black art'. I didn't understand it at all. And even the machine physicists had to work at it very hard, round the clock.[14] But if it was opaque to me, then so it was too for the crew. For the physicists embodied skills that the crew did not. And the physicists barely embodied some of those skills, or the job would not have been so difficult.

The crew resented this state of affairs. Perhaps they resented it in principle, I don't know. But they certainly resented it in practice: hence the barbed 'need to know' comment that I quoted above. It was told that the machine physicists were only doling out little snippets of knowledge. The big picture – the information needed, I don't know, to 'fly' the LINAC, or to understand where the process of tuning it had got to – this was not being passed on to the lower orders. So the technicians did not embody the skills of physicists. And, in the face of opposition, orderings of vocational ranking were being performed and embodied.

But, but ... did the crew really want to know enough to be able to commission the LINAC? Did they really want to *lead the life* of a machine physicist? My guess is not. But it doesn't really matter whether my guess is right or not. What's important is this: performed skills are tied up with embodied desires. And only occasionally is the lack of skill determinant in the last instance.

As, for instance, when the nurses and the doctors have all gone home, and someone knows how to do heart massage. Or not.

It would be best to talk of ourselves, of agents, as complex embodied networks or economies of skill/desire. And to say of those networks or economies that they embody and perform many ordering stories. But this is the easy part for a sociologist. From Weber onwards we have all recognized that talk, texts, body language embody/perform organizational arrangements. But what about other materials? Why stick to bodies? That is, why stick to human bodies? This is the actor-network part of the question. Actor-network writers (but also Michel Foucault too) tell us that if agents are network effects, then we aren't going to make too much sense of those effects, unless we look, too, at other materials. I want to press this relational materialism, and argue that other materials perform and embody hierarchical ordering modes too. I want, that is, to say that they embody implications for agents and the bodies that carry these around.[15]

For instance, we might say that the control desk of the NSF implies a set of roles. VDUs and light pens *ask* to be used in a certain way. And figures that appear on the VDUs are like instructions: they *ask* for the crew to take certain actions. I write 'ask', but I could write 'tell'. That is, I could write 'tell' if the crew were 'competent' enough to decode the instructions that were built into them – though, to be sure, what counts as 'competence' is itself a matter for contest. But put the (ordering) fact that materials may be used in different ways aside for a moment, and stick with the order, that is, the orders of the designers. If we do this, then Madeleine Akrich (1992) and Bruno Latour (1992) suggest that we might think of machines as 'scripts'. There are scripts for the components of the machine – roles to be played. But so, too, are there scripts for those who surround the machine. So here we might say that 'competent' crew members are those that are able to act the scripts built into the machine by the designer: and, of course, enact (and embody) the rankings in the orderings implied by the (designers' version of the) machine.

But (again a familiar point) members of the crew don't know the scripts written into the (new) controls of the LINAC. Indeed, as I have noted above, the machine physicists are pretty unclear about these too. Thus one way of describing what the latter are up to would be to say that they are using *other* scripts to write *this* script. And, as they write it, they are writing it into themselves, but also into VDUs, readouts, mimics, protocols, and all the other bits and pieces that will form a part of the control panel of the LINAC once it is up and running. And they are also, at any rate in the end, going to try to write it into the crew members who will operate the LINAC when this becomes routine.[16]

It is obvious that crew members, machine physicists, or passers-by such as myself could ignore the design scripts, find ways of abusing the machinery, and use it to embody an alternative set of ordering patterns. This is the stuff of labour-process studies; they tell of workplace resistance and industrial sabotage. Not to mention youth-culture studies of glue sniffing and ram raiding. But the question is, do they *actually* do so? Do we ignore the intended scripts of the NSF control room? The answer is, sometimes we do. Here is a simple example. As ill design would have it, the crew kitchen was the most convenient way into the control room from one part of the the building. And people tended to use it as a passage: members of the crew themselves (but that was all right, because it was their kitchen); the machine manager (but what could the crew say about this, even if they didn't like it?); and then random outsiders, such as myself (at one point later on in the ethnography one crew member told me that I shouldn't be using it as a passage).[17]

Did the crew similarly 'misuse' the control panels, ignoring the 'official' scripts written into these by the designers? The answer is, I don't know (if they didn't tell me, I wasn't likely to be able to work this out for myself). But I expect they did, because we all seek to resist the orderings that are laid on us at least some of the time. What I *can* say is this: most of the time the NSF Tandem operates very well; I watched crew members fine-tuning it; I watched them discussing with users and managers about how best to fine-tune it; and I watched as users and managers looked over their shoulders while they were working at the controls.

So again, what I'm trying to do is to resist arguments from the last instance. I am happy with the instincts of most sociologists who want to say: 'No, technology is not determinant in the last instance.' This is right. But I only feel *quite* happy. And this is because, unless we are very careful, when we say this what we are really saying is that it is the *social* that is determinant in the last instance. But this is an impoverished version of the social: warm bodies, selves, their words, their gestures; and maybe their texts. And what I'm saying instead is that it doesn't make much sense to tease this heterogeneous and seamless web apart.

So this is another version of the debate about agency. It is to say that nothing is determinant in the last instance. And to say instead that patterns or arrangements of machines, of bodies – and we could add texts, and architectures, and conversations and many more – perform/embody incomplete orderings.[18] This is what I have tried to tell. Most of the time there is no last instance. There is no simple story. Instead there are modes of ordering, performances, embodiments. And they tell of the organization of agents and their rankings.

4 TECHNICAL HEROISM

Managers have their modes of ordering; and they perform and embody these. But there are quite other ordering patterns being told too. Sometimes the same places embody different ordering arrangements. Or they tend to stabilize these.[19] The Tandem in the NSF runs 24 hours a day, and 7 days a week. So the crew work shifts and, in general, this suits them. This isn't because they are workaholics, for they aren't. Mainly it's because of the pay – it is better paid than equivalent non-shift work. But I think it also has to do with autonomy.

And also because of the embodied skills that I talked of above. The
pride in a job well done.

Once the 'day-drones' go home, the atmosphere in the building
changes. There is the machine. There are two or three experi-
mentalists. There is the odd in-house scientist working late. But
after five the car park rapidly empties and the building *feels* empty.
Empty, remote, but full of powerful noises like – I don't know –
an ocean liner.

This is the moment when crew members take unsupervised responsibility for running many million pounds worth of machinery.
So they sit in the control room; they monitor the behaviour of
the machine and fine-tune its performance; they walk round the
building from time to time to make sure that all is well; they pursue
personal projects on pcs; they drink coffee; and they cook meals in
the small kitchen that adjoins the control room.

I have watched the crew relax after 5.00 p.m. They don't relax
into sloth, but into a special kind of routine, of responsibility, and
into a kind of identification with the machine and the building.
It can be a good time to be in the control room. Gradually the
number of visitors drops off. The machine manager wanders quietly
through with his briefcase, looks over the shoulder of the crew,
satisfies himself that all is well, and disappears home. At this moment there is the sense of a self-contained completeness. Autonomy,
responsibility, isolation, trust – these are some of the terms that come
to my mind. Plus the feeling that the crew is in for a long night's
haul. And that they *are*, somehow, the building.

I *know* that this is a romantic story. But notice two things: it cele-
brates the crew as heroic agents; *and* it performs/embodies organizational rankings.

Here's another heroic story. Actually, it is a part of a much longer
story about commissioning a recalcitrant ion source. The source
generates ions – negatively charged atomic nuclei to feed to the
accelerator. The accelerator won't work without it. The ions come
from a small 'pill' bombarded with a beam of positive caesium ions.
It's a delicate arrangement, and all sorts of things can go wrong.
For instance, it may be poisoned by spraying caesium over its inside
surface.

On the day of my story this had happened. The crew had applied
the remedy, but it didn't seem to be working. After a lot of techical
work which I won't describe here, they decided to try to commission
another quite different source – the 'Alton'.

The original version of this story runs to many pages. But, as I've
edited, I've cut it down to these few paragraphs. And I've just written
the words I use above: 'a lot of technical work which I won't describe
here'.

I've already noted that the people I spoke to at Daresbury said
things like: 'You wouldn't be very interested in that. It's technical
detail.' Or they distinguished in their own practice between the technical and the managerial. But now I'm doing the same: let's say that
I am performing/embodying the ordering of the two cultures in this
script. And performing a pattern of ranking which says something like:
'Technical work is essential, but uninteresting and low status.' In fact
just like the machine physicists as they struggled to commission the
LINAC.

First, however, they needed to find a pill to put in it. By now, with
the building largely empty, there was no question of phoning the
appropriate technician or scientist and getting one sent up. So one
of the crew members went hunting, and after a considerable period
reappeared with a plastic box of sulphur pills. He looked gloomy.
None of them was very satisfactory for they all had neat holes
drilled in their faces – a sign of extensive use. But they picked
through them anyway, to find the least unsatisfactory. And the
same member of the crew went back to the eighth floor, installed
it, and started to pump the 'Alton' ion source down to vacuum.

But then there was another snag. My notes observe: 'they can't
find [the] water pipe connections – so they can't start [the Alton]
up because it isn't cooled'. By this time it was 7.20 p.m. The crew
had been working for nearly four hours, they were beginning to get
tired, and they were also starting to get fed up. Obviously someone
had cannibalized the water hoses to get another piece of equipment
working. But until they could be found they were stuck. And tens
of millions of pounds worth of equipment was standing idle. So
they tried to call the fitter at home. He might know where the
pipes had gone. But they couldn't get through: his line was engaged!

True stories; romantic stories of heroism, autonomy and creative
puzzle-solving. The point of these stories is to show that *the modes
of ordering performed by the crew members at the NSF aren't so different
from those performed by the top managers.* All this work involves skill,
all of it demands a form of enterprise. Perhaps (I'm not so certain
about this) it demands a kind of vision too. But the data, and experience in general, suggest that outsiders tend to delete the work
– and particularly the heroism – that is involved in the efforts
of others. And they tend, in particular, to delete the work of
subordinates: to assume that technical or low-status work gets done
'automatically', as if people were programmable devices.

Of course, there may be differences. It may be that vocational
puzzle-solving by technicians looks more like *bricolage* than the
similar puzzle-solving by scientists. If this is right then it is not,
I think, because scientists are not practised *bricoleurs*.[20] Rather it
is that their bricolage is inserted into *a different network of desire*.
Patrick Snowden:

> scientists are the world's worst and best. They are interested
> in doing their own science, so they are *ruthless* about it. [I
> was working with a particular scientist once, when we were
> having difficulty with the equipment.] He came to me and said:
>
> 'I might as well be dead.'
>
> 'I beg your pardon?' I said.
>
> 'I might as well be dead. If I am not writing papers, then I
> might as well be dead .... To be second in science means that
> you might as well not do science.'

Patrick seems ambivalent about the vocational economy of desire.
But it certainly receives a better press than working-class instrumentalism. But here's another class-relevant difference: if *bricolage*
by technicians sometimes looks like the opportunism of enterprise,
then it is enterprise of a more restricted kind. Partly this is a
matter of the *materials* that we use. Professional *bricolage* uses 'special'
materials, symbolic and otherwise.[21] And partly I think it is a matter
of sheer brass effrontary: while *bricolage* is content to tell of its
heterogeneity, enterprise graces itself by saying that the bits and
pieces that it combines together 'truly' form a whole.

In any case, for the technician, the economy of desire is limited,
the endless promiscuous lust of the Big Man is absent.[22] So the
similarities between the embodied ordering modes of the scientists
and those of the technicians are real. But so, too, are the differences.
And the differences turn around hierarchy and the attribution of
agency. For the economies of skills and desires of those who are
told that they are second-class agents and those who are performed
and perform themselves as second-class agents are different.

> When we tell ordering stories we simplify and 'punctualize'. As we
> embody and perform ordering modes, so, too, we delete. This is
> what agency is about. It's what ordering is about: ignoring; simplifying;
> fixing what is complex for a moment in a stable form; reifying.
>   Symbolic interactionists such as Leigh Star (1992) speak of 'deleting
> the work'. So deletion is unavoidable. The real issue is deletion *plus*
> ranking. And, of course, the perennial desire to turn orderings into
> orders.

And a part of that difference has to do with the compartmentaliza-
tion of desire. Technicians tell of *wanting* to be distant from the
organization. Of wanting, sometimes unsuccessfully, to leave it
behind them when they go home: they tell of autonomy, of being
left to get on with a responsible job like running the machine over-
night. They don't necessarily mind being ignored: 'Experimenters
can get very wrapped up in their work, and be abrupt. Most of
them aren't interested in the complexity of the source.' But they *do*
mind when there is interference, or lack of recognition of their skill
and responsibility. And, when this happens they create and perform
their own stories, stories to do with resistance, for instance like this
from the Synchrotron Radiation Division:

> The job is badly paid compared with local industry. And people
> aren't given any interest in the job. All that the [last] manage-
> ment was concerned with was cutting costs. And it was them
> who introduced the business of clocking in and clocking out.
> And they were always switching overtime on and off. They
> can't have it both ways. They *want* dedication. But the con-
> ditions are terrible.

And they tell stories that celebrate the technical incompetence of
managers and scientists. And they tell stories that neatly combine
resistance with management incompetence:

> *Christine*: They simply haven't thought it through at all. They're
>   going to close down the machine so that the maintenance
>   period will fall over the bank holiday. And that will mean that
>   they will have to pay a lot of extra overtime or, more likely,
>   they will have to extend the maintenance period because they
>   won't be able to get people to come into work over the bank
>   holiday.
> *John Law*: Did they ask you about it?
> *Christine*: Nah! They never ask us our opinion about anything!
> *John Law*: Did you think of mentioning it to management?
> *Christine*: No. They don't want to hear from us.
> *John Law*: So they'll just go ahead with it?
> *Christine*: No. In the end, they'll work it out for themselves!

Note this: the story *also* meshes in with, embodies, or re-enacts
the hierarchical simplifications and deletions of the ordering modes
performed by management; it re-enacts the passivity, the lack of
skill, and the absence of grace that these recount and perform even
though the story also tells of (the possibility of) creative puzzle-
solving by the technicians. But it does so in a different context –

one in which the ordering arrangements of management are stood on their head. It is those who claim to distribute agency and its rewards who become the butt of the joke.

> Working-class instrumentalism; working-class resistance; two of the great myths of sociology; performed, in varying modes by sociologists and the people whom they study. Shades of 'Sambo', the loyal but lazy plantation slave?[23] Of learning to labour?[24] But there are other working-class stories that haven't perhaps quite achieved the same mythical status in sociology. Like pride in a job. Or commitment to puzzle-solving.

When the ordering patterns of ranking overlap, perform, and are embodied in boundary arrangements like those that I've described in this chapter, their effects are powerful indeed: this is the lesson that I want to take away from this chapter. For the sociologists of order have a propensity to say of the sociologies of ordering that they cannot 'deal with' hierarchy, or power. But this seems to me to be entirely misleading. It is, of course, the case that some sociologies of ordering have ignored hierarchy: I tend to agree with those who have suggested that the sociology of scientific knowledge has been relatively uninterested in either gender or class.[25] But this is, at least in substantial measure, a contingency: the remnants, perhaps, of the optimistic form of liberalism that I discussed in the last chapter.

But optimism is no longer appropriate – indeed it has been outgrown – and at their best such modest sociologies as symbolic interactionism, actor-network theory and figurational sociology are all about hierarchy. They are all about distribution, unfairness and pain. And, most importantly, they are all about how these are done in practice. So when the sociology of order complains that inequality is absent what I now hear is a different kind of complaint: an objection to the fact that the sociologies of ordering do not buy into a reductionist commitment to some final version of order; that they are not, for instance, committed to a particular theory of class or gender exploitation; that they refuse to adopt what some feminists call a 'standpoint epistemology';[26] that their materialism is relational rather than dualist; that there is no a priori distinction between the macro-social and the micro-social. These complaints are right, but I don't believe that they are justified. For ordering sociologies, whether legislative or interpretive, prefer to explore *how* hierarchies come to be told, embodied, performed and resisted. But to choose to look at hierarchy in this way is neither to ignore it, nor to deny it. Rather, it is to tell stories about its mechanisms, about its instances, about how we all do it, day by day.

NOTES

1 Feminist writing has started to help us listen out for some of the silences. See, for instance, Rowbotham (1973), and more recently Star (1991). For male commentary, see Law (1991a); and another matching male analysis, Staudenmaier (1988).

2 He makes use of the metaphor in his celebrated paper on ideology and ideological state apparatuses. See Althusser (1971b: 146).

3 I'm substantially persuaded by Steve Shapin that personal contact is a much more important tool in social ordering than sociologists generally assume. (For arguments leading to this conclusion see the analysis of the character of witnessing in Shapin and Schaffer 1985 and Shapin 1989.) It is possible that the advent of the mass media have reshaped the character of charisma, reducing the importance of personal contact, and replacing it with something quite different such as 'television presence'. Or telephone voices. But changes in the modes of communication – the processes that Anthony Giddens calls 'disembedding' – have had complex effects on other forms of ordering. For instance, in enterprise, it appears that for certain purposes face-to-face contact remains essential. (Why else would there be 'smoke-filled rooms' or 'corridors of power'? Why else would it be important to go to Winchester School, and on to Balliol?) And if vocation rests upon apprenticeship, then, notwithstanding the arguments of the proponents of distance learning, then face-to-face contact remains crucial here too.

4 Most of us have stood at those biographical great divides, places like the rift valley of the Dead Sea, places where the personal landscape really looks like the maps that the social geographers draw. For me, and I suppose for others interpolated in the performances of vocation, credentialling rites of passage have felt this way. The day of my Ph.D. oral exam was consequential both for my ranking in profession, and for my character as an agent.

5 A 'wiggler' is a very strong magnet, inserted in the electron beam, which produces a particularly strong beam of light for experimental purposes.

6 To speak of workaholism is to introduce my own twist into the story and impute another commonality. But I do this partly because I notice the commonality; and partly because I want to refuse a moral told in all these ordering modes: that work is an ultimate good.

7 For a classic essay, see Thompson (1967).

8 If we spoke of discourses we would say that the control room and its occupants perform (and embody) interdiscursive arrangements.

9 See Shapin (1989) for a fine, historically sensitive, understanding of the hierarchical character of the work of technicians.

10 For commentary and criticism of what they call the 'dominant ideology thesis' see Abercrombie and Turner (1978).

11 Barry Barnes (1988) says something similar, though he makes his argument in a different idiom, suggesting that all agents are empowered by virtue of their participation in the social.

12 These terms are current in post-structuralist writing. See, for instance, Baudrillard (1988a); Foucault (1981); and Featherstone (1991). For a particularly interesting analysis and discussion, see Bauman (1992).

13 Society is a distribution of knowledge: so says Barry Barnes (1988: 57). It's a good way of telling it. Though it's incomplete.

14 They also worked against the clock, not because time was directly relevant to them (for they were, in some sense, out of time), but because they were only scheduled a small number of shifts to do their commissioning. If they overran then they were faced with irate users.

15 I will develop this argument more fully in chapters 7 and 8.

16 What a dead give-away that word 'routine' is! It speaks of the ranking of machines and of people, all in the same breath. Routines are practised by the *Untermenschen*. 'I am pleased that I am an epsilon ...'. Steve Woolgar (1991) puts it very well, this simultaneous process of designing a machine and the agent who will operate it. Talking of personal computers, he speaks of 'configuring the user'.

17 So it was that I was performed/re-embodied as an outsider rather than an honorary member of the crew after a period spent away from the NSF in other parts of the Laboratory.

18 If we said this, then we could start to explore the strangenesses of impure orderings. Can a machine embody skills? Can it embody desires? Before you laugh, remember that Sherry Turkle tells of the stories that children tell about these questions.

19 For instance, Leigh Star and Jim Griesemer (1989) write about boundary objects – objects that overlap into and play a role in a number of different social worlds. And Madeleine Akrich (1992) writes of scripts and counter-scripts.

20 A *bricoleur* is an odd-job man, someone who makes, makes do, and mends, with whatever there is to hand.

21 Have not middle-class professionals sometimes been tempted to laugh at the sheds made out of corrugated iron and tea chests that appear on allotments? But think about what has been mobilized to make such a shed!

22 Are we not in the presence of what Durkheim (1964) would have called anomie – for he wrote of the way in which desires grow unchecked. The difference is this: now we'd want to say that desire is a social construct too.

23 This example is explored by Elkins (1959).

24 The title (and the idea) comes from Paul Willis (1977).

25 See, for instance, the commentary by Sara Delamont (1987).

26 See, for instance, Harding (1986: 136ff).

7

Dualisms and Gradients: Notes on the Material Forms of Ordering

1 MODE OF ORDERING, MATERIAL AND MODERNITY

Zygmunt Bauman has observed that:

> Ours is a self-reflexive world; self-reflection, monitoring the outcome of past action, revising the plan according to the result of the reflection, re-drawing the map of the latter as the situation keeps changing in the course of and under the influence of action, re-evaluation of the original purposes and adequacy of the originally selected means, and above all an ongoing re-assessment of the plural and uncoordinated values and strategies, have replaced to a great extent the deterministic push of tradition both on the organizational and the individual level. (Bauman 1992: 90)

Translated into my jargon, what he is saying is that in the era of modernism: the recursive networks of the social embody and so, though only ever with partial success, shape themselves by means of reflexive strategies; that they tend to generate places or nodes from which the future might be ordered; and that they tend to generate locations, arrangements or patterns of which it might be said 'these are reflective, planful, thoughtful places, places where one can take stock',[1] and that these planful, thoughtful places bring together and (more or less unsuccessfully) seek to reconcile different modes of ordering.

If this is right it suggests, to misuse George Orwell, that while all networks are recursive, some struggle by self-reflexive means to be

more recursive than others.[2] Again, it suggests that modes of ordering may be seen as *strategies or modes of recursion*. That is, they
may be seen as particular expressions or embodiments of the modern
project. And specifically, it suggests that they might be also be treated
as particular strategies for implementing, or seeking to implement,
Cartesian dualism: that they are bootstrapping arrangements for
generating (and performing discontinuities between) consciousness
and its surroundings, or between mind and matter. Finally, it suggests
a genealogy for the modernist concern with (a particular version
of) heroism – that in which the hero becomes the embodiment of
recursive agency *par excellence, homo clausus* who resolves the mind-
body problem in favour of mind over matter.

Like writers in a number of traditions including those cited above,[3]
I take it that there are good methodological, theoretical and ethical
reasons for rejecting root distinctions between the macro-social and
the micro-social, mind and body, and the agent and social structure.
The argument from symmetry is that we should try to do our level
best to avoid such dualisms. But on the other hand we shouldn't
throw out the baby with the bathwater. In particular, to turn away
from dualism doesn't mean that we should ignore the ordering strains
towards dualism built into the modern project. Instead, we should
seek to treat dualism as a social *project*, a sociological topic, rather
than treating it as a resource. Accordingly, the argument is that
modernism more or less successfully (though partially and precariously)
generates and performs a series of such divisions. It works itself, for
example, some way towards creating the effects that we call 'mind',
or 'organisation', or 'decisionmaking' or 'management' or consciousness. But *how* does it do this? If dualism is to be turned into a
topic, then this is the crucial question.

In earlier chapters I have tried to lever open this question in two
connected ways. First, I have pointed to a series of ordering strategies, or modes of reflexivity, that (I have argued) are carried in,
and performed by, management activity in Daresbury Laboratory.
My assumption is that versions of these strategies are found elsewhere:
that they are not peculiar to Daresbury. It is this that makes the
Daresbury case-study of general rather than specific interest. Each
of these (and, to be sure, all sorts of other) modes of ordering
implies, characterizes, and in part performs places of reflexive privilege. Each, that is, suggests and (in some measure) performs what
Bruno Latour, in the language of actor-network theory, calls a
centre of translation.[4] So each may be treated as a strategy for
generating reflection and control – *as a strategy for generating the
practice of mind or its analogues.*

Second, and more than is usually the case in social theory, I
have tried to press the importance of materials, and the case for
relational materialism. The argument is quite straightforward. It is
that if you scratch the surface of what we tend to think of as the
social, then we will find that this is materially hetereogeneous. The
argument is that *the social is almost never purely social.*

For me these two analytical insights cannot be prised apart. This
is important: *mode of ordering and material need to be taken together.*
I don't want to look at strategies without at the same time looking
at the material character of their ordering. This is because, to the
extent that it is accomplished at all, *reflexivity is a strategic effect
generated by creating distinctions between materials.* In other words, to
practise reflexivity is to practise a series of strategies for generating
differences in durability, and ordering the relationship between the
materials so generated. And specifically, to monitor and to plan an
order is to do three related things:

1 to find ways of simulating and exploring the properties of the more
   durable in materials that are less durable;
2 to find ways of making some materials more durable than others;
   and
3 to find ways of linking the more durable to the less durable, such
   that the latter stand for and represent the former.

I'm saying, then, that it won't do to treat with ordering mode
or strategy as a 'purely social' phenomenon. Indeed, if we put on
one side its predilection for hideous purity, I believe this is the most
fundamental problem of contemporary social theory: its tendency
to imagine that the social is purely social. For patterning mode or
strategy is not simply a matter of ordering the interaction between
social agents, nor indeed of constituting those agents (though both
of these are, of course, important). To view it in this way misses
out the most important part of the argument: to repeat, it misses
out on the way in which the material is a relational effect too.
Indeed, I follow Bruno Latour here: my hunch is that it is the
generation of material effects that lies at the heart of the modernist
project of self-reflexivity. Modern minds and modern centres of
translation are different, but we cannot separate these from the circumstances of their material production.[5]

Look at the figure on page 140. Let's be very careful. Don't let's
interpret it in a mechanical fashion.

**Remember that in a modest and ironic sociology modes of ordering
are defeasible imputations. Remember that in their instantiations, as**

1 2 3 4 ... n

Thought
Talk
Material   Action
Text
Technology
Architecture
Etc

Mode of ordering

they butt up against one another, they work and rework one another: we have, I hoped, escaped from the timeless limbo of synchronic linguistics. Remember, also, that there are other modes of ordering too: those that I've identified are not found everywhere; that they are strategies imputed to the networks of the social, nothing more. But if ordering modes aren't given by nature, then neither are materials. So remember also, as I've just being arguing, that in the networks of the social materials are effects — strategic effects. The list in the figure above is arbitrary. It could be otherwise. For materials are not given in the order of things.

So long as we can avoid a mechanical reading the figure is handy because it points to the kind of space for sociological inquiry that I'd like to see opened up. This space is theoretical, but also empirical. In particular, it's a space which generates a series of more or less empirical questions about the production of dualisms and asymmetries. Here are some of these questions:

How are modes of ordering *carried*?
How do they *pattern themselves* within the networks of the social to generate and characterize particular material relations?
How are the latter related to those generated in *other ordering patterns*?
How do they tend to generate the *privileged places* where the monitoring and the revisions that we call 'decisionmaking' or 'consciousness' result?

I take it that these are the kinds of empirical questions about the production of dualism opened up in a modest and pragmatic relational materialism, and I now want to touch on some them.

2   THE HETEROGENEITY OF DUALISM

Let's start by remembering that a place like Daresbury Laboratory is a physical place, an arrangement of non-human materials. For instance, it is stuffed full of machinery, scientific machinery, and much of this is on an industrial scale. The NSF tower stands 200 feet high, dominating the Mersey valley for miles around. You can see it from the main London to Glasgow railway line. And if you crane your neck and know exactly where to look, you can just see it from the M6 motorway on the Thelwall Viaduct. The tower is tall because it contains the monstrous van de Graaf generator which accelerates atomic nuclei and fires them at other atoms. And it's upright because they didn't want to risk lying it down on its side in case it sagged.

The NSF is at the top of the site. If you walk down the slope of the access road you come to the large, rather shabby, nondescript industrial building which houses the SR Accelerator. This is a large ring with a circumference of nearly 100 metres. It's housed in a huge hall, and it works by shining intense beams of light down tangential tubes to its many experimental stations. With its gantries and catwalks, it's 15 feet – in places 20 feet – high. And if you clamber over the Ring, up and down the stairs, as you can when it is not in operation, you can see the klystron and the high-voltage control equipment at its centre. The klystron, which is 8 feet tall, is the power source which lies at the heart of every television transmitter, and it is this which pumps out the RF (radio frequency) radiation which keeps the electrons moving round the ring.

These are the giant machines at Daresbury, these and the mainframe computers. If you ask a scientist what Daresbury is about, it's most likely she will tell you about work that uses the SR Accelerator, the NSF van de Graaf, or the supercomputers. But these are just the tip of the mechanical iceberg. Everywhere you go, there are machines. Computer terminals, Macintoshes, Sun stations, cameras, photocopiers, telephones, printers, lathes, drills, milling machines, pumps of all sizes and descriptions, cranes, bending magnets, trolleys, vacuum cleaners, coffee-dispensers, centrifuges, ovens, refrigerators, calculators, shredding machines, faxes, transformers, circuit-breakers, TV monitors, public-address systems, water de-ionizing plants, compressors. Truly, it's difficult to ignore the machinery at Daresbury. That is why the Lab is there. Because of the machinery.

In my story the architecture, the machinery and the social relations of the Lab all go together. They *all* perform and embody modes of ordering. They're inextricably entwined. There is no possibility of separating them out at all.

How many ways can I say this without being boring? Without stating the obvious? Bruno Latour (1988b) reminds use that even pure mathematicians (why should I say 'even'?) work with the tools of their trade. Everything we do, from epistemology to digging the garden, is

> a trade with its own tools. We need to break down the dualism of
> head and hand, the idea that the less embodied the intellect, the
> better it is.

This is why I believe that the stories which we tell of ordering will
be the poorer if we try to treat them separately from the materials
in which they are carried.

> I've talked of ordering modes, and I've named a few of them. But
> what about the others, those of which we do not tell? Now, or ever?
> Did you ever read *The Ship Who Sang*? Who can tell what songs
> machines sing to themselves?
>   You accuse me of romanticism? Perhaps you are right, though I
> would prefer to say that I am a mystic. I believe that there are songs
> which are sung which we have not heard. But my romanticism is also
> a principle of method. I prefer to be cautious, to find ways of telling
> stories of ordering than blaspheming with stories of pure order, even
> sociological pure order.

There are various ways of telling the story, but since I'm particularly interested in dualisms I want to get a lever on this by
thinking of the spatial organization of the Lab, and the ordering
performances and materials which generate the distinction between
backstage and frontstage. Here, for instance, is one restricted place:
Andrew Goldthorpe's office. Though it's not palatial, it's somewhat
larger and better appointed than the average office at Daresbury.
But, though the walls and the door are standard issue, they perform
somewhat differently here: they tell of ranking, though they don't
do so by themselves. For the performance is also told by a gate-
keeper, his secretary, and her presence in an ante-room. And the
general absence of the lower ranks.[6]

But Andrew's rank is strategically performed in a series of materials. No. I don't want to say that it is *reducible* to the materials
that I've just mentioned. This is the trouble with sociological myth-
making: it tends to want to reduce too soon, to ask *why* someone
is the boss, or why there is a boss at all, rather than asking *how*
bossing is performed.[7] Thus if Andrew's office were gutted by fire
and he were obliged to set up in the users' coffee room I guess
that he'd *still* be performed as the Director. But what would happen
if they took away his phone? And his secretary? And the stream
of papers that crosses his desk? And what would happen if he
were no longer able to travel south to London or to Head Office
at Swindon? Or receive visitors? Would he still be Director then?
And what would it mean if he were?

> There are pretenders to half the thrones of Europe. Did you know that
> the last of the Bourbons lives in internal exile north of Paris, waiting
> for the call?

This is what I want to say: all these materials and endless others *together* perform Andrew Goldthorpe as Director of Daresbury.[8] But this isn't quite right either, for the Directorship is not reducible to whatever lies *outside* the skin either: it's obvious to those who watch him that Andrew is very smart. And very skilled. Like the rest of us, he *embodies* a set of relations, a set of memories, a set of preferences. The myth of high office is embodied in a series of performances, a series of materials, and a series of spatial arrangements, corporeal and otherwise. None is necessarily crucial, but *if we take them together then they generate the effect.*[9]

Here's another restricted space: the major computer room at Daresbury. Here there are more walls. And locked doors. And air conditioning. For in some ways the computer is more demanding than Andrew Goldthorpe. People may need quiet in order to think. But when the computer tries to organize its thoughts it needs a supply of pure air at a specified temperature. Together with a strictly controlled regime of electricity, of programs, and of data.

> In telling it this way I'm not trying to be rude about Andrew. What I'm trying to do is to see what happens if we tell a short story about a machine in terms similar to those we would use when talking of a person. If this *sounds* dismissive, this is because we do not usually tell stories in this way. We prefer to tell that people are different in kind. We continue to prefer dualisms to gradients.[10]

So the fans of the air conditioning perform the separation of the computer from its environment, as do the walls and doors. But there's more to tell about the computer, for they say that it is 'sensitive', that it does not appreciate disturbances. Thus it carries confidential data – files that can only be restored with difficulty. And they say that it's so powerful that access is also restricted on grounds of national security. Here's the conclusion: where the computer goes, most of us do not – which is, I think, a dualist performance from the storybook of administration, but one that is told in steel and passwords, slivers of silicon, and the wording of the Data Protection Act and the Official Secrets Act. And isn't it also embodied, somewhat differently, in vocation? For which scientist wishes to lose her precious data?[11]

At Daresbury there are many stories about places, machines and people. Some of these are told in the language of safety, a language that often turns out to be a dialect of administrative ordering. For instance, there are places where people cannot go when the SR Accelerator is working because it is said that they are full of lethal X-rays and intense magnetic fields.[12] People take these hazards very seriously. And the business of defining them and separating them from people is performed and embodied in a series of interacting materials.

> This is the place I'm trying to get to: that we should feel comfortable talking of the *heterogeneity* of our arrangements. That we should feel comfortable in thinking of ourselves as the *effect* of a process like heterogeneous engineering.
>
> I want to get to the place described by Steve Woolgar. I want to say that the business of defining what is to count as an agent is *performed*, actually performed, in these safety regulations. Don't forget this: Marie Curie performed safety differently; and with it agency. And so did I when I looked through the X-ray scopes at the bones in my feet in the shoe-shops of my childhood. That's the analytical point: the boundary between agents and machines is an *effect*. The nouns are all verbs as well. Consequences. Or, if you prefer, the bits and pieces that we tell as being incorporated within the person (paracetamol? heart pacemakers? cars? clothes? laptop computers?) are not stable.
>
> But there's a moral point too. Sure, we're all in the process of defining and redefining what it is to be a human being. But it is best to be cautious. Do not believe those who tell you simple stories about that boundary. Remember that Hitler told hideously simple stories too.

For instance, after it has been serviced, the crew switch the SR Accelerator on. But first they search the machine area to make sure there is no one there. One day I was with the crew as they climbed and crawled round and through the labyrinth of pipes and devices that makes up the ring. And I followed them down the ladder into the underworld of dimly lit corridors which carry the ducts and cables that pass beneath the machine.

I hadn't understood this before, but I learned that day that the search by the crew is neither casual nor random. It's systematic, and that system has been carefully planned. Indeed the crew have no choice in the matter. They are required to press a series of buttons at different places in the search area in the appropriate order. And they have to press designated *pairs* of those buttons simultaneously.

> I believe nuclear missiles are armed and fired by means of similar protocols. Perhaps it is that where we cannot trust either machines or people by themselves to perform their scripts, together they turn in a more satisfactory performance?
>
> But no. That cannot be right. Charles Perrow[13] tells us hair-raising stories about the disastrous errors made by complex arrangements of people-and-machines. Three Mile Island sang its own song, and when it sang we learned the hard way that our scripts are never complete, that ordering is a fallible verb.

If the search goes wrong — for instance if the sequence in which the buttons are pressed isn't right — the crew has to start again. But if the search is 'successful' then the crew leader watches the TV monitor and sees the two searchers leaving the machine area. He watches as they close the security gate behind them. And he checks the control console to see whether they have done this properly — for sometimes they have to slam it to make the contact. Then, and only then, the interlock falls into place and it is possible to power up the magnets, switch on the klystron, and inject electrons into the ring.

Here's the moral: whatever's going on to distinguish between the inside and the outside, to generate the places of privilege, it depends upon a delicate dance of people-and machines. Parts of this network are embedded in the bodies of the technicians — and in their actions. Some are built into the circuits, the switches, and the relays of the SR Source safety system. But, for the moment, it's the *continuity* which impresses me most, the continuity between the different materials of the network as they perform the gradients that strain towards dualism.

3 PRIVILEGE, ARCHITECTURE AND THE BODY

Let's talk about the materials of another privileged place, another place which enacts the organizational equivalent of Cartesian dualism. Once a month the top managers — the Daresbury Management Board (DMB) — meet in Andrew Goldthorpe's office. The six managers sit round a conference table, usually for between one and two hours. They bring papers that have been circulated beforehand, and in its usual order of business the DMB works its way through an agenda which refers to these papers. Sometimes additional items are included in the agenda, perhaps because they are late but more usually because they are so informal that it doesn't occur to the administration to agenda them — as, for instance, in the reporting and discussion of intelligence gathered by one or other of the managers. Occasionally items are not put on the agenda because they are sensitive, and it is thought better not to commit them to paper at all.

So the DMB meeting is not unusual. Anyone who works in an organization will instantly recognize its general form: the cocktail of paperwork, talk and personalities that generates the discussions and conclusions that make up the modern managerial meeting. And neither would that observer be surprised to find that, in a small group of middle-aged men who know each other (and one another's foibles) well, talk oscillates between the formal and the informal, between what is serious and what is not.

However, though the form of the DMB meeting is unremark-able, the DMB is none the less taken to be a special place. If we choose to inscribe it in administrative ordering, then it is the senior decisionmaking committee in the Laboratory. So few people (including many senior and responsible managers) participate. And it is also worthwhile stating the obvious: outsiders do not observe or listen in to what goes on. Thus the membership and the privacy − the sense of backstage privilege − is also reproduced in the topography of the meeting.

I have mentioned that this meeting takes place in Andrew Gold-thorpe's room. I've also mentioned that for most members of the Laboratory, most of the time, this is a pretty inaccessible space. To say this is not to make a personal comment about Andrew Goldthorpe himself. He's generally friendly and few people think that he is stuck up. Rather it is an observation about a hierarchical role. For in any of the modes of ordering that I've identified, to be the director of a large organization is to be distinguished and set aside from others. So, whatever he says, when he is at work Andrew speaks of hierarchy. But this is not all: in the way I have noted above, the *office* also speaks of and tends to embody hierarchy.[14] Direct access *is* possible, but most people never go into the room because they have no business there. And those who do mostly pass through an ante-room and check with the secretary before entering.

Now I need to make a more personal comment: if the room is not exactly a sacred space, I nonetheless experienced it as rather special. I've noted that it is quite large, but I haven't so far said that the interior decor and furniture also speak, at least to me, of organizational power.[15] Of course, we need to be cautious. It is no more acceptable to attempt a mechanistic decoding of the fur-nishings of a room than it is to interpret any other text in this way.[16] Even so, like other materials, the decor and furniture of a room embody, perform and instantiate nodes of ordering, together with the distributions and hierarchies that these tend to carry with them.[17] So, albeit quite modestly by contemporary standards, Andrew Goldthorpe's office spoke to me of power.

Physically, it is furnished with a version of the accoutrements that are thought appropriate for the managing directors of large organiza-tions in the 1990s. There is a rather superior carpet. There is a large 'executive desk' with a VDU and a keyboard, together with (one or more) telephones. There are several easy chairs, grouped around a low coffee table. And there is a conference table, with six upright but comfortable chairs. This is not the shiny idiom of sprayed metal and plastic to be found in lower-status offices. Instead, the predominant effect is of oiled wood and attractive rough-textured cloth.

So the room speaks of hierarchy. But the hierarchical roles of which it speaks can be broken down.

1 there is the *individual* work of Andrew Goldthorpe (and high status executives in general); this is done at the (large) desk;
2 there is the collective work of chairing *meetings*; this is done from one end of the conference table; and
3 there is the *informal* work of meeting equals, or at any rate people who are to be put at their ease. This, which involves diluting or denying the effects of hierarchy, is done by sitting in the easy-chairs round the coffee table.[18]

For nearly a year I sat in on the meetings of the DMB. I didn't sit at the conference table. Instead, I lodged in one of the easy chairs next to the coffee table. So I was removed from, and physically lower than the members of the DMB. Why was this? What was going on?

There's a straightfoward answer that is partly correct: all the places at the conference table were taken by members of the DMB, and there wasn't room for me. But it was more than this. For instance, throughout, I experienced the overwhelming sense that I did not *properly* belong there at all. Obviously, I wasn't a member of the DMB and I had no rights to speak. But despite the fact that I was in one of the easy chairs, I usually felt uncomfortable or even anxious. So why was this?[19]

The answer partly lies in the very character of ethnography: the ethnographer is *always* inscribed in a place where she does not properly belong. She is always a stranger, always partly foreign. This was how I experienced it. But this is only a beginning. For instance, I usually felt much less anxious in other meetings. So why?

I think any answer comes in several parts. First, there's an issue to do with familiarity: I often knew people in the other meetings better than (some, at least, of) the members of the DMB. Second, I need to say that I'm frightened of people in powerful positions. Quite simply, I embody and perform a series of hierarchical effects: deference, anxiety, a sense of a lack of personal worth.[20] But the DMB brought together the most powerful people in the Lab, so I found that frightening. I guess that this is probably the most important factor.

What happens if we use the body as an instrument for sociological research? Jan Low says that bodies get deleted from ethnographies.

> I hadn't thought about it before in this way, but I think she's right. In general they do. But if we want to turn dualisms into effects, gradients, and ask how they are performed, then the corporeal becomes a part, just another part, of that performance. And our bodies become just another way of understanding our performance. As Jan indicates, it's in this light that we need to consider why the body disappears from ethnography: why we don't for instance, write that we are shit scared; or, for that matter, caught up in admiration, infatuation, or love.[21]

Third, there was something about the *way* in which my status as an outsider was acknowledged. When I first attended other meetings I was normally introduced by the chairperson. And if people asked me to say what I was doing, I tended to respond by saying that I was 'a fly on the wall' looking to see how scientists and engineers 'really make decisions'.

> This kind of comment often led to jokes: people might laugh and threaten to swat the fly on the wall; or they might transmute what I'd said and refer to me jokingly as 'the fly in the ointment' or 'the flea in the ear'.
>
>   I guess we don't need to go far into the character of this kind of humour to note that it is, amongst other things, a way of acknowledging ambivalence. It is, surely, a way of dealing with anxiety, of recognizing that something is out of place. And it is a way of bringing that anxiety out in the open. At any rate, whatever it did for others, the acknowledgement of that ambivalence reduced *my* anxiety.

By contrast, at the DMB they knew who I was before the study started. I don't remember ever being introduced formally to the DMB, and certainly I didn't speak to them collectively about what I was up to. And subsequently, they almost always ignored me. In this respect it wasn't so different from any other meeting, except that I was rarely acknowledged and included by the ambiguity of humour.[22] Instead, however, I was distanced from the meeting in terms of height (I was low, they were high), spatially (they were at the conference table whereas I was not), and by the inappropriate informality of the easy chair and the coffee table.[23] And on the very rare occasions when a member of the DMB *did* speak to me, it was usually the Laboratory Secretary, John White who did so in order to remind me that the business was confidential:[24] to remind me, in effect, that I was an outsider.

Treat this as an observation rather than a complaint: here, more than anywhere else in the Lab, I felt that I did not belong. To attend this meeting generated a corresponding corporeal effect in me: that of anxiety, and a constraining need to be on my best behaviour, an anxiety which is just another material part in the performance of dualism.

What I've just written might be treated as a whinge, a complaint. But it's not intended as such. I hope that it is really to do with treating the body as an instrument for sociological research.

My sense of anxiety is consistent with the sociologies of both Norbert Elias (1983) and Pierre Bourdieu (1986). In figurational sociology it would be interpreted as a need to conform to the civilizing process, a calculative need to suppress any tendency in the direction of the spontaneous expression of emotion.

But perhaps Pierre Bourdieu's notion of habitus is even more useful here. Though I scarcely think that I am proletarian, nor even petit bourgeois, the situation that I describe makes me think immediately of his memorable observation that 'The petit bourgeois is a proletarian who makes himself small to become bourgeois' (1986: 338). The DMB was a place where I tried to make myself as small as possible.

This then, was my experience: that the DMB was a special place and time, one set aside. It was a powerful place, somewhat sacred. It was a reflexive and consequential place. Dualisms were being performed. But this is only a part of the story. There was something else going on which scarcely fits with this at all.

When I first attended the DMB I arrived with a set of dualist assumptions, bodily, but also (as it were) more cognitive. For instance, I thought, without having thought about it very much, that this was the place where the *real* decisions were made, where the *real* action was. And I thought, as I drove to Daresbury to attend my first meeting of the DMB: 'Now I'll find out what's *really* going on at the Lab.' But here is the oddity, the anomaly, the inconsistency. Despite my dualist presuppositions I was rapidly disillusioned. I've mentioned this before: in practice I only rarely experienced the business in this way. Sometimes – no most of the time – *the DMB seemed to be where the action was not.* Indeed, often it seemed downright mundane. So why was this? What was going on?

First, an ethnographic observation:[25] a lot of the DMB business had to do with administrative or infrastructural matters. One of the reasons for this is quite straightforward. For many purposes Daresbury wasn't a single laboratory at all,[26] and this was reflected in the business of the DMB. Think of it as the Daresbury Ministry of Foreign Trade and this catches a certain truth, for much of the business had to do with the administrative (or political) interaction with Head Office or other off-site bodies. Then roll Sir Humphrey Appleby's Department of Administrative Affairs[27] into the mix and you net about 80 per cent of the business: overheads, conditions of service, organizational charts, manpower ceilings, systems of budgeting, demands from Head Office ... these were the stock in trade of the DMB. And, on the whole, they weren't wildly exciting.[28]

I don't doubt that my feeling that the work of the DMB was mundane is in part a reflection of the modes of ordering that I carry. Though I've tried to resist this, I find it too easy to perform administration as a more or less trivial overhead.[29] And it is difficult to map more than about 20 per cent of the business of the DMB on to the patterning of vocation, enterprise or vision.

But this is only a part of the story. Think, again, of the dualist theory of agency carried in these ordering modes. The latter tell that certain heroic places and persons are special, set aside, particularly energetic, creative, visionary, skilful, and the rest. Sometimes, to be sure, we are sceptical about these suggestions. But, though we may struggle with these dualist myths, most of the time I find that I at least am caught up in them.

I've described the way in which that dualism is inscribed in me above: as a body, I *experience* the privilege of dualism as I move from the centre to the periphery; and, as it were, cognitively I *expect* to see it being performed.[30]

So what happens if we find ourselves in a special and privileged place? There are various possibilities. But if we come with a dualist habitus, then there's a good chance that we'll feel let down for we suddenly find that the heroes who rule us are not 'really' heroes at all; that they are no more competent than us; that they see no further than we do; that they are smallminded or corrupt; or that they have mortgages and gum disease; we learn that they are not omniscient, that there are limits to their self-reflexivity too; we learn, though they may *tell* it otherwise when they gloss what they are up to, that *their* version of the modernist project is little more successful than our own; we learn, in short, that there is a *gradient* between the reflexive parts of the networks of the social and the rest, not a dichotomy. Here is the bottom line: *we start to learn that dualism is an effect.*[31]

Perhaps we all *live* in banality but *tell* of heroism or infamy?[32] Such a bifurcation would be consistent with the commitment of the modernist project to reflexive dualism. So we'd discover that heroes, generated as they are in Bruno Latour's 'secondary mechanism' are *always* somewhere else, inhabiting the pages of fairy tales.[33]

So my position is this: most of the real work of the Laboratory is not done in the DMB; its done elsewhere. No: it's not done *somewhere* else in particular — for this would be to rehabilitate heroic dualism in some other form. Instead we need to say that it is done *everywhere* else. Work is distributed through the networks of the social, through the laboratories and the control rooms, the workshops and the kitchens, the offices and the seminar rooms. So the DMB is not special. Or, if it is special, then it is because it deletes the other work, and speaks for it. It's because the networks in which it is embedded strain towards the impossible apogee of dualism. So the inquiry is re-focused, as we look at the material gradients that perform dualisms. We start to look at the place, the time, the props. We start to look, as I've tried to above, at the way in which dualisms are written into our own bodies. And we start to look at the materials of representation.

4   PAPERWORK AND PRIVILEGE

There are patterns of ordering, modes of reflexivity, expressions of the modern project. These modes tell of themselves, they perform themselves, and they embody themselves in different materials. And, as a part of this, they gather experience about the universe, they process it, they distribute it, and they display it. But the way in which they do this, the way in which they strain towards dualism – what counts as experience, how it is assembled, how it is reproduced or represented – all of these depend upon the character of the mode of ordering in question.

> If we want to talk sociologically, we can say that a mode of ordering is also a mode of representation, or a mode of reflexivity. Or, at any rate, it implies a mode of representation. If we want to talk philosophically, we can say that it embodies and performs a practical epistemology.

How is experience assembled? What is it that is created and included? What is excluded, unknown, unheard? These are material questions about the practical epistemology of organizing. Paperwork, talk, visual depiction, models, computer simulations – all of these perform and instantiate the gradients that strain towards dualism. For the practices of representing are many and varied.

> The invention of linear perspective. Chiaroscuro. A visual language for geology. False colour on digital maps. Logarithms. Cubism. Traffic lights. Leitmotivs. Language. Heavy metal. X-ray diffraction patterns. Cartoon strips. Fractals. Computer code. The Speech for the Prosecution. Radar displays. Cell phones. Proportional representation. The silent worship of a Quaker meeting. Graphology. The Queen's Speech. The political funerals in the South African townships. Candles, clinking keys, Union Jacks, masonic handshakes, string quartets. Truly, the list is endless.

Visual, verbal, textual – we shouldn't get too hung up about the statistical or mathematical forms of representing. What's important is the jump from bits and pieces in one medium or form into bits and pieces in another, another which is said to 'stand for' or 'speak on behalf of' the first: it's this jump that performs the strain towards dualism.

So there are differences in materials, just as there are differences between the modes of ordering that are performed in the materials. But there are also similarities, common themes to all modes of representing.[34] Here's the first. I want to say that all these stories, wherever they derive from, and whatever it is that they tell, have this in common: that they are *simplifications*. Obviously, the mode of simplification varies. Is there talk of heroes and villains: of Little Red Riding Hood and the Big Bad Wolf? Or is this the kind of story in which heroes are effaced in due process, in duties and legalities? Answer: it depends on the ordering mode in which the story is told. The character of agency – and all the other materials of drama – will vary. But – this is the basic point – *no story ever tells it all*. It wouldn't be a story if it did.

> One of the stories that they started to tell in the Laboratory shortly before I arrived was about 'manpower'. And particularly about the way in which it was used. I think that this derives from the patterning of enterprise. Suddenly, people aren't clerks. They're resources. And they have to be deployed. But, to make the best decisions about deploying them, first you have to know where they are, and how they spend their time. So that's the simplifying principle.
>
> I wasn't there when this system was first designed. So I don't have any data about it. But they must have said to one another: what shall we bother with? How much detail do we need? What can we do without? And, if we take our critical distance, then we can guess that even to think of telling the 'story of manpower' in the first place meant that all sorts of other stories that might have been told were not.
>
> But the same is true for my story too. It's a heroic simplification. And the simplification could have been done in other ways.
>
> So these are practical questions. Every time we tell a story we have to solve them. But they're the same questions as those addressed by political philosophers: questions about how the views/activities of many may be translated into a just, a legitimate, or at any rate a workable, electoral system. To tell a story is to practise a form of political philosophy. It's to define and perform rights, or the absence of rights.[35]

So much is concealed. For all stories, looked at from another point of view, another mode of ordering, are also heroic attempts at *suppression*. This is the second point. All sorts of bits and pieces – events that *might* have been told – these are excluded, deleted, suppressed, forgotten, ignored or considered irrelevant. For instance, a manpower booking system doesn't need to tell of most of the 'details': it doesn't need to tell whether a scientist, an engineer, or a shop-floor worker is a man or a woman. In this context the work of men and women is subsumed to the gendered category of manpower. Human resources are de-gendered. Or non-gendered. That's how enterprise sees it, at least until it reaches a place where its (male) human capital is starting to dry up. Or it needs gender-specific services. [36]

So every story strains towards dualism by being partial, every story deletes almost everything. If we are offended by the partiality of a story, then we may say that it is ideological. [37] Or false. Or that it doesn't correspond to the way in which things 'really' are. But beware! What *counts* as truth, or correspondence, or impartiality? This has been a great battleground between the protagonists of different myths of hideous purity, each claiming special access to the truth. But now we have the means to tell it differently, to say that what we tell as the truth is lodged within one mode of ordering or another. Or, perhaps better, that it's lodged and performed within the interdiscursive places which we all inhabit, those places where the different orderings lap up against one another to explore their limits and their boundary relations. We no longer have the luxury of stepping outside a mode of ordering.

'No longer'? Well, of course, we never did. We only *thought* that we did, for the hideous claims to epistemological purity echoed as the myths were performed. And each sought to drive its rivals into the marginal and destructive places inhabited by distraction. But perhaps, now, we might do a little better. Perhaps we can understand, in this post-sociology of knowledge, that truth is lodged in ordering patterns and their values, as well as in experience. And that performance brings these things together. So perhaps we can accept that there are truths, but that our truths are also modes of deafness. This is why we might tell fragmentary stories, and sing songs in the centre of the sociological clearing. That way, we might hear truths being told in other ways in the place where, in the past, we were only allowed to write accounts that would pass as 'scientific'. That way we might hear that objectivity comes in other forms too.

We can't step outside an ordering mode. But this shouldn't paralyse us. It shouldn't stop us seeking for truths. Or telling our own stories about how truth may be distinguished from power. It shouldn't stop us, as George Fox put it, speaking truth to power. For we are all interpolated, one way or another, in the ordering production of truth. Which is a fancy way of saying that we aren't floating around in mid-air. We're anchored somewhere. So we *still* have grounds for telling stories. Local grounds. Grounds that carry and embody values that we hold dear.

So every story, each representation, is selective. But to put it this way is already misleading. In particular, it's to assume that what is to be selected exists before it is selected, like tins of soup sitting on a supermarket shelf.

> Here are the kinds of questions that we need to think about. Do heroes exist independently of the stories that are told of them? Does consciousness exist before the stories that it tells and performs? Does it exist outside the stories that are told of it? Or the votes? Or the electors? Or the manpower bookings? Or the manpower codes that make the manpower bookings possible?
>   Think about the managers and the accountants as they sit down to design a set of codes, deciding what is important, and what is not, what can be properly grouped together, and what cannot. Like the drafting of an Electoral Reform Bill, this is a process of design, the design of an asymmetrical and dualist world.

So there's more than selection. If I were to put the point, coldly, in the language of social science I would say that selection presupposes *coding*. It depends on a process in which events or activities are converted from one form into another: from what is represented, to whatever it is that is going to try to do the representing.

> The symbolic interactionists know this well. For many years they have talked of the importance of labelling and the attribution of deviance. And there is fine work by ethnomethodologists on the decisions that go into social science coding.[38] But the point is a general one. It doesn't particularly have to do with social science.

The equation joins what is represented to what is going to try to represent it. But both the terms in this equation are shaped in the process of designing the equation itself.

> We tend to want to say: 'These things existed already. It's just that we didn't know about them.' This was the complaint about the symbolic interactionist theory of labelling, that it didn't have anything to say about 'primary deviance'. Or we tend to want to say 'We knew they were there, but we didn't have the means of collecting the data.' This is the form of justification of almost every piece of research, scientific or social scientific, when it goes out to seek funding.
>   But if we speak in this way we beg an important question: in what sense did these things 'really exist' *before* we started to represent them?

So I'm saying that representation tries to shape whatever it represents. But please don't misunderstand me. I'm not saying that there is nothing there to shape. I'm not saying that you can dream up any old story and expect it to be as good as any other representation.[39] Instead, what counts as a successful story, a successful representation — this depends on the ordering mode that is being performed. But, wherever we look, we find that some representations are 'successful' whereas others are not. That is, some manage to code up and represent parts of their environment, whereas others do not.

> Bruno Latour puts it this way: he says that those who claim to represent sometimes succeed and sometimes they do not. This is an empirical matter — and it's a matter of degree. It's to do with the relationship between who or what is spoken *for*, and who or what is spoken *to*. (And sometimes these are the same).
> Suddenly, in Europe, the Marxist parties no longer speak on behalf of the proletariat. What used to be the proletariat — or was *told* as being the proletariat — has found other spokespersons and tells other stories. The conditions that used to allow the General Secretary to speak for the proletariat have dissolved. But for a long time, though I might have wished it differently, this was not the case.

Here's another way of putting it: representations, whatever their provenance, are always the *product of ordering work*. They're a *part* of ordering. And they are produced *in* ordering. It's the same story again. A recursive Foucauldian story. A story of processes, of verbs straining to perform material gradients, not the nouns of dualism.[40] For representations have to find a middle way. They don't just select between the myriad bits and pieces that happen to be lying around and shake them up together in a bag to form a picture. Neither do they invent such bits and pieces, *de novo*. Instead, the components of a picture are *built up*. With difficulty. Often painfully. On the basis of what is already being performed out there.

I've got good data on this from the Laboratory. It has to do with the manpower-booking system. James Goody is the Laboratory Finance Officer:

James Goody: [The manpower-booking system] is still not very successful. For the month of August we still had 40 plus cards outstanding at 3.00 p.m. today. This is about the norm. The people vary, [though] there are one or two persistent offenders.

Peter Baron: That's about 10 per cent.

Hugh Campbell: All the cases I've investigated have been due to legitimate absence from the Lab.

Jim Haslehurst: But that's not an excuse. The cards are out a long time in advance, and we've asked supervisors to fill them in.

Hugh Campbell: It's difficult to find a way of operationalizing it.

This talk is all about ordering – the ordering of representation. Hugh Campbell says 'It's difficult to find a way of operationalizing it.' I guess that Hugh approves of the manpower-booking system, at least in principle. He knows that that if the Laboratory is to perform properly – that is, if it is to perform self-reflexively – then as a part of this it's going to need to know how it deploys its manpower. But, at the same time, perhaps there is sweat in that statement. Or irritation. At any rate, I guess that there's a profound sense of the gap that opens up between the telling of a story – the story of manpower bookings – and the way it is performed in practice. And, at the same time, there's also a sense of the work that goes into the coding – of the gap between what people would tell about their own doings, and what they have to *report* themselves as doing for the purposes of the manpower booking system.

> This is the problem. The working day is a hodgepodge of bits and pieces – performances within a dozen different stories and three or four different modes of ordering. But the manpower-booking form has to simplify. If it didn't, there'd be no possibility of coding up the results that come into the Finance Office at the end of each month. So the form divides the time up into half-day chunks. And it defines – I don't know – perhaps thirty different activity codes.
>
> So here's the employee's task: to jump from the hodgepodge of the experienced day to the chillingly clear categories provided by the form. Sometimes this may be easy. For instance, if you've sat in a committee meeting about the design of the Second Wiggler all morning, then the code you should be putting down is fairly clear. But what about those mornings that were broken up in a dozen different ways? Under these circumstances, even if the spirit is willing the flesh may well be weak.
>
> Unsurprisingly, the ordering of the system of representation starts to experience its limits: forms are not filled in; or they are filled in wrongly.

This is what the manpower-booking system is all about. It's about a set of statistics to do with 'effort', statistics that may be laid on the desks of senior managers each month, so that they can see at a glance, how manpower has been deployed. And this business, the ability to see *at a glance*, is terribly important. The effect of surveillance is not achieved, unless everything comes together. Here's a different example, not to do with manpower booking:

Jim Haslehurst: You don't give us a printout of the actual receipts received on this chart.

James Goody: I could do.

Jim Haslehurst: That would mean we could see what expected receipts we needed to worry about.

Michel Foucault is right. Metaphorically, a good system of representation is a bit like a perfect set of optics. It transmits (in fact translates and creates) the essentials: 'Am I alone in finding Part 4 not transparent? I find it confusing. Every time there is a change I have to read everything, and all the footnotes.' But it also brings them together to create a focal point: 'The *overall* nature of these family trees is just what you need to see, at a glance ... .' And again:

Giovanni Alberti: Let me ask you a question. Do you get *this*? [He gestures to a substantial computer printout].

Stephen Nicholson: We *don't* get a summary.

Stuart Fraser: This is the Stuart Fraser special summary. I think it would help if you did. That gives you the global summary.

So it is that a focal point, a nerve centre, is generated:

Giovanni Alberti: This [chart] is supposed to be a communal fact. It is being circulated. You can add your own corrections, and pass it on.

Stephen Nicholson: But we can do it on the *computer*.

Giovanni Alberti: Yes. Okay. But we need a *central* one. And I propose that the central one is the one on my Macintosh. And you can all get into my Macintosh.

So everything comes together in one place. And how things appear to be is compared at that place with how things ought to be. So it is that action becomes possible. For instance, to return to the case of the manpower-booking system, without summary and focused representation, the following kind of conversation would not be possible:

Andrew Goldthorpe: The manpower [used] was low [when we looked at it] in December. It was said that it would pick up. We aimed to use 19 man years, and we actually used 7 in-house man years.

Patrick Snowden: No. The 19 includes contract labour.

Andrew Goldthorpe: Okay. How does it break down?

Patrick Snowden: With contract labour we got 2.4 man years. So in all [we got about] 9.5 man years.

Andrew Goldthorpe: Okay. But contract effort is counted in £s. So [when the report is made to] the LMC [Laboratory Management

Committee] it gets it (1) in £s, and (2) in direct man years. [In any case] we planned for 19, not 10. And next year we planned to use 29, and we will have to use 39. So there is a big gap developing. I think that means we've got a problem developing. Is that right?

The details don't really matter. What is important is two things. First, that the conversation is an example of all the features of the modern world pointed to by Zygmunt Bauman in the quotation with which I started the chapter. In other words, it is all to do with self-reflection, self-monitoring and revising. But second, it is only possible because of all the work that has gone into the manpower-booking system. If the meeting is a privileged place where dualism is performed, it is because of the work that has gone into that manpower-booking system, because of the networks of ordering, simplification, juxtaposition and concentration that it embodies.

The managers are endowed with self-reflexivity not because they are special. I've tried to argue that they are not. Rather, if there is self-reflexivity, consciousness, the formation of a dualist effect, this is because they are at one end of a gradient of materials. They're in a place where they deal with docile and tractable materials. These materials *represent* all sorts of events spread out through time and space. They *juxtapose* what would otherwise have been separate. They *summarize* what might have been said in a great many more words or figures. And they *homogenize* what would otherwise have been performed and embodied in a variety of different materials and a range of modes of expression. These are the materials that generate, albeit precariously and reversibly, the very possibility of discretion. They are, in short, the kinds of materials that generate the dualisms of modernity. That produce organization.[41]

NOTES

1 Or, in actor-network jargon, I could say that the networks tend to form and carry recursive 'centres of translation'. See Latour (1990).
2 This is a restatement of the argument made in the last chapter, that there are, indeed, hierarchies and asymmetries, but that it is a mistake to start off assuming very much about their character.
3 Again, I am thinking of the 'usual suspects' from symbolic interaction (Mead 1934); figurational sociology (Elias 1983); actor-network theory (Latour 1990); historical sociology (Abrams 1982); structuration theory (Giddens 1991); and post-structuralism (Foucault 1979; Cooper and Burrell 1988).
4 See Latour (1987); and in particular, his superb essay 'Drawing things together' (1990).
5 And neither, to be sure, should we conflate mind with whatever goes on between our ears.

6 This is standard sociological fare. They tell stories like this in gender studies, and in organizational theory.

7 We like nouns too much, and we don't listen enough. What would happen if we listened in verbs instead? And told uncertain stories to match?

8 Of course I could tell a similar story of John Law, the current Professor of Sociology at Keele University. Or anyone else. We're all the way we are – what we are – because we have assembled together a whole lot of bits and pieces.

9 When I think in these terms, I think of the Ceauçescus. And the end of their hideous performance in Romania.

10 *Morally*, it's a good starting point to tell that people are special (though it is only a starting point because there are other inhabitants on the planet too). But *analytically*, the habit stops us telling all sorts of interesting stories about both machines and people and machines. This is the point: we're all people-and-machines. But the language makes it difficult to say this. And even more difficult to explore it. For this point explored in different ways, see Law 1991a; Star 1988, 1991; and Woolgar 1991.

11 But here's a difference. Andrew Goldthorpe is allowed – perhaps he is *required* – to sign the Official Secrets Act, but it is told that computers cannot. Here's agency performed again. That's the point: agency is *performed*.

12 If I say that some areas are 'said to be unsafe' or 'told to be lethal' this should not be taken to reflect scepticism on my part. So though it is true that I have never seen an ionizing radiation, I have the greatest respect for the stories in which these are described; and I regularly argue with my dentist about the X-rays of my teeth that he likes to take. So I believe, all right. I'll perform this ordering pattern. But what I'm doing is being detached. I'm trying to use the same language to talk about different kinds of ordering. Only this time I'm not doing it about machines and people, but about ordering arrangements to which I happen to subscribe, and those to which I do not.

13 See his hair-raising book, *Normal Accidents: Living with High-Risk Technologies* (Perrow 1984).

14 For a superbly illuminating analysis of the role of architecture in a social figuration see Norbert Elias' (1983) discussion of the relationship between the Palais de Versailles and the court society of Louis XIV.

15 For this point explored historically, see Adrian Forty's entertaining *Objects of Desire* (1986), and in particular ch. 6.

16 This is John Thompson's point about the 'fallacy of internalism' (Thompson 1990: 24–5).

17 To be sure, it is sometimes possible to freeze such hierarchies administratively, and then to satirize them by talking about (supposed) civil-service rules which define the size of desk, the size and the quality of the carpet, and the number of pictures on the wall appropriate to this grade or that.

18 What happened to individuals interpolated in subordinate positions in the hierarchy who are summoned to the office of the Director? This is a fourth role, but I don't know the answer to this question at Daresbury, because I was never in that situation. Elsewhere, if the hierarchical difference is not extreme, they tend to sit facing the Director with his desk between them – unless there are extensive documents to be examined, in which case the encounter moves to the conference table.

19 I'd like to thank Jan Low for sharing some of her own observations about the physical and spatial organization of management meetings. Talking with her has persuaded me to take my own bodily experiences as a fieldworker more seriously than I would otherwise have done.

20 This is only a part of the story, of course: I also think that I embody worth in other ways. But this – I mean my own particular habitus – isn't really the point.

21 A part of the answer doubtless lies in the 'civilizing process' described by Norbert Elias (1983) – that is in the way in which we have learned, historically, to suppress animality.

22 This is not strictly true. Elsewhere I cite a couple of occasions when my presence was used as a foil. In one of these (which I mention in the next chapter) to do with a matter of security and confidentiality, the humour of the exchange rested very precisely on who was inside (and could be trusted) and who was not. In the other the sociologist was cast in the role of the outsider.

23 I'm grateful to Jan Low for pointing to the hierarchical effects of height.

24 It was, of course, quite proper for him to do so. On a very few occasions the DMB found itself discussing business of a particularly confidential character.

25 I will leave on one side the issue of ethnographic panic which I mentioned in chapter 2.

26 Daresbury is (or was at the time) essentially three laboratories rolled up into one: the Nuclear Structure Facility, the Synchrotron Radiation Facility, and Theory and Computational Science, the third and smallest division which I have not discussed in this book. These were all on one site, and they shared support facilities. In addition, for certain administrative purposes they were treated as a single unit by Swindon Head Office. Again Andrew Goldthorpe, for reasons of bureaucratic politics, often presented 'the Laboratory' case. To that extent, then, the Laboratory was a reality. But there were many other ways in which it was not. In particular, at the level of the *science*, the three divisions, and in particular the NSF and the SRR, had little to do with one another.

27 This refers to the BBC2 television series 'Yes Minister', which features an imaginary Whitehall ministry, and the interactions between ministers and senior civil servants.

28 Don't get me wrong: I'm not intending to sneer. Usually these were matters vital to the wellbeing of the Laboratory: if the overheads were wrong, then there might not be any heating, or the demineralized water supply might fail. And then the scientific work of the Lab would grind to a halt. But they were only *indirectly* vital: they were 'overheads' or 'infrastructure'. They didn't necessarily have much directly to do with enterprise, with the business of seeking out new resources. And they were of similarly little immediate relevance to the conduct of decent scientific work.

29 Giovanni Alberti expressed this feeling pithily after one such meeting. As he walked down the corridor on his way out he muttered in my ear: 'I'm going to go and do some work before I lose the habit!'

30 I'm in good company. Philip Abrams, who used his historical sociology to erode agency–structure dualism, also talks about the same difficulty, the way

in which he experienced himself as an agent separated from structure (Abrams 1982: 227).

31 Talking of Watergate, Baudrillard (1988b: 173) observes 'The denunciation of scandal always pays homage to the law. And Watergate above all succeeded in imposing the idea that Watergate *was* a scandal.' His argument is that Watergate was *not* a scandal. Rather 'it is a scandal-effect concealing that there is no difference between the facts and their denunciation (identical methods are employed by the CIA and the *Washington Post* journalists)'. He ties this carapace of legal denunciation to a post-modern interpretation of the character of capital: 'its instantaneous cruelty; its incomprehensible ferocity; its fundamental immorality'. Baudrillard's conclusion is that this carapace (and attempts to use it) should be abandoned. Despite the similarities, I'd like to draw a distinction between this position, and my own. First, I don't want to draw an a priori distinction between capitalism and whatever might have preceded it: I take it that the Other is always present; that ordering always experiences its limits; second, I don't want to assume a dichotomy between the ordering denunciation and what it denounces; as I've argued above, such differences as there are are better seen as gradients; and third, as a pessimistic liberal, I want to press a distinction between reason and power despite the fact that any such distinction is a convention.

32 Hannah Arendt wrote of the banality of evil. The DMB isn't evil. Far from it. But much of its business is certainly banal (though that doesn't mean to say that it's unnecessary). For more thoughts about dualism, the division between backstage and front, and the character of disillusion, see Law (1992b).

33 I have developed this argument in more detail elsewhere, distinguishing between the technical and the social, and arguing that the social is a residual untameable category which protects the control-integrity of the technical. See Law (1992b). See also Bruno Latour's (1987).

34 This analysis draws upon Bruno Latour's (1990) crucial paper, 'Drawing things together'. But see also Law (1986b, 1986c).

35 For this point developed, see Law and Whittaker (1988); and Latour (1991a).

36 Which it often does. For recent discussion, see the papers gathered together in Savage and Witz (1992).

37 This is how the sociology of knowledge started. As a magnificent political critique, in the writing of Karl Marx. Ideology was partial. But it was a form of distorted partiality, serving the interest of a ruling class. But – here the complexities start – it isn't of course, pure dream either. Otherwise people wouldn't believe it. Ideology has to work for them too.

38 See, for instance, Becker (1963); Cicourel (1964); and Garfinkel (1967).

39 Either this is a form of solipsism. Or (perhaps this amounts to the same thing) it is a large step in the direction of the hideous purity of order. It was said of the Ceauçescus that when they toured a town the Securitate first stocked the local supermarket with all the goods that were never usually available. Only non-Ceauçescus knew other forms of story-telling, and understood – or whispered that they understood – that the cornucopia of Romanian socialism was a ludicrous fiction. Fortunately, we are not obliged to perform the fantasies of most practising solipsists.

40 This is why the sociology of knowledge is too simple. We can't separate out representations from the context in which they appear and say that one produces the other.

41 Bob Cooper and Gibson Burrell (1988) talk, revealingly, of the 'production of organization', and Bob Cooper has explored the relationship between that process and the character of representation in terms similar to this. See Cooper (1992).

8

Enterprise, Trust and Distrust

This chapter is about heroism and enterprise. It's about some of the ways in which enterprise seeks to order and perform its worlds, its blind spots and its failures, the ways it interacts with other modes of ordering, and the ways in which it represents the world. In particular, it's on the way in which it strains towards a particular form of dualism, a dualism that is enshrined in a division between frontstage and backstage.

In order to explore the implications of this divide I focus primarily on matters of external relations, and consider aspects of the way in which Daresbury Laboratory situates itself in relation to the outside world. First I explore the character of impression-management. I argue that (a particular form of) impression-management is central to enterprise, and from this go on to suggest that this generates scepticism and *distrust*. But there's an oddity here, an oddity that I explore by considering the character of organizational intelligence-gathering. My suggestion is that at *elite* levels enterprise is a thoroughly informal mode of ordering: that it turns around face-to-face interaction between powerful agents. But such face-to-face interaction, and the lobbying and the intelligence-gathering that goes with it, rests on (and again helps to reproduce) a form of *trust*. So the oddity is this. Corrosive scepticism and trust – the two seem to co-exist within enterprise.

1 PERFORMANCE AND DISTRUST

One day Andrew Goldthorpe reported to the DMB that the Prime Minister was to visit the Laboratory. He said that she was on her way to Liverpool, and would spend an hour or so at the Lab on her way.

> Mrs Thatcher: a name to conjure with! But is this a clue to dualism? Is it that in enterprise — and perhaps in other modes of ordering too — those places that perform *external relations* tell of themselves as important?

Andrew spoke of the need for absolute security:

Adrian Smith: What about confidentiality? Can people know?

Andrew Goldthorpe: Keep it in this room. [Though when you are getting things ready you can tell people] that we are expecting a visit by some VIPs.

Giovanni Alberti: Then, if there *is* a leak, Andrew only has to shoot four innocent people!

Andrew Goldthorpe: Yes. That's right. Or we can blame John [Law]! [Laughter]

Giovanni Alberti: No. Much more likely it is the nig-nog Italian!

Security was paramount. It was told that people would check every inch of her itinerary beforehand; that they would hide in bushes, and crawl through drains. It was one of those moments when John White reminded me that I was not to talk to others about what I'd heard. And indeed, I told no one what I had learned until after the visit. Not even my partner. And this was partly that I'd given my word. And partly it was because if the IRA *did* manage to blow up Mrs Thatcher at Daresbury then I wanted to be able to look the man from MI5 straight in the eye when I told him that I had spoken to absolutely no one.

> A moral: in the command for silence speaks due process, a mode of ordering performed into bodies and arrangements for a visiting VIP, identity unknown. I watched it being performed, and found that few (said that they) knew until the day before. And, like everyone else, I performed state security too.

The issue of security *was* important.

> I'm not arguing. The issue of security was important. But *why* was it important? Here's an other part of the answer: the *IRA* performed it as important too. Let's rephrase that. The IRA plays at ranking as well. It lionizes heroes and denounces villains. Like the rest of us it reflects and performs the collapse of a network of bits and pieces into a single spokesperson, a star, a heroine. Assassination is nothing more than the continuation of heroism by other means.

So the issue of security was important. But when the managers told of the importance of the visit, they spoke in other terms:

Andrew Goldthorpe: We have to play it very carefully. I have no instructions about what she wants to do and see. But I thought that she should see something, and not be talked *at*.

And, again (I've already quoted this, but here it is, back in context):

Andrew Goldthorpe: We have to give the message about how good and positive we are − what good work we are doing. And, though our work is good, we are also going out energetically and getting additional resources and customers. The message must be *good*!

One person can speak for a whole government. This is heroism, the performance of dualism, on a huge scale! And, like the IRA, Daresbury helped to perform that collapse, the elision of network, its identification with a person. No. In the first instance I'm not complaining, simply reporting. In the political economy of enterprise there is no alternative.

They wanted to tell stories about Daresbury to the Prime Minister. They wanted to tell of energy, of excellence, of the active search for resources. They wanted to tell heroic stories; they wanted to speak of enterprise. And they wanted to do this because this is what they thought she wanted to hear. And because they thought that if she heard what she wanted to hear, this might make it easier for them to attract scarce resources in the future.

Of course, they didn't want to tell lies, and I don't think that they *did* tell any lies. On the other hand, representation is always a simplification and a deletion. So, as I hinted in the last chapter we need a complex model of the economy of truth. And we have to accept that what counts as truth in one mode of ordering may count as evasion, or falsehood, or misunderstanding in another. So when they spoke of the forthcoming visit of Mrs Thatcher they spoke, in part, of Politics, capital 'P'. Should we hide alternative realities? Should we perform other kinds of ordering patterns? The managers played, like political spin-doctors, with these questions − with the relationship between stories of enterprise and those of vocation or vision as they reviewed possibilities at the DMB:

John White: We need to avoid [simply giving] the impression that 'aren't we a lovely lab! Everything is rosy!' And she goes away thinking that there are no problems.

In fact *everyone* in the room told stories about the science budget. I'll rephrase that. Like every other scientist that I know, all the senior managers at Daresbury worked on the assumption that the science budget *is* a problem; they lived with that problem daily; they spent a large part of their working lives trying to deal with the shortage of resources; they performed and embodied that shortage; sometimes they even joked about it. But, when it came to talking with the Prime Minister they were also deadly serious. Which meant that some things were better left unsaid. I cited this in chapter 4:

Andrew Goldthorpe: There is no gain in giving negative messages. If she asks, okay, but if we complain she will say that it is Swindon's problem.

> This is a classic move in enterprise; to devolve responsibility; and to require *others* to perform. The redistribution of agency. On the little things the hero is no longer an agent! In Barry Barnes' language, the power turns itself into an authority. And in the language of Michel Callon, the agent turns itself into an intermediary.[1]

'There is no gain': this is the vocabulary of the storybooks of enterprise. And, in the calculus of enterprise Andrew was right. I've said it already: backstage whingeing *may* be acceptable, though there are limits. But when we arrive on stage we hold back our complaints. Heroes, enterpreneurs, don't cry – unless, of course, there is some gain in crying.

> It's one-sided, but I'm not sneering or complaining. At least, I'm trying not to, for the sight of opportunistic moralizing is singularly un-edifying. Let's be a little kinder: we know the downs, the stresses. We know them perfectly well, because we live them. But sometimes it is possible to address some of these ordering dissonances if we are also successful entrepreneurs; which, to be sure is why they have us by the short-and-curlies![2]

I've spoken of heroes and entrepreneurs. But I've also spoken of stages and performances. Indeed, Goffman's dramaturgy is a singularly appropriate metaphor for exploring the strain towards dualism carried within enterprise.[3] For instance, it talks of a lot of effort – over weeks and months – to create a single important strategic performance. This is a process of concentration: of converting a great deal into not very much. Or a process into an event.

> Here's one of the features of that concentration: it's letting a few words, a few minutes, and a few people, stand for lots of people working over months or years. But I think it's the same elision, the same process that generates and performs external relations: if Mrs Thatcher *stands for* the government, or the DMB *stands for* Daresbury, so a performance *stands for* all the hidden work. All perform the deleting work of ranking. All perform the heroism of a star system. All perform a version of dualism.

How should we mount a performance? How can we mount a *convincing* performance? How can we mount a performance that conveys the bright-eyed, bushy-tailed optimism of enterprise? How should we go about mounting a performance that will attract and hold an audience? These are strategic questions.

> When we perform Holy Communion are we trying to *impress* God? Or, for that matter, one another? Or neither? When a surgeon performs an operation, how much has this to do with impression management? When we fill in the application form to pay our road tax, how much do we care whether the clerk thinks that we are wonderful?
>
> Goffman's metaphor is appropriate, but I take it that we need to tease it apart: to ask about performance in its different guises; to think about the different modes of ordering in which it is inserted, which it performs. And to think about their different kinds of political economy.

As the Daresbury managers anticipated and planned for Mrs Thatcher's visit these were the questions they rehearsed. And the answers weren't obvious:

John White: I have been to lots of labs which were empty apart from a pump going 'pup, pup, pup, pup' in the corner. You need to have bodies *doing* things, even if it is artificial.

John is right: at the place where a lionized spokesperson meets the performance that is intended to impress, it's very easy to mount something that falls flat, or simply goes wrong. For heroism demands heroic performances. And enterprise demands enterprising performances. It takes art and effort to mount one that will really *work*. It takes art and effort, and perhaps some luck, to ensure that the material gradients that carry the strategy look like dualism on the day.

Think about what that means: 'one that really *works*'. What should count as 'working'? There are whole sociologies about this, about the conflicts between different groups about what should count as 'working'.[4] And there are pollsters and specialists who make it their trade to design and hone effective performances.[5]

Daresbury is a relative beginner in some of these games. The art of *enterprising* dissimulation is not one that is well developed among civil servants or scientists. But the Lab is trying hard. John says: 'You need to have bodies doing things, even if it is artificial.' He tells of the need to mount something that *looks* good. This is backstage/frontstage territory. But it is a particular version of that dualism, for I want to say that when the orderings of enterprise are performed they drive a *moral* wedge between backstage and frontstage.

Indeed, they build a division that is both moral and epistemological between the 'real' and the 'artificial'. Or between what is presented, and what 'really goes on'.

> There are places where this kind of division doesn't matter. For instance, in Shaftesbury Avenue. There all is artifice. That is what theatre is *about*: artifice. Audiences judge the quality of the artifice as artifice. Or, more grandly, they talk of the 'willing suspension of disbelief'. But there are other places, like laboratories, or the myths about twentieth-century marriage, where artifice is said to be out of place: where moral dualism is said to be wrong; where frontstage is supposed to reflect what goes on backstage. Or where any division between frontstage and backstage is said to be inappropriate.

Daresbury is like most other laboratories in this respect. It's a working place. It works, but it works in the first instance by performing the vocational ordering. Since it is a user facility in practice it deals with more visitors than many labs. But they are – or they were – just that: 'users'. That is, they too tend to perform and embody the vocational puzzle-solving. So Daresbury may deal with more bodies than many labs. But it isn't so used to non-vocational performances:

Peter Baron: I'm disappointed by the attitude of some of our younger people. They enjoy their work, they are paid to do what they enjoy, but they *don't describe* what they are doing [to non-scientists]. I think this is a very sad state of affairs.

Giovanni Alberti: On the rare occasions that I'm doing my own thing, the last thing I want to do is to *tell* someone what I'm doing! I have a lot of sympathy with them ....

Another crueller way of putting it would be to say that, in the past it didn't much matter if the plant was dull and those who worked there were ugly. Or vice versa. Excitement and beauty were't the commodities in which the laboratory traded. And, since enchantment was achieved by other means, local presentation could have taken the form of the standard factory cliché: the division between the front gates with its patch of lawn and tired rose bushes, and the back entrance with its security and its weighbridge. Though, in fact at Daresbury there is only one main gate (though with a barrier), and the Lab looked – it looks – more like a university campus than a factory.

Here's the argument. A Lab is not live theatre: it's more like a film studio. When it tells stories of itself to outsiders, it 'normally' does so by shipping texts or artefacts out of the front gate. And these are consumed (or not) *elsewhere*.

When Bruno Latour and Steve Woolgar talked of the economy of the laboratory they spoke of 'the cycle of credibility' (Latour and Woolgar 1979: 187ff.). They said that texts are converted (or not) into grants. I think that they are right, but now I'm trying to tease out some of the ordering arrangements that are performed in that cycle.

And as for open days, visits – it is told that these are overheads, displays, more or less necessary diversions from the serious work of the organization. As Giovanni Alberti says: 'The last thing I want to do is to *tell* someone what I'm doing.'

That was 'before'. But now enterprise tells a different kind of story. It tells of the need to scramble for resources. It tells of the need to *perform* for those resources. It tells of competition, of the need to mount a performance that will impress those upon whom the Lab depends, those who already embody and perform enterprise. Annual reports, news releases, submissions to committees – there are many ways in which it is starting to tell of enterprising performance. But it also tells of the need, in some measure, to do this *in person*, on site – for if it did not, then why would a visit by someone like Mrs Thatcher be so important?

We have started to move from the rose bushes outside the front gate of the works. We've started to elaborate, perform and embody a much more complex syntax of organizational performance. Red brick, tinted glass, cedar chips round the bushes, indoor plants, hi-tech easy chairs, pastel shades, phones that warble discreetly, atriums (or is it atria?), whiteboards, devices that photocopy what you write on the board: these are the kinds of syntactical elements that spring to my mind.

I take it that this syntax doesn't have much to do with science. Or anything else, in *particular*. Mainly it has to do with itself. For isn't it a form that appears, with minor variations, in the front offices of the better-funded Labs, in Ramada Inns, in the Visitor Centre at Sellafield, in the offices of venture capital companies, and in the executive lounges of airports? So here's a guess: we're witnessing the enactment and embodiment of a kind of lingua franca, a spatial, architectural and stylistic Esperanto of enterprise as it hits the road and flits tirelessly across the time zones; as it goes frontstage to perform to itself. Did I say tireless? But this is quite wrong. Bruno Latour is right: movement is never tireless. It takes time. Or it is tiresome, tiresome for those who make it easy for others (see Latour 1988b). And, before we fall for the language of local and global, let's not forget that Esperanto is a pretty local form of globalism!

But there's another twist to this story about performing enterprise. I want to say that the dualism between backstage and frontstage – the division between reality and artifice – performs and embodies a *theatre of distrust*. Here's a story about that theatre.

Many people living in the vicinity of the Lab believed that it had something to do with atomic weapons: for why would it have a 'Nuclear Structure Facility' if this were not the case? But the Lab took – it takes – its relations with its neighbours very seriously. And it sought to reassure them that it had nothing to do with bombs and, more generally, that there was no danger of radioactive pollution. As a part of this, parties of locals, including councillors, were taken on tours of the Laboratory, and the science being done was carefully described.

Perhaps this is apocryphal. But I was told that on one occasion a group of locals passed some service ducting between buildings that had been opened up for maintenance to reveal a network of pipes and cables. And the guide overheard one of the visitors saying significantly to another: 'You see what I mean! These tunnels stretch for *miles* in all directions.'

It's important, I think, to unpack the logic that lies behind this theatre of distrust. Doesn't it run something like this?

'Look how impressively I perform.'

'But you perform to impress me. So your performance is an artifice. What does it hide? What *really* lies behind smooth talk, the pastel shades, and the tinted glass?'

'But come backstage and have a look. You'll see that my performance isn't *really* an artifice.'

'How nice. But you're *still* performing. What are you hiding? What *really* lies behind the smooth talk ...?'

And so on.[6]

Many have told stories about distrust. Brian Wynne has written about Sellafield's credibility problems. He asks, who will believe what they say when they claim that it is all safe? If you already distrust them, then is not their very *appearence* of honesty an artifice? Erving Goffman similarly tells stories about strategic games, and of the endless potential for paranoia once we set out down that path. And Richard Sennett tells of the self-revelatory games of intimacy where what is uncovered immediately loses its value,[7] games of emotional strip-tease where the currency suffers from hyperinflation. There have never been referents, realities in the last instance. We have always recounted ordering stories about orderings. But without an economy of distrust this did not matter, or it mattered differently, in part because we not only recounted ordering stories, but we performed them too. So I'm persuaded by Anthony Giddens' (1990, 1991) diagnosis. These are versions, symptoms, products of the reflexive project of modernism: they point to what happens when it points its ordering scepticism on itself.

So Daresbury works. It embodies and performs a series of ordering arrangements. And it doesn't, by and large, depend on the carriage trade. It isn't like a road-house on the A1. But this poses problems when people who aren't scientists coming to work at the Lab *do* visit: what to do with the visitors who arrive at the gates? And what, in particular, to do with the stream of more or less important visitors – visitors interpellated in the story-telling of enterprise?

In scientific vocation people perform for their peers at specialist meetings, or in the pages of arcane journals. Numerous examples suggests that those who 'go public' are thought of as untrustworthy, or immoral. In administration people perform for the guardians of legality and due process. In vision people are driven to perform by the need for grace. But in enterprise, people perform because they need to secure resources. So when resources are scarce, and performers are many, every performance becomes important. This is how it was told at Daresbury.

Mrs Thatcher's visit was the VIP visit of the year. So the general problem – what to do with VIPs – was writ even larger than usual. What, then, *should* she see? The visit was to be very brief; there would be no time to walk her all round the Laboratory. And, in any case, Mrs Thatcher was told as partaking of the properties of a heroine.

Hugh Campbell: I've spoken to people at Cambridge, and she will divert from the programme if she wants to, and dive into a laboratory if she sees anything interesting.

Andrew Goldthorpe: Yes! I was involved when ISIS was opened. She is energetic. And she *listens* to you.

This is the dualism of heroic enterprise; she is told as an active agent, resourceful, self-starting, interested, concerned to gather intelligence. But this is important: she's suspicious too. Knowing that the Lab would seek to mount an impressive performance, she also knows that it would seek to conceal.

Mrs Thatcher as heroine: an ordering story performed and embodied for over a decade in British politics. And here was Daresbury, doing its bit, performing that ordering. Performing rank. Indeed, performing rank just like the technicians whom I talked about in an earlier chapter.
    Would I have done differently? No. Of course I wouldn't! I may hate it, but I am also a part of that pattern too. The only question is this: what happens when the fragmentation becomes so destructive that we cannot bear it any more? When the hegemonic claims of enterprise have wounded all the other voices?

So the managers talked about the visit in a practical manner, to be framed and performed within the heroism of enterprise. The issue was: how to hold the attention of an active agent like Mrs Thatcher? How to hold the attention of a prime minister known to be restless, energetic and sceptical? How to shoehorn a network of multi-ordering bits and pieces into a concentrated performance of enterprise? And how to draw a veil over all the bits and pieces that might not tell the right kind of story?

> How to attract an audience? How to *hold* that audience? This is the question that the managements in Shaftesbury Avenue pose themselves. But here the economics of performance are different. Endless re-runs of 'The Mousetrap' will not do. On this point, at least, vocation and enterprise can agree.

The members of the DMB talked about Mrs Thatcher's programme and arrived at a provisional agreement: that she should see some hardware, but not too much:

Andrew Goldthorpe: She should *see* the SR Ring. But it is too big to walk all round. But she should see a station.

Giovanni Alberti: The problem is, the area is a pile of steel and concrete. It is a mess. It is not [meant] to be *seen*.

Andrew Goldthorpe: Okay. So the problem is, what about the *presentations*?

The scenery *is* important. The SR Ring is not a wooden O but perhaps it is a reasonably convincing stage set.

> When they first started drafting out designs for the SR Ring, surely they did not script it as a backdrop for prime ministerial visits. Surely it was intended to perform and embody quite other ordering arrangements. So, it's not ideal, but since it is *there*, it may as well be used to perform other versions of the social ordering. At least within limits.
> Here's a tension: the syntax of entrepreneurial architecture — the cell-phones and the tinted glass — can't tell of the *specificity* of what goes on beyond the plate glass. Or, to put it more soberly, if performance in enterprise rests on the composition of the balance sheet, then the balance sheet cannot tell of things that are not account-able. Other more awkward measures may be needed — like concrete and steel.

But so too, indeed more so, is what goes on in front of the scenery. For the SR Ring is not very malleable. It cannot be reshaped for the convenience of prime ministers, at least not in the short run. But talk is cheap, a long way down the gradient of malleable materials:

Andrew Goldthorpe: Okay. So the problem is, what about the *presentations*?

Giovanni Alberti: I can give my usual bullshit talk about biology.

Andrew Goldthorpe: So that's not a problem. Who else?

Giovanni Alberti: Freddy Saxon can talk about surface science.

Of the 250 people who work in the SR Division, the suggestion is that only a very few will talk to Mrs Thatcher. This isn't the fault of the Laboratory. It's what happens when a laboratory responds (it has no choice) to the logic of enterprise: there is selectivity; and deletion too! Freddy Saxon and Giovanni Alberti will speak for the Division: they will be turned into its spokespersons.[8] So Freddy and Giovanni will be the stars, the heroes of the division. Or they will *play* the role of stars on the stage of the SR Accelerator.

Again we are reminded: heroism is dualist. It demands heroes. So it is that heroes are created. And the work of hundreds is subsumed to their heroism.

And they are chosen to speak because it is thought that they will perform, and perform convincingly, even when the greatest embodiment of enterprise in the nation, the Prime Minister herself, is the audience. And, as a part of that, because they have good scripts – two 'hot areas' in SR science, and (at least in the latter case) in industrial R&D too.

So heroism values heroes, and their actions. The syntax of its economy, the grammar of its performances, is epistemologically and morally dualist. It generates stars who perform to a backdrop of hi-tech baubles, pastel shades and cedar chips. In its external relations it performs a profound form of elitism.

But something else is going on too. Go back to the exchange reported above, to the talk about talk. This assumes that talk is cheap and malleable. It can be shaped and reshaped, switched on and off. It is, as it were, easy to switch in mid-sentence to perform enterprise. Or relatively easy, at any rate. But the switch also demands a change in register. So it is that Giovanni Alberti talks his talk down. He talks of 'bullshit ...'. What is this talk of bullshit?

Bullshit is false; it pretends to something that it is not; it misrepresents; it is superficial. It tells of the cynical rhetoric of the entertainer; or the con-man; enterprise with more than a touch of the sardonic. Indeed, Giovanni Alberti was a master of the sardonic: 'Are you sure you really want an Italian nig-nog to talk to your Prime Minister?' This kind of talk trades on a distinction between presentation and reality, dwelling in and subsisting on the exciting space that opens up between them.

> Social theory has been here before. I'm thinking of Erving Goffman's essay on role distance,[9] his description of the adolescent fooling around on the child's roundabout to show that he is not really 4 years old. Agency and performance: the two are separate, but yet are joined together.
>
> Roland Barthes was here before us too (see Barthes 1973). I'm thinking of his image of the image of the black soldier on the front of *Paris Match*. He's in the uniform of the French army, saluting the tricolour. Barthes has it that the image is part of a second-order semiological system: it is a myth. But is there a reality behind the image? Is there a way of communicating that is not myth? Barthes told us that there was. But in the high modern Hall of Mirrors they tell it differently.
>
> Here is the question for me: are there ways of telling/ordering that lie somewhere between? Between, that is, the fecklessness of endless re-presentation in the Hall of Mirrors; and the hideous purity of the infrastructural last instance? Where some other kind of authenticity is possible?
>
> In this book I've been trying to respond to these questions by saying 'Yes': that there are places like that. Here's one way of telling about them; I think that they are the spaces which we *inhabit*, the agents we *are*. Spoken in vocation, Giovanni Alberti's talk *is* a misrepresentation for no one would tell it that way; spoken in enterprise it is a proper representation; no, better, it is an proper embodiment of that mode of ordering; except that the political economy of truth in enterprise subsists upon and serves up a diet of distrust.
>
> Enterprise unwillingly suspends belief; post-modernism willingly embraces disbelief. That is the difference. But there are other ways of telling too, provisional beliefs, provisional forms of trust, places for a modest and pessimistic commitment to liberalism.

Here's the rest of this story. That day the DMB agreed a programme for the visit. It ran in part like this. The Prime Minister would arrive. She would be greeted by the Chairman of SERC. She would walk with the welcoming party from the administration block to the SR Source and visit a couple of experimental stations. She'd listen to brief presentations by Giovanni Alberti and Freddy Saxon. There would be a photo-opportunity. And she would depart in the limousine for Liverpool.

That was the plan. People in the Lab were told to prepare talks. They were told that VIPs would be in the party – Swindon and the Department of Education and Science were mentioned. They started to put together their posters. And they started to rehearse. Indeed the whole visit was rehearsed several times. People played the role of the Prime Minister and the other visiting VIPs such as the Chairman of SERC, while the managers and the scientists tried out their speeches. So it was that the performance was refined, and timed, and the welcome polished up.

I was told that the rehearsals were important. Here is Andrew Goldthorpe after a quite different but very important visit by the Council of SERC:

> The visit went *extraordinarily* well. We've done ourselves a lot of good by sending people away with a good *feel* about the place. The presentations were uniformly excellent .... These things *really* matter. They *really* matter. Which is why I was such a pain at rehearsals. I'm sorry about that. But it matters! They went away *extraordinarily* impressed.

Here's the moral. It has to do with material gradients again. Talking about and *designing* performances is relatively cheap. That's why draftspersons are employed. It's cheaper to make mistakes beforehand than it is to make them on the day. And it's cheaper to perform those mistakes in ephemeral media than it is for real, when all the bodies are assembled together, or the aircraft has already been built.

Rehearsals are relatively cheap too. Then the mistakes and the infelicities are made to an empty house, rather than to one stuffed full of critics on the first night. Rehearsals, mockups, tests – these are all ways of talking about the process of scaling up. Or the economics of translation: of translating from talk and text into bodies and machines. Of enrolling and marshalling the necessary bits and pieces.

Bruno Latour says that we laugh at politicians because they make their mistakes in public, in real time. I'd prefer to say that they make a few of their mistakes in public, and in real time. The politics of concealment, the politics of backstage, the politics of only going public with the performance when you think you've got it right, are just as finely honed in Downing Street as they are in an aero-engine design office.[10] Until, of course, the hubris of imagined order overtakes the uncertainty of ordering and distraction is turned into self-destruction.

And on the day? Well, I didn't go to Daresbury on the day of the Prime Minister's visit.

I owe you an explanation for this. And probably I should have gone. But here's why I didn't.

(1) Ethnography would have been difficult; I would almost certainly have been pinned down, kept far distant from the party. (2) I didn't really *want* to watch the visit; too much was at stake for the Lab and I was nervous for it, nervous like the managers, and for some of the same reasons. (3) I didn't want to risk the smallest chance of getting in the way and screwing the performance up for the Lab. And (4), as I noted in the last chapter, I too embody hierarchy. So I was frightened

of Mrs Thatcher — of the (admittedly remote) possibility of having to perform for her myself.

Those who were there told that the visit passed off well for the Lab. And they also told of the Prime Minister's energy, her interest, and her sheer professionalism. They said, for instance, that Freddy Saxon's presentation was excellent — most impressive. But that at the same time Mrs Thatcher managed to position herself *between* Freddy and his poster so that it looked as if she was telling *him* about the science. So it was that, for the photographers at least, she performed herself as dualist heroine, speaking *for* science and *for* the lab, rather than being spoken too.

2 INTELLIGENCE-GATHERING AND TRUST

I've tried to show that enterprise embodies and seeks to perform a profound epistemological dualism: it rests upon (and seeks to create) a division between frontstage and backstage. Frontstage, there are bright-eyed, bushy-tailed performances. And backstage there is all the effort that goes into mounting those performances. But the dualism is not only epistemological, but also *moral*. For what goes on frontstage is also a form of impression-management, and it slides easily into dissimulation, or suspicion of dissimulation. So it is that in enterprise the syntax of performance gets divided from the syntax of reality, and the need to perform starts to erode the possibility of trust.

There's a lot more that could be said about this. For instance, I've concentrated primarily on live theatre and only touched upon the way in which this syntax is embodied and performed in other material forms — in the cedar chips, the potted plants, and the glossy annual reports and brochures. But enterprise performs in other ways too. Remember its organizing principle: it has to do with opportunism, with seeking out resources, combining them, and creating performances that will secure further resources. So enterprise is also, and fundamentally, to do with discretion, the discretion to make the most of circumstances, to react, to anticipate and avoid difficulties. Thus it strains towards creating options, the options that give point to the self-reflexive project of modernity.[11]

Thus *inside* the organization, the buzz words are delegation, performance, efficiency and responsibility. But there is also a strain towards surveillance. How do you get the best out of your people? The enterprise strategy is to give them resources and require that they perform. And then it is to monitor performance. It is to monitor performance for two reasons: first, to see how well they are performing; and second, to foresee, so far as possible, if anything is going to go wrong. The strain, in other words, is towards a self-reflexive space, a place of discretion. And it's towards the disciplinary surveillance of subordinate performance.

> This is a dynamic that tends, once again, to generate epistemological and moral dualism. Performance, suspicion, surveillance of performance — within enterprise the three tend to go together and propel one another.

But what happens *outside* the organization? Listen to this. We're at the Laboratory Management Committee:

Andrew Goldthorpe: I believe we need to get money from the EEC, and that the DES budget will be docked [in order to pay for the EEC] Framework Programme .... [And I believe that] *individuals* should build contacts with Brussels.

Peter Baron: We need to influence the *future* shape of the programme.

Adrian Smith: Yes, we need also to add *referees*, to help them build a network of decent referees.

Giovanni Alberti: They operate by *verbal* communication, not written. Therefore you need to contact people. You are a nonentity otherwise.

Adrian Smith: Pressing the flesh ....

Giovanni Alberti: And you need to know who is influential.

Adrian Smith: [What worries me is that we're missing out. The British] have three women [working on it part time.] The French have [a whole office working on it?] full time.

Andrew Goldthorpe: Do we need *one* person [at Daresbury] to be a contact person? If so, its a new job.

Here there's an intimate link between, opportunism, intelligence-gathering and impression-management. Opportunism demands intelligence, but intelligence-gathering is told as participative and interactive. It involves talking with people. It's to do with finding out about and putting oneself *on* the map. It's about learning, *and* creating a good impression. Its about building and manipulating networks. But there's another feature of this exchange: the idiom of intelligence-gathering and impression-management is said to be *personal* and *unroutinized*. Giovanni Alberti and Adrian Smith are making the same point: even more so than in the United Kingdom, it's who you know in Brussels that counts.

> I was always very naive about this. I didn't seem to know anyone who counted, very much. And, to the extent that I thought about it at all, I imagined that people made their way by virtue of their native excellence. Of course, I should have known better. Even (perhaps especially?) in the functionalist sociology of science, they knew better: Robert K. Merton (1968: 439–59) talked of the Matthew effect when he described recognition in science: 'To them that have shall be given.'

Andrew Goldthorpe, Giovanni Alberti and Adrian Smith are pressing the importance of informal exchanges with key outside players. They're saying that intelligence is gleaned in the course of personal exchanges. They're saying that, sometimes at least, paperwork plays second fiddle to informal talk over a glass of straight malt whisky. But why should this be?

This is the argument. Enterprise is dualistic. As I've tried to argue, there's an epistemological and (more importantly) a *moral* gap between backstage and frontstage. So it places a premium on performance, and performances. These re-present the organization to others. Or, to put it differently, they help to define the boundary relations between institutions – their rates of exchange. But if performances embody a set of dualist arrangements, then so too do key per-*formers*, the stars who can speak for their institutions. For to 'speak' is already an achievement, to speak 'on behalf' is more difficult, but to speak successfully on behalf is tricky indeed. That's the gradient – the slippery slope between fantasy and heroism that has to be climbed.

But in the multi-ordering stories of organization those who speak successfully are told, and performed, as those with rank. So it's a ranking effect too: the top performers are precisely that – the top performers. They speak for and capitalize on all the backstage work. So the dualism that drives the star system also pushes towards its own version of a 'last instance'. In this last instance it is the agents/stars/heroes at the top of the organization who can be trusted to represent their institutions. *But in public, enterprise demands incurable optimism* (even though everyone knows that it's incomplete at best, and dissimulation at worst).

> I've tried to write about this already. Where is there room for tears? Or for day-dreaming? Or for love? One of the reasons I find enterprise so hard, is that if I want to cry, or dream, or love, or do the moral thing, I cannot *tell* this unless I dress it up as opportunism. We *all* know realities to which enterprise does not have access.

Here's the finding: in enterprise it is only in private that the mask of optimism, the difference between backstage and front, begins to slip.

> Barney Glaser and Anselm Strauss (1965) talk of contexts of aware-
> ness, of who knows what, of who knows who knows about what, and
> of the rules for acknowledging who knows who knows about what.
> They're telling terrible stories about the terminally ill. But their ter-
> minology works just as well here.

So what happens backstage between the stars, when the malt whisky comes out? Of course, I don't really know. Why not? The answer's obvious: I'm never there, of course! But, what I *think* goes on is a kind of horse-trading informed by an acknowledgement, perhaps more or less tacit, of *realpolitik*. Everyone is in the same boat. And that is the basis of a kind of trust.

> Trust? What is this trust? They trust each other like a bunch of
> predators! But this is the point: they are predators that have to live
> with one another. There is, as they say, honour amongst thieves.

And it's informed by *realpolitik* because backstage, where everyone is in the same multi-ordered boat, the pull towards consistent pre-sentational optimism is that much weaker. The stars are off the record. So they may speak (not write, but speak) to one another in the different backstage idiom of enterprise.

> *That's* the point: they speak; they do not write. For this is 'big man'
> territory. The pressure is towards the personal, the informal and the
> verbal, towards intelligence-gathering and trading.

But I think there's a second enterprise-relevant reason for the importance of informal contacts between stars. This has to do with *change*. In the stories that it performs enterprise inhabits a changing world. I've said it already: opportunism is the order of the day. And the object of intelligence-gathering is to cotton on to possibilities as quickly as possible.

> Christine Tiler tells me that it's a matter of 'second-order learning',
> and surely she is right. But we don't have to go to the literature on
> organizational behaviour to find a definition of second-order learning.
> Here's one, plucked from my field notes:

The successful project manager is the one who knows how to *find out* how to do it.

But these possibilities − are they clear to the audience that watches the public performances. Or, for that matter, the readership that receives the paperwork? Surely the answer is that they are not. You need to know about them of course. Indeed, you need to know how to read them suspiciously and symptomatically. That's all a part of the dualism of enterprise, for you know they're a carapace, a front-stage performance because you've treated paperwork in that way yourself:

Giovanni Alberti: The big thick [report] has got to be there. But they're not going to read it. They'll only read the little thing.

Gordon Pike: They'll *weigh* it!

Or you've used the paperwork as a kind of ratchet or anchor:

Giovanni Alberti: We can turn a blind eye [to the fact that this paper is late]. We can [accept] it and move fast.

Karen Jones: We can incorporate it in [the minutes of] yesterday's meeting.

Giovanni Alberti: Rules are for the guidance of wise men and the obedience of fools.

Or you've avoided putting in paper altogether:

Karen Jones: Do you want to [report to the committee on the large-scale laser] orally, or write a report?

Giovanni Alberti: I would prefer to do it orally, because that way there is a chance people will forget what I said.

Karen Jones: Do you think a matter that important *should* be oral?

Giovanni Alberti: That is an even better reason for doing it orally!

Peter Baron: I entirely agree. I would not put anything on paper unless they absolutely force you to.

But it's not only that the paperwork is a kind of public performance that may mislead. It's also that it trails hopelessly behind. At best it tells stories about what may (perhaps) have been going on weeks or months ago. By the time the budget allocations arrive it is far too late to act. By then they have been set for weeks in the concrete of due process. Flexibility, room for manoeuvre, discretion – the core concerns of the modern reflexive project – have long since disappeared.

So intelligence-gathering is a case of reading between the lines, of picking up on hints, of detecting possible trends and changes before they become common currency. And this is verbal, it's face-to-face, and it takes place especially between stars and heroes who speak (I use the word advisedly) informally for, and putatively exercise discretion over, their organizations.

> Just let's remind ourselves: the stars perform enterprise and embody it. But a major part of the star system is ordered, performed, and reproduced, in the smoke-filled rooms of which I am telling.
> Two thoughts on this. First, if the star, the hero, the 'big man' consistently comes home empty-handed, then he is no longer a star or a big man.[12] It's true that the organization performs and embodies other modes of ordering too. So the followers may not abandon ship overnight as they might in the stories that are told about New Guinea. But soon the 'cowboy' is being re-told as a 'civil servant'. And the complaints start to circulate.
> Second, there is the matter of dispositions, of habitus.[13] For a part of this business — the part that is performed by the body, and embodied within the skin — is the (seemingly) effortless capacity to 'be' right. Not to be a parvenu. Not to exhibit a failure to understand what everyone understands. Not to feel out of place in high places.
> I bristle in the face of this effortless superiority. And I make myself small. But I know that others bristle at me.

So I'm telling that enterprise (and its opportunism) generates pressures towards informality and personal contact at all, but possibly in particular, at elite levels. At root, the issue is one of trust: in a dissimulating and dualistic world, whom can you trust? Perhaps the answer is no one. But if you interact with stars from the same kind of organizational context, if you know one another's past track record, if your future fates are bound up together, and you are relieved of the dualist need to maintain a publicly consistent face, then perhaps everyone can subscribe to a currency of unrecorded wheeling, dealing, and political bargaining.

> Steven Shapin describes the importance of personal contact between 'gentlemen' and the historical formation of the scientific Laboratory. I think he's saying that scientific trust rested upon *personal* interaction.[14] I think this is an argument about social ordering, but also about the hierarchy of the senses: they say that seeing is believing; but perhaps not clinical, panoptical, seeing. Perhaps it needs to be seeing, as it were, in the round, back-stage, where one can hear and smell, and feel too.

3   A NOTE ON FACE-TO-FACE INTERACTION

What should we make of the dualism of enterprise, of the moral distinction between backstage and frontstage? And what, in particular, should we make of the apparent importance of the personal contacts that take place backstage, of the wheeling and the dealing that take places in the smoke-filled rooms?

One possibility is this: it is to say that in the last instance there really *is* something special and privileged about personal contact. It's to say that at the end of the day the heterogeneous networks of the social are, as it were, cemented together by virtue of face-to-face contact between individuals. This, I guess, is what Erving Goffman assumes. And Anthony Giddens builds it, in an entirely different manner, into his analysis of ontological security.

I'm not ready to cope with the arguments of these authors. Possibly they are right. All I want to do here is to point to another possibility, and one which is more consistent with relational materialism. This alternative suggests that the face-to-face interaction between humans achieves its importance as a function of the way in which materials – somatic, textual, technical and architectural – are told and performed. It says, in other words, that the importance of the somatic is a function of the character of the mode of ordering, and in particular of the way in which the latter performs and embodies human agency.

Where does this leave our understanding of face-to-face interaction – or for that matter interaction that is mediated? Any answer to this question will demand a whole inquiry in its own right. Nevertheless, the way in which it might go is reasonably clear. We might expect face-to-face interaction to tend to be particularly important where the theory and practice of agency stresses the importance of opportunism. It would, in other words, tend to be important in those strategies, such as enterprise, which generate contexts of distrust.

The reason for this simple enough. In face-to-face interaction, as Erving Goffman brilliantly indicated, it is relatively difficult to put on a dissimulating performance. This is because body is a network of materials that gives off many signs. Thus, notwithstanding the development of the civilizing process, ordering the expressions 'given off', the slips of the tongue, and all the rest, is relatively difficult. This is because the strain towards backstage and front, between the dualism of mind and body is ruthlessly tested in a context of distrust. The smallest lapse is liable to give the game away. So I'm suggesting that it is this, this process of ruthless testing, that gives the body, and the interactions that take place face-to-face, their particular moral significance in enterprise.

I don't believe that the dynamics of the smoke-filled room rest on face-to-face interaction alone. For it is also important to this kind of wheeling and dealing that it does not pay to chase after short-term profits. Here there is a degree of trust not because the dualism between front-stage and back-stage is effaced, but because those who negotiate know that they will have to negotiate again tomorrow, and the next day too.[15]

In other modes of ordering, bodies and their unmediated interaction acquire quite a different significance. For instance, in vocation the problem is not one of trust: professionals, or so the story tells, are in principle to be trusted. The issue turns rather around the question of skill. So in vocation, bodies become networks of gestures, actions and the rest, which reveal their skill, or perhaps, if they are neophytes, their lack of skill. So a body tells of skill, in part at least in the process of face-to-face interaction. But more importantly still, vocation tends to assume that skills are transmitted in the course of face-to-face interaction. So writing and reading – all the sociotechnologies of mediated interaction – may have their place, but they also have their limits too. Even telling is only a part of the story: in the end the materials of the body are, as it were, drilled directly by means of emulation and practice.

I'm not certain about the role of face-to-face interaction, and the proper character of agency in the case of administration. But for vision the body is the vehicle of grace. So the issue is – how is bodily grace and charisma transmitted? Does it depend on face-to-face interaction? Or can it flow down the channels of mediated communication? I don't know the answers to any of these questions, though it does seem likely that television, and possibly recorded music, may create, shape and transmit grace. Nevertheless, I guess that face-to-face interaction plays an important role: I saw it in the Laboratory, and I've experienced it elswhere: the touch, the look, the smile, the comment, these often seem to be important channels for those of us who wish to touch the hem. And if this is even partly right then, of course, bodies and interaction between bodies acquire a significance quite unlike their role in other modes of ordering.

NOTES

1 Though the two authors approach the matter of agency and discretion in different ways using different idioms, their conclusions are not so far apart. See Barnes (1988) and Callon (1991).

2 It's a version of the old question: is it better to argue from the inside, or to fight from the outside? Do we sell out if we don't speak out? Do we sell out if we *do*. In the last instance there is no moral high ground. Only shifting morals, shifting circumstances, and shifting resources for ordering. No: as I tried to argue in chapter 5, this is not a counsel of despair. We may hold some things to be sacred. Like, for instance, resistance to hideous purity.

3 Erving Goffman, as is well known, developed his argument through a luminous set of books. My favourites include *The Presentation of Self in Everyday Life* (1971), *Asylums* (1968), *Encounters* (1972) and (particularly relevant in the present context) *Strategic Interaction* (1970).

4 This sociology extends into the analysis of technology. What counts as a working artefact is also a matter for negotiation. See Akrich (1992) and Bijker (1992).

5 And there is a theatrical agent in London that specializes in lifelike noises. Are you thinking of coconut halves banged together to sound like horses hooves? Believe me, that's kids' stuff!

6 This problem also affects ethnography. Did I ever get backstage? Inserted into some modes of ordering this question would not necessarily be problematic. But in enterprise it is.

7 See Goffman (1970); Sennett (1972); Wynne (1990).

8 This is the theory: all the other voices will be stilled, and the Lab will speak with one voice through its designated spokespersons.

9 Reprinted in Goffman (1972: 73–134).

10 See Latour (1983). For the other part of this argument explored at some length, see Law (1992b).

11 It is interesting to note that a number of sociologies assume that power (or having power) is close to, perhaps equivalent to, having discretion. And again, that discretion is closely, sometimes definitionally, related to agency. Clearly, such definitions are bound up with the modern project if not more specifically with enterprise. See, for instance, Hindess (1982); Barnes (1988); Callon (1991).

12 For a grid-group analysis of the dynamics of 'big man' social ordering see Mary Douglas (1973).

13 The notion is developed by Pierre Bourdieu. See, in particular, Bourdieu (1986).

14 See Shapin (1989); but also Shapin and Schaffer (1985).

15 Here I'm talking strictly of face-to-face interaction. Certainly there are quite other kinds of ordering tactics.

9

Postscript

It remains to be said that the author of this
report is a philosopher, not an expert. The latter
knows what he knows and what he does not
know: the former does not. One concludes, the
other questions – two very different language
games. I combine them here with the result that
neither quite succeeds.

Jean-François Lyotard, *The Postmodern Condition*

1   REACTIONS

I worked this book for over 18 months, and it went through two
major drafts. Finally I reached a point when I concluded that it
might be publishable. I could have carried on writing and rewriting.
Which author has not felt the need to carry on tinkering? So I knew
that there were warts. But I'd also come to realize, in the process
of writing, that there would always be warts: ordering, I'd learned,
is a process rather than a something that can be achieved.

This was the moment when I sent copies of the manuscript to
the publisher. Academic readers would look at it and approve it,
reject it, or suggest possible alterations. I also sent it to a number of
colleagues and friends seeking their reactions and comments. And,
after a little delay I submitted it to the management at Daresbury.

The ethnographer has a duty to her fellow anthropologists: I'd
lived with this sense of duty for nearly three years. But she is also
supposed to report back to her 'subjects', perhaps to incorporate
their reactions and responses in the final version. At any rate, this

is what other ethnographers I knew had been doing. So, with my heart in my mouth, I submitted it to the managers along with four questions. First, I asked the Daresbury Management Board to agree that it could, indeed, be published: that it wasn't likely to harm the Laboratory. This request was in conformity with the initial ground rules we'd agreed: I needed their *nihil obstat* to go to press at all. Second, I asked whether I could name the Laboratory. Thus in the version that I submitted to them I'd called it 'Shrewsbury Laboratory'. But I hoped – and expressed the hope – that I might avoid this pseudonym. The reason for this was partly because I wanted to dedicate the book to the men and women of Daresbury. And it was also in part because disguising the site – in any case impossible in the case of those who knew the Laboratory well – meant distorting various parts of the story, for instance to do with the character of the SR Ring and its science. A third question followed on from the second. If they were willing to have the Laboratory named, I wanted to know whether they would mind if I used people's real names. Or should I hide people behind pseudonyms? And fourth, I asked for their reactions. What did they think of the book? Did it make sense? Had I got anything wrong that should be put right?

I spent an anxious few weeks waiting for responses to these questions. Since you have the book in your hands you know that they were happy both for the book to be published, and for Daresbury to be named. 'Publish and be damned' said John White, summing up the DMB reaction on the phone. On the question of names, they were happy for me to abandon the pseudonyms so long as the individuals I mentioned were themselves agreeable. The message, then, was that I should contact people and ask them.

Which is what I did. And everyone whom I spoke to said: 'Fine. I have no problem.' Or words to that effect. Except for one manager. He said that he didn't mind being named. Not at all. But, he noted, I'd said people would be anonymous when I spoke to them. And since I'd said that, wasn't it possible that there was both an ethical problem, and a problem of measurement? People might have spoken differently had they known that I hoped to attribute comments.

I reflected on this. I don't remember promising anonymity. What I *think* I said was that if quotations were attributable, then I'd ask people if was okay for me to use them. On the other hand, I don't doubt his word. The conclusion was obvious: I should use pseudonyms. And in any case, the conversation also made me reflect on the fact that junior people, on hearing that the senior managers didn't mind being named, might feel that they were constrained to agree. Which made me feel doubly uneasy.

That unease was compounded by his measurement point. The manager in question is trained in quantum mechanics, a branch of physics that is particularly sensitive to observer effects. Its principle of indeterminacy says that an observer may measure either the position of an elementary particle, or its momentum, but not both: so intervention influences what can be measured. It's true that the networks of the social are not like the wave functions of quantum mechanics. In particular, I don't have a simple theory about what the decision to measure in one way or another might have on the character of the data gathered together into my stories. Nevertheless, since the sociological value of the study isn't linked to real names, I can see no strong reason for using them. So it is that the names remain pseudonyms.

And the fourth question, the Daresbury reaction on the character of the book itself? Well, here I had a variety of responses. For instance, I was told that parts of it were very 'sociological'. Or, more bluntly, that it was 'bloody hard going'. I thought that this was fair comment. I'd woven theory and data together, and in places the result assumes a fair degree of sociological knowledge. On the other hand, I was pleased when I was also told that I'd captured something important about the character of the Laboratory. And I was also pleased when one scientist told me that he'd been par-ticularly sympathetic to my attack on the horrors of purity. One or two people said that they'd gone through, looking for the quotations and trying to work out who had said what. I had sympathy with this: I might have done the same in similar circumstances. And, interestingly, no one objected to the 'personal' style, though I'd been more worried about this than anything else.

One manager – Giovanni Alberti – told me that he'd taken the book on holiday. He seemed to have read it quite carefully. He said he hadn't understood it all, and he didn't feel like searching for a reference library in order to understand the sociological terms. Then he went on:

Giovanni Alberti: I've just got one general comment. Now that I've read it, I'm not very clear what the conclusion is. What the the bottom line is. It would be nice if this was clear for the general reader.

This comment indexed some of my fears, for instance about the complexity of the argument. But it also illustrated a clash between modes of ordering. For notions like the 'bottom line' derive, or so I've argued, from enterprise. In enterprise people are practical. They come to conclusions. They make hard choices. And suddenly I was being asked, in the language of enterprise, to justify the book. After a moment, the conversation continued like this:

John Law: The bottom line is that there *is* no bottom line. What I think's happening at Daresbury in management — though I guess it goes on everywhere — is a bit like juggling. You've got all these balls up in the air, and the art of management is to keep them all up in the air at the same time. And to do that you have to keep on moving. You never come to rest. So that's how I see an organization like the Lab. It's a lot of different ordering principles. Not one. And the work of ordering is never finished.

Giovanni Alberti: It would help if you could say something like that in the conclusion. Help naive readers like me.

Well, that, then, is the bottom line. Or a bottom line. And I think that for many purposes Giovanni is right to ask for a bottom line. Why should the reader not go away with something firm, something to hang on to? And yet, I feel uneasy both about his question and my answer. For instance, the latter is a response posed in human terms: it sounds as if I'm saying that there are human managers; and then that they have to juggle conflicting demands and principles. This captures something about the argument. On the other hand however, that division — the division between human agents and the networks of the social — is precisely one of the dualisms that I'm trying to resist.

That, then, is a specific problem if we talk of 'bottom lines' in the way that I did. But there are more general problems too. Why do we feel the *need* for a bottom line, when the argument is precisely about the *absence* of a bottom line? Why do we still respond to modes of ordering that demand discrete and relatively simple conclusions that can be transported from one place to another? How might we create alternative modes of ordering, alternative ways of writing, where these demands are no longer made? Graham McCann, the author of a reflexive biography of Marilyn Monroe, writes:

Myth emerges out of the author's need and the reader's desire for wholeness and order. Irony emerges out of the tension between the impulse to correct in the biography and its generation of new myths about the subject. (McCann 1988: 207)

McCann is wrestling with the same general problem. This is that if we choose to write about something, then we have opted willy-nilly for some kind of a call to order. Perhaps a provisional call. Perhaps one that is modest. Perhaps one that exemplifies its limits in the juxtaposition of fragments. But, whatever the caveats, the act of writing is one of putative legislation.

2 REFLECTIONS

The reactions of my colleagues and friends to the book were mixed. On the whole, people were interested in the 'substance' of the argument, its 'theory'. They tended to agree with the arguments about purity – though not necessarily with some of the epistemological implications of that argument. Some felt more comfortable with the notion of the mode of ordering than others, while others raised questions of a 'macrosocial' character. But most of all, there was comment, and disagreement, about the self-referring character of the book. Some appreciated it. More were uncertain. And one or two of my friends, colleagues and critics intensely disliked it.

Critical comments about reflexivity came in three main forms. First, some noted – and I'm sure that they are right – that irony is possible without self-reflexivity. For instance, there are fine studies where machines are given voices, and proceed to enter into debate with humans. Or places where humans attempt to deconstruct each other. In the present book there is a certain amount of the latter – places where the modes of ordering butt up together – though I don't give voice to machines to any great extent, and I now wish I had done this more. But what drives this first comment isn't really that other forms of irony are possible. Rather it is that it is better not to be self-reflexive at all. On this I remain agnostic. This book is self-reflexive, though only to a degree. And as a part of this reflexivity, it makes the argument that if we are committed to what I've called pessimistic liberalism then there are reasons for redrawing the distinction between the private and the public in academic writing. More of this in a moment.

The second major criticism about reflexivity concerned the character of the personal voice developed in the book. The argument was that it is possible – indeed perhaps important – to maintain a distinction between the author as a person, and the author as a voice, or a set of voices. This is not a distinction which was particularly clear to me when I began the study. So, re-reading the text as a part of the final revisions, I now find places where I agree with the critics. In particular, I believe that in places what I write is theoretically humanist: where I talk about 'I' and 'me' rather than reconstituting the author as a textual and interdiscursive effect. As a result, in the final editing I've cut out a number of such 'personal-humanist' passages, thereby continuing a process that had already started in earlier drafts. But the process is incomplete.

One of my colleagues, Gordon Fyfe, caught the non-humanist character of authorship rather well. He observed that there is a real sense in which the author of this book is Keele University in the 1980s. This was a decade in which Keele (along with other universities) was rapidly (though incompletely) re-ordered in terms of enterprise, and it was thus a period in which there were various tensions and conflicts between different modes of ordering. So the argument is that such tensions at Keele are also told, through the medium of this study, in Daresbury Laboratory. I think this is right, though it is also more complicated. For instance, we need to make something of the fact that it wasn't Keele that sat down and wrote the book. Or, to put it in another way, we need to make something of the way in which other performances, individual and collective (for instance derived from social theory) also participated in the writing.

What, then, is the role of the 'personal' in self-reflexive writing? A short digression. I've read enough self-reflexive studies to know that these can be most irritating. Leaving aside the fact that they may appear cute, many self-reflexive texts are strangely self-contained, sealing themselves off from comment and criticism. The initial reason for deploying and criticizing arguments within one text may be to show that the latter is incomplete. But often enough it is the opposite effect that is achieved. I wanted to avoid such self-insulation in the present study: the object was to empower the reader, not to dis-empower her. And I chose to try to do this in a way which I now think is in part humanist – that is by laying *myself*, as a person, on the line. I didn't want to try to cover all bases. Rather I wanted to say: 'I came from this place; these things happened to me. This is what I make of them. I may well be wrong. And even if I'm right, I don't know how far what I've said applies elsewhere.' Thus I wanted to emphasize both the context of the work, and the continuities between the author and his subject-matter. To be risky with myself.

That, then, was how I started out thinking about the 'personal'. But this is not (at any rate) completely successful. For the critics can (and have) said: 'You say you're being honest. But of course you're not really being honest. You exclude all sorts of important matters, personal and otherwise.' And this is right: I have to reply by saying 'Quite so.' But the important point is this: it is to respond by trying to shift the grounds of the argument. In particular, I want to argue that both my attempts at honesty *and* the suggestion that I've failed are constituted *within humanism*. In which case the next question would be: don't we need, therefore, to detach the notion of 'honesty' from its connection with the 'personal'?

This leads to a third kind of criticism about self-reflexivity. This has to do with power. Several of my colleagues said things like this: 'It is all very well you writing like this. You're a Professor. You're well established. But I'm not. I still have to get my Ph.D. So I can't possibly write like that.' The complaint, then, is that this kind of writing is an elite game. It is that people in my position can choose to ignore the standard conventions of academic writing. But most people have to crank the handle and produce papers and reports. So they don't have the luxury of writing like this, even if they want to.

This is very interesting. As I've said, I started out writing the book self-reflexively because I wanted to redraw the boundaries between the private and the public. The object was to move academic writing from a self-contained realm in which good theory and data stand up for themselves. Instead I wanted to empower the reader within the processes of order*ing*, rather than insist that she insert herself into a logic of completed order. Thus I wanted to de-mystify, de-reify, and make local. The third criticism, however, suggests that the effect of writing in this way is to create another kind of ideal realm, one in which authors are free from the constraints of position and can *afford* to expose the difficulties in their arguments. In this (imaginary) realm readers respect signs of uncertainty in one another. But (so the criticism runs) this is unrealistic. For most people in the real world uncertainty is taken as a sign of weakness. Which has devastating effects on those who try it, unless they already have high status. In other words, it ignores the imperfect conditions which make writing – and unconventional writing – possible in the first place.

Perhaps I should plead guilty to this. It's possible that I've tended to forget that I'm a professor, and that since I'm pretty secure I can *afford* to make academic mistakes. On the other hand, it's also worthwhile observing that both the initial accusation and this response are located within the orderings of humanism. Or, to put it slightly differently, both combine a *description* of a state of affairs (that people like professors embody and perform certain kinds of privilege and power) together with a moral vocabulary. The latter (inevitably?) takes a more or less personal form, and has to do with the responsibility of the powerful for the state of affairs within which they are located. But this is not a combination given in the order of things. For though the *description* is possible within both humanist and non-humanist orderings, a vocabulary of ethics makes best sense within humanism because it tends to personalize responsibility for unjust asymmetries in power. Or, rather, it tends towards a vocabulary of personal responsibility and irresponsibility – a vocabulary that is combined with a sociological concern with explanation only with difficulty – and only (I think) within a humanist vocabulary.[1]

What happens if we think about this in a non-humanist way? There are various possibilities. The most obvious is to say that privilege is an effect generated by modes of ordering. And to show how this is done. Indeed, I've tried to do this, particularly in chapter 6. Another, which I haven't consistently considered, may offer more political promise. This is to note that many parts of privilege are generated in the relationship *between* modes of ordering. Here the argument is that orderings always discover their limits. They run into the sands of intractablility. But this means that the *very possibility* of a project of the search for order is maintained by jumping between necessarily inconclusive ordering modes. When one runs out, when it is no longer performable or tellable, *then another takes its place*. This mirage – a commitment to an imagined order or master-narrative, rather than to the inconclusive ordering of little narratives – is thereby sustained. But this is a point of political leverage. It is a place where play, in the post-modern sense of the term, becomes possible. For if the privileged perform and embody a mode of ordering that, self-reflexively, *also* tells that it is a mode of ordering, then possibly, just possibly, this new way of being will become more performable by those who are less constituted in privilege. It will start to spread.

I don't believe that this will be easy. And neither do I take it that it is simply a matter to do with academic debate. Politics, administration, vocation, theory, all of these areas offer possibilities for, but also resistances to, orderings that tell that they are orderings. But – this is the argument – one possibility is for those who are told as privileged to perform their multidiscursive writing as weak, inconclusive, and limited, in the hope that this will make it easier for those who are less privileged in turn to perform their writing as orderings rather than orders. Which will rework what counts as privilege – perhaps, or so is the hope, fragmenting it. At any rate, this is why I believe in the importance of a non-humanist understanding of personal provenance. And why I remain committed to the idea that a sociology of ordering might write itself in an ordering mode, rather than as an order. Though how best to do this remains a puzzle.

What, then, should we be seeking? What are the merits of 'weakness'? What sense does this have in a non-humanist world? In earlier chapters I followed Richard Rorty and Judith Shklar by saying that the worst thing we can do to one another is to be cruel. But what does this mean in practice? As I wrestled with this question I distinguished between optimistic and pessimistic liberalism. I suggested that the former agrees that all is not perfect, but believes liberal democracy (or its intellectual analogue in the form of the academic community?) to be the least worst system that we've got. Pessimistic liberalism might agree with the 'least worst' argument. But it's also much more cautious. This is because we're constantly discovering that we're cruel in ways we never dreamed of.

I argued for a pessimistic form of liberalism in chapter 5. But now I want to make a further step in that argument, and distinguish between its possible humanist and non-humanist forms. The humanist version would note that there are endless voices waiting to be heard, just as there are endless stories about our cruelties to which we have not yet listened. So the object – and it is an endless and incomplete process – is to extend the territory covered by the democracy of voices. To extend the list of cruelties which we have heard, and to which we seek to respond. And to patrol, with vigilant sensitivity, the constant incursions into the territory of voices, in- cursions made by those who seek to silence, or to deny that this or that amounts to cruelty. This, then, is a form of principled weakness. It is one in which those who do have voices seek to be weak precisely because they are committed to the chronic process of trying to listen out for cruelties; and the voices which tell of these.

But what happens if we try to imagine pessimistic liberalism in a non-humanist mode? The answer to this question is that I'm not certain. But I do have one or two ideas. The first is that this 'democracy of voices' is broadened. In particular, we find that it is not simply human voices to which we have to attend. Microbes, trees, fish, weather-patterns and ultraviolet radiation – these are the kinds of voices waiting to be heard. There are the voices of the dead, of the spirits, and of the gods. And, so too, are there cyborg voices – the monstrous voices of those that are denied a voice because they are mechanical, machine-like. Or because they are part human, part device. This, then, is the first dissolution of humanism – it extends beyond humans. It is not speciesist. Others may speak too.

The second move has to do with entities and voices. For humanism takes it that there are entities – in the first instance, human entities. And it tells that they have voices. They may be, and very often are, silenced voices. So it is that feminism has shown us that they may be voices without vocabularies, voices that cannot find a name for themselves and speak of their experiences. In the first dissolution of humanism this assumption is preserved: it says that entities (though no longer simply human entities) are there. And that 'they' 'have' voices, if those voices can be discovered. But the second dissolution says that voices, and the 'entities' of which they speak, are effects or products. This is relational materialism: neither are given in the order of things.

This is horribly complicated. It means, for instance, that it is no longer clear, even in principle, what a democracy of voices would look like. Who or what is to be included? Unanswerable question. What do we mean by 'who' or 'what'? Entities are not pre-constituted. They aren't lining up, waiting to be granted their voices so that they may tell us that we have been cruel. They aren't even there, waiting to be found by the pessimistic liberal as she searches through the dark and disenfranchised places of the world. Neither are 'we', those who tell and speak, any more entitled to claim that we should be numbered among the fundamental particles of the social universe – for we too are precarious relational effects.

This, then, is a negative argument. I don't know where it leads. But let me put the negative argument as positively as I can. If entities and their voices are complex and contingent effects, then the liberal idea of a terrain – a singular meta-place where those who are allowed come to speak and tell of cruelties – starts to lose its appeal. Indeed, as Annemarie Mol notes, the very language is wrong. For the notion of an ideal speech situation – a space where entities meet together having agreed to obey a single set of discursive rules – is not so much another mode for disenfranchising most entity-effects (as would be the case in liberal theory). Rather, by striking at the heart of liberal theory, it suggests the need for alternative political metaphors. So how might the non-humanist liberal respond? What, in her theoretical and political imagination, can replace the ordered and united terrain where truth is properly distinguished from power, where cruelty is constituted and combatted?

It would seem that if the answer is not a single space, then the (plural) answers will be diverse. Taking many forms. Told, performed and embodied in many different ways. In many different places. For many different entities, near-entities, and proto-entities. So the conduct of the search for cruelty will be very local. And in this new politics the arguments and expressions of these (quasi-)entities as they debate the character of cruelty will be quite specific. And when local conclusions are, for a moment, reached, those conclusions will be transferable only with effort, difficulty, care and caution from where they were created. For what reduces cruelty in one place may simply increase it in another. There will, then be no one gathering place, no privileged forum, no single calculus of cruelty. For a single calculus will instantly deposit us back in the hideous purity of a unitary if well-meaning liberalism. Instead there will be many ways of reckoning. And many ways of linking reckonings together.

This, then, is our task once we set aside the search for the certainties of modernity. It is to find decentred, distributed, but rigorous ways of knowing and being. Ways of knowing and being appropriate to a world that wants to live at peace with the knowledge of its incompletenesses.

NOTES

1 I'm aware of Bauman's arguments about the way in which sociology reduces the moral to the social, and feel uneasy about both the phenomenon itself and his solution. But I don't know why, so I can't deal with the issue here. See Bauman (1989).

References

Abercrombie, Nicholas and Turner, Bryan S. (1978) 'The dominant ideology thesis', *British Journal of Sociology*, 29, 149–70.

Abrams, Philip (1982) *Historical Sociology*, Shepton Mallett: Open Books.

Akrich, Madeleine (1992) 'The de-scription of technical objects', in Wiebe E. Bijker and John Law (eds) *Shaping Technology – Building Society: studies in sociotechnical change*, Cambridge, Mass.: MIT Press, 205–240.

Althusser, Louis (1971a) 'Ideology and ideological state apparatuses', in Louis Althusser, *Lenin and Philosophy and Other Essays*, London: New Left Books, 123–73.

Althusser, Louis (1971b) *Lenin and Philosophy and Other Essays*, London: New Left Books.

Barnes, Barry (1977) *Interests and the Growth of Knowledge*, London: Routledge and Kegan Paul.

Barnes, Barry (1986) 'On authority and its relationship to power', in John Law (ed.), *Power, Action and Belief: a new sociology of knowledge?*, *Sociological Review Monograph* 32, London: Routledge and Kegan Paul, 180–95.

Barnes, Barry (1988) *The Nature of Power*, Cambridge: Polity Press.

Barthes, Roland (1973) 'Myth today', in Roland Barthes, *Mythologies*, Saint Albans: Granada, 109–59.

Baudrillard, Jean (1988a) *Selected Writings*, Cambridge: Polity Press.

Baudrillard, Jean (1988b) 'Simulacra and simulations', in Jean Baudrillard, *Selected Writings*, Cambridge: Polity Press, 166–84.

Bauman, Zygmunt (1989) *Modernity and the Holocaust*, Cambridge: Polity Press.

Bauman, Zygmunt (1992) *Intimations of Postmodernity*, London: Routledge.

Becker, Howard S. (1963) *Outsiders: studies in the sociology of deviance*, New York: The Free Press.

Becker, Howard S. (1971a) 'Notes on the concept of commitment', in Howard S. Becker, *Sociological Work: method and substance*, London: Allen Lane, 261–73.

Becker, Howard S. (1971b) 'Whose side are we on?', in Howard S. Becker, *Sociological Work: method and substance*, London: Allen Lane, 123–34.

Becker, Howard S. (1982) *Art Worlds*, Berkeley: University of California Press.

Benhabib, Selya (1990) 'Epistemologies of postmodernism: a rejoinder to Jean-François Lyotard', in Linda J. Nicholson (ed.) *Feminism/Postmodernism*, New York: Routledge, 107–30.

Beniger, James R. (1986) *The Control Revolution: technological and economic origins of the information society*, Cambridge, Mass.: Harvard University Press.

Bijker, Wiebe E. (1992) 'The social construction of fluorescent lighting – or how an artefact was invented in its design stage', in Wiebe E. Bijker and John Law (eds) *Shaping Technology – Building Society: studies in sociotechnical change*, Cambridge, Mass.: MIT Press, 75–102.

Bijker, Wiebe E., Hughes, Thomas P. and Pinch, Trevor J. (eds) (1987) *The Social Construction of Technical Systems: new directions in the sociology and history of technology*, Cambridge, Mass.: MIT Press.

Bloor, David (1976) *Knowledge and Social Imagery*, London: Routledge and Kegan Paul.

Blumer, Herbert (1969a) 'Society as symbolic interaction', in Herbert Blumer, *Symbolic Interactionism: perspective and method*, Englewood Cliffs, New Jersey: Prentice Hall, 78–89.

Blumer, Herbert (1969b) *Symbolic Interactionism: perspective and method*, Englewood Cliffs, New Jersey: Prentice Hall.

Boltanski, Luc and Thévenot, Laurent (1987) *Les Économies de la grandeur*, *cahiers du Centre d'Études de l'Emploi* 31, Paris: Presses Universitaires de France.

Bourdieu, Pierre (1986) *Distinction: a social critique of the judgement of taste*, London: Routledge.

Bowker, Geoff (1988) 'Pictures from the subsoil, 1939', in Gordon Fyfe and John Law (eds) *Picturing Power: visual depiction and social relations*, *Sociological Review Monograph* 36, London: Routledge, 221–54.

Bowker, Geoff (1992) 'What's in a Patent?', in Wiebe E. Bijker and John Law (eds) *Shaping Technology – Building Society: studies in sociotechnical change*, Cambridge, Mass.: MIT Press, 53–74.

Brannigan, Augustine (1981) *The Social Basis of Scientific Discoveries*, Cambridge: Cambridge University Press.

Braudel, Fernand (1975) *The Mediterranean and the Mediterranean World in the Age of Phillip II*, 2 vols, London: Fontana.

Braudel, Fernand (1985) *Civilization and Capitalism, 15th–18th Century*, 3 vols, London: Fontana.

Burns, Tom, and G. M. Stalker (1961) *The Management of Innovation*, London: Tavistock.

Callon, Michel (1980) 'Struggles and negotiations to define what is problematic and what is not: the sociology of translation', in Karin D. Knorr, Roger Krohn and Richard D. Whitley (eds) *The Social Process of Scientific Investigation: sociology of the sciences yearbook*, vol. 4, Dordrecht and Boston, Mass.: Reidel, 197–219.

Callon, Michel (1986a) 'Some elements of a sociology of translation: domestication of the scallops and the fishermen of St. Brieuc Bay', in John Law (ed.) *Power, Action and Belief: a new sociology of knowledge?*, *Sociological Review Monograph* 32, London: Routledge and Kegan Paul, 196–233.

Callon, Michel (1986b) 'The sociology of an actor-network: the case of the electric vehicle', in Michael Callon, John Law and Arie Rip (eds) *Mapping the Dynamics of Science and Technology: sociology of science in the real world*, London: Macmillan, 19–34.

Callon, Michel (1987) 'Society in the making: the study of technology as a tool for sociological analysis', in Wiebe E. Bijker, Thomas P. Hughes and Trevor J. Pinch (eds) *The Social Construction of Technical Systems: new directions in the sociology and history of technology*, Cambridge, Mass.: MIT Press, 83–103.

Callon, Michel (1991) 'Techno-economic networks and irreversibility', in John Law (ed.) *A Sociology of Monsters? Essays on Power, Technology and Domination*, Sociological Review Monograph 38, London: Routledge, 132–61.

Callon, Michel and Latour Bruno (1981) 'Unscrewing the big Leviathan: how actors macrostructure reality and how sociologists help them to do so', in Karin D. Knorr-Cetina and Aaron V. Cicourel (eds) *Advances in Social Theory and Methodology: toward an integration of micro- and macro-sociologies*, Boston, Mass.: Routledge and Kegan Paul, 277–303.

Callon, Michel and John Law (1982) 'On interests and their transformation: enrolment and counter-enrolment', *Social Studies of Science*, 12, 615–25.

Chandler, Alfred D. (1977) *The Visible Hand: the managerial revolution in American business*, Cambridge, Mass.: Belknap, Harvard University Press.

Cicourel, Aaron V. (1964) *Method and Measurement in Sociology*, New York: The Free Press.

Cicourel, Aaron V. (1974) *Theory and Method in a Study of Argentine Fertility*, New York: Wiley.

Clegg, Stewart R. (1989) *Frameworks of Power*, London: Sage.

Clifford, James (1986) 'Introduction', in James, Clifford and George E. Marcus (eds) *Writing Culture: the poetics and politics of ethnography*, Berkeley: University of California Press, 1–26.

Collins, H. M. (1975) 'The seven sexes: a study in the sociology of a phenomenon, or the replication of experiments in physics', *Sociology*, 9, 205–24.

Collins, H. M. (1985) *Changing Order: replication and induction in scientific practice*, London: Sage.

Cooper, Robert (1987) 'Information, communication and organisation: a post-structural revision', *The Journal of Mind and Behavior*, 8, 395–416.

Cooper, Robert (1992) 'Formal organization as representation: remote control, displacement and abbreviation', in M. Reed and M. Hughes (eds) *Rethinking Organization*, London: Sage, 254–72.

Cooper, Robert (1993) 'Technologies of representation', in Pertti Ahonen (ed.) *Tracing The Semiotic Boundaries of Politics*, Berlin: de Gruyter.

Cooper, Robert and Burrell, Gibson (1988) 'Modernism, postmodernism and organizational analysis: an introduction', *Organization Studies*, 9, 91–112.

Dalton, Melville (1959) *Men Who Manage: fusions of feeling and theory in administration*, New York: John Wiley.

Delamont, Sara (1987) 'Three blind spots? A comment on the sociology of science by a puzzled outsider', *Social Studies of Science*, 17, 163–70.

Derrida, Jacques (1976) *Of Grammatology*, Baltimore and London: Johns Hopkins.

Douglas, Mary (1973) *Natural Symbols: explorations in cosmology*, Harmondsworth: Penguin.

Douglas, Mary and Isherwood, Baron (1979) *The World of Goods: towards an anthropology of consumption*, London: Allen Lane.

Duncan, Hugh Dalziel (1962) *Communication and the Social Order*, Totowa, New Jersey: Bedminster.

Duncan, Hugh Dalziel (1965) *Culture and Democracy*, Totowa, New Jersey: Bedminster.

Duncan, Hugh Dalziel (1968) *Symbols in Society*, New York: Oxford University Press.

Durkheim, Émile (1915) *The Elementary Forms of the Religious Life*, trans. Joseph Ward Swan, London: George Allen and Unwin.

Durkheim, Émile (1964) *The Division of Labour in Society*, New York: Free Press.

Elias, Norbert (1978a) *The History of Manners*, Oxford: Blackwell.

Elias, Norbert (1978b) *What is Sociology?* London: Hutchinson.

Elias, Norbert (1983) *The Court Society*, Oxford: Basil Blackwell.

Elkins, Stanley (1959) *Slavery*, Chicago: Chicago University Press.

Featherstone, Mike (1991) *Consumer Culture and Postmodernism*, London: Sage.

Featherstone, Mike, Hepworth, Mike and Turner, Bryan S. (eds) (1991) *The Body: social process and cultural theory*, London: Sage.

Forty, Adrian (1986) *Objects of Desire: design and society, 1750–1980*, London: Thames and Hudson.

Foucault, Michel (1974) *The Order of Things: an archaeology of the human sciences*, London: Tavistock.

Foucault, Michel (1976) *The Birth of the Clinic: an archaeology of medical perception*, London: Tavistock.

Foucault, Michel (1979) *Discipline and Punish: the birth of the prison*, Harmondsworth: Penguin.

Foucault, Michel (1981) *The History of Sexuality: volume 1; an introduction*, Harmondsworth: Penguin.

Fyfe, Gordon and John Law (eds) (1988) *Picturing Power: visual depiction and social relations*, Sociological Review Monograph 36, London: Routledge.

Garcia, Marie-France (1986) 'La Construction sociale d'un marché parfait: le marché au cadran de Fontaines en Sologne', *Actes de la Recherche en Sciences Sociales*, 65, 2–13.

Garfinkel, Harold (1967) *Studies in Ethnomethodology*, Englewood Cliffs, New Jersey: Prentice-Hall.

Garfinkel, Harold, Lynch, Michael, and Livingston, Eric (1981) 'The work of a discovering science construed with materials from the optically discovered pulsar', *Philosophy of the Social Sciences*, 11, 131–58.

Giddens, Anthony (1976) *New Rules of Sociological Method: a positive critique of intepretative sociologies*, London: Hutchinson.

Giddens, Anthony (1984) *The Constitution of Society*, Cambridge: Polity Press.

Giddens, Anthony (1990) *The Consequences of Modernity*, Cambridge: Polity Press.

Giddens, Anthony (1991) *Modernity and Self-Identity: self and society in the Late Modern Age*, Cambridge: Polity Press.

Gilbert, G. Nigel and Mulkay, Michael J. (1984) *Opening Pandora's Box: a sociological analysis of scientists' discourse*, Cambridge: Cambridge University Press.

Glaser, Barney G. and Strauss, Anselm L. (1965) *Awareness of Dying*, New York: Aldine.

Goffman, Erving (1968) *Asylums: essays on the social situation of mental patients and other inmates*, Harmondsworth: Penguin.

Goffman, Erving (1970) *Strategic Interaction*, Oxford: Blackwell.

Goffman, Erving (1971) *The Presentation of Self in Everyday Life*, Harmondsworth: Penguin.

Goffman, Erving (1972) *Encounters: two studies in the sociology of interaction*, Harmondsworth: Penguin

Goody, Jack (1977) *The Domestication of the Savage Mind*, Cambridge: Cambridge University Press.

Habermas, Jürgen (1972) *Knowledge and Human Interests*, London: Heinemann.

Hackett, Edward J. (1990) 'Science as a vocation in the 1990s: the changing organizational culture of academic science', *Journal of Higher Education*, 61, 241–79.

Hammersley, Martyn and Atkinson, Paul (1983) *Ethnography: principles in practice*, London: Routledge.

Haraway, Donna (1990) 'A manifesto for cyborgs: science, technology, and socialist feminism in the 1980s', in Linda J. Nicholson (ed.) *Feminism/Postmodernism*, New York: Routledge, 190–233.

Harding, Sandra (1986) *The Science Question in Feminism*, Milton Keynes: Open University Press.

Harvey, David (1990) *The Condition of Postmodernity: an enquiry into the origins of cultural change*, Oxford: Blackwell.

Hennion, Antoine (1989) 'An intermediary between production and consumption: the producer of popular music', *Science, Technology and Human Values*, 14, 400–24.

Hesse, Mary B. (1974) *The Structure of Scientific Inference*, London: Macmillan.

Hindess, Barry (1982) 'Power, interests and the outcome of struggles', *Sociology*, 16, 498–511.

Hughes, Thomas P. (1983) *Networks of Power: electrification in Western society, 1880–1930*, Baltimore: Johns Hopkins University Press.

Hughes, Thomas P. (1986) 'The seamless web: technology, science, etcetera, etcetera', *Social Studies of Science*, 16, 281–92.

Keat, Russell (1991) 'Introduction: Starship Britain, or universal enterprise', in Russell Keat and Nicholas Abercrombie (eds) *Enterprise Culture*, London: Routledge. 1–17.

Keat, Russell and Abercrombie, Nicholas (eds) (1991) *Enterprise Culture*, London: Routledge.

Knights, David and Morgan, Glenn (1990) 'The Concept of strategy in sociology: a note of dissent', *Sociology*, 24, 475–83.

Kuhn, Thomas S. (1970) *The Structure of Scientific Revolutions*, Chicago: Chicago University Press.

Latour, Bruno (1983) 'Give me a laboratory and I will raise the world', in Karin D. Knorr-Cetina and Michael Mulkay (eds) *Science Observed: perspectives on the social study of science*, London: Sage, 141–70.

Latour, Bruno (1987) *Science in Action: how to follow scientists and engineers through society*, Milton Keynes: Open University Press.

Latour, Bruno (1988a) *The Pasteurization of France*, Cambridge, Mass.: Harvard University Press.

Latour, Bruno (1988b) *Irreductions*, published with Bruno Latour, *The Pasteurization of France*, Cambridge, Mass.: Harvard University Press. 151–236.

Latour, Bruno (1988c) '*The Prince* for machines as well as for machinations', in Brian Elliott (ed.) *Technology and Social Process*, Edinburgh: Edinburgh University Press, 20–43.

Latour, Bruno (1990) 'Drawing things together', in Michael Lynch and Steve Woolgar (eds) *Representation in Scientific Practice*, Cambridge, Mass.: MIT Press, 19–68.

Latour, Bruno (1991a) *Nous n'avons jamais été modernes: essai d'anthropologie symétrique*, Paris: La Découverte.

Latour, Bruno (1991b) 'Technology is society made durable', in John Law (ed.) *A Sociology of Monsters? Essays on Power, Technology and Domination*, Sociological Review Monograph 38, London: Routledge, 103–31.

Latour, Bruno (1992a) 'Where are the missing masses? Sociology of a few mundane artefacts', in Wiebe E. Bijker and John Law (eds) *Shaping Technology – Building Society: studies in sociotechnical change*, Cambridge, Mass.: MIT Press, 225–58.

Latour, Bruno (1992b) *Aramis, ou l'amour des techniques*, Paris: La Découverte.

Latour, Bruno, and Woolgar, Steve (1979) *Laboratory Life: the social construction of scientific facts*, Beverly Hills: Sage; repr. Princeton: Princeton University Press, 1986.

Law, John (1984) 'How much of society can the sociologist digest at one sitting? The 'macro' and the 'micro' revisited for the case of fast food', *Studies in Symbolic Interaction*, 5, 171–96.

Law, John (1986a) 'On the methods of long-distance control: vessels, navigation, and the Portuguese route to India', in John Law (ed.), *Power, Action and Belief: a new sociology of knowledge?*, *Sociological Review Monograph* 32, London: Routledge and Kegan Paul, 234–63.

Law, John (1986b) 'Laboratories and texts', in Michael Callon, John Law and Arie Rip (eds) *Mapping the Dynamics of Science and Technology: sociology of science in the real world*, London: Macmillan, 35–50.

Law, John (1986c) 'On power and its tactics: a view from the sociology of science', *Sociological Review*, 34, 1–38.

Law, John (1987) 'Technology and heterogeneous engineering: the case of the Portuguese expansion', in Wiebe E. Bijker, Thomas P. Hughes and Trevor J. Pinch (eds) (1987) *The Social Construction of Technical Systems:*

new directions in the sociology and history of technology, Cambridge, Mass.: MIT Press 111–34.

Law, John (1991a). 'Introduction: monsters, machines and sociotechnical relations', in John Law (ed.) *A Sociology of Monsters? Essays on Power, Technology and Domination, Sociological Review Monograph* 38, London: Routledge, 1–23.

Law, John (1991b) 'Power, discretion and strategy', in John Law (ed.) *A Sociology of Monsters? Essays on Power, Technology and Domination, Sociological Review Monograph* 38, London: Routledge, 165–91.

Law, John (1992a) 'Notes on the theory of the actor-network: ordering, strategy and heterogeneity', *Systems Practice*, 5, 379–93.

Law,. John (1992b) 'The Olympus 320 engine: a case study in design, development and organisational control', *Technology and Culture*, 33, 409–40.

Law, John and Bijker, Wiebe E. (1992) 'Technology, stability and social theory', in Wiebe E. Bijker and John Law (eds) *Shaping Technology – Building Society: studies in sociotechnical change*, Cambridge, Mass.: MIT Press, 290–308.

Law, John and Callon, Michel (1992) 'The life and death of an aircraft: a network analysis of technical change', in Wiebe E. Bijker and John Law (eds) *Shaping Technology – Building Society: studies in sociotechnical change*, Cambridge, Mass.: MIT Press, 21–52.

Law, John and Lodge, Peter (1984) *Science for Social Scientists*, London: Macmillan

Law, John and Mol, Annemarie (forthcoming) 'Notes on materialism', *Politica y Sociedad*.

Law, John and Whittaker, John (1988) 'On the art of representation: notes on the politics of visualisation', in Gordon Fyfe and John Law (eds) *Picturing Power: visual depiction and social relations, Sociological Review Monograph* 36, London: Routledge, 160–83.

Lynch, Michael, and Woolgar, Steve (eds) (1990) *Representation in Scientific Practice*, Cambridge, Mass.: MIT Press.

Lyotard, Jean-François (1984) *The Postmodern Condition: a report on knowledge*, Manchester: Manchester University Press.

McCann, Graham (1988) *The Body in the Library*, Cambridge: Polity Press.

MacKenzie, Donald, and Wajcman, Judy (eds) (1985) *The Social Shaping of Technology: how the refrigerator got its hum*, Milton Keynes: Open University Press.

MacKenzie, Donald, Rudig, Wolfgang and Spinardi, Graham (1988) 'Social research on technology and the policy agenda: an example from the strategic arms race', in Brian Elliott (ed.) (1988) *Technology and Social Process*, Edinburgh: Edinburgh University Press, 152–80.

Malavé, José (1992) '*Systems, networks and structures*', unpublished Ph.D dissertation, University of Lancaster.

Mannheim, Karl (1953a) *Essays on Sociology and Social Psychology*, London: Routledge and Kegan Paul.

Mannheim, Karl (1953b) 'Conservative thought', in Karl Mannheim (ed.) *Essays on Sociology and Social Psychology*, London: Routledge and Kegan Paul, 74–164.

Marx, Karl (1889) *Capital: a critical analysis of capitalist production*, vol. 1, London: George Allen and Unwin.

Mead, George Herbert (1934) *Mind, Self and Society*, Chicago: Chicago University Press.

Merton, Robert K. (1957) *Social Theory and Social Structure*, New York: The Free Press.

Merton, Robert K. (1968) 'The Matthew effect in science', *Science*, 59, 56–63.

Mills, C. Wright (1959) *The Sociological Imagination*, Oxford: Oxford University Press.

Mol, Annemarie (1991) 'Wombs, pigmentation and pyramids: should anti-racists and feminists try to confine 'biology' to its proper place', in Joke J. Hermsen and Alkeline van Lenning (eds) *Sharing the Difference: feminist debates in Holland*, London: Routledge 149–63.

Morgan, Gareth (1986) *Images of Organization*, Beverly Hills: Sage.

Ong, Walter J. (1988) *Orality and Literacy: the technologizing of the word*, London: Routledge.

Parsons, Talcott (1951) *The Social System*, New York: The Free Press.

Perrow, Charles (1984) *Normal Accidents: living with high risk technologies*, New York: Basic Books.

Polanyi, Michael (1958) *Personal Knowledge: towards a post-critical philosophy*, London: Routledge and Kegan Paul.

Popper, Karl R. (1959) *The Logic of Scientific Discovery*, London: Hutchinson.

Popper, Karl R. (1962) *The Open Society and Some of Its Enemies*, London: Routledge and Kegan Paul.

Poster, Mark (1990) *The Mode of Information: poststructuralism and social context*, Cambridge: Polity Press.

Rock, Paul (1979) *The Making of Symbolic Interactionism*, London: Macmillan.

Rojek, Chris (1985) *Capitalism and Leisure Theory*, London: Tavistock.

Rorty, Richard (1989) *Contingency, Irony, and Solidarity*, Cambridge: Cambridge University Press.

Rorty, Richard (1991) *Objectivity, Relativism and Truth*, Philosophical Papers, Volume 1, Cambridge: Cambridge University Press.

Rowbotham, Sheila (1973) *Women's Consciousness, Mans' World*, Harmondsworth: Penguin.

Sapolsky, Harvey M. (1972) *The Polaris System Development: bureaucratic and programmatic success in government*, Cambridge, Mass.: MIT Press.

Savage, Mike and Witz, Anne (eds) (1992) *Gender and Bureaucracy*, Sociological Review Monograph, Oxford: Blackwell.

Sennett, Richard (1972) *The Fall of Public Man*, Cambridge: Cambridge University Press.

Shapin, Steven (1989) 'The invisible technician', *American Scientist*, 77, 554–563.

Shapin, Steven and Schaffer, Simon (1985) *Leviathan and the Air Pump: Hobbes, Boyle and the experimental life*, Princeton: Princeton University Press.

Star, Susan Leigh (1988) 'Introduction: the sociology of science and technology', *Social Problems*, 35, 197–205.

Star, Susan Leigh (1989) *Regions of the Mind: brain research and the quest for scientific certainty*, Stanford: Stanford University Press.

Star, Susan Leigh (1990) 'What difference does it make where the mind is? Some questions for the history of neuro-psychiatry', *Journal of Neurology and Neuropsychology*, 2, 436–43.

Star, Susan Leigh (1991) 'Power, technologies and the phenomenology of conventions: on being allergic to onions', in John Law (ed.) *A Sociology of Monsters? Essays on Power, Technology and Domination*, Sociological Review Monograph 38, London: Routledge, 26–56.

Star, Susan Leigh (1992) 'The sociology of the invisible: the primacy of work in the writings of Anselm Strauss', in David Maines (ed.) *Social Organization and Social Processes: essays in honor of Anselm Strauss*, Hawthorne, New York: Aldine de Gruyter, 265–84.

Star, Susan Leigh and Griesemer, James (1989) 'Institutional ecology, "Translations" and boundary objects: amateurs and professionals in Berkeley's Museum of Vertebrate Zoology, 1907–39', *Social Studies of Science*, 19, 387–420.

Staudenmaier, John, Sj (1988) *Advent for Capitalists: grief, joy and gender in contemporary society*, The Tenth Nash Lecture, 1987, Saskatchewan: Campion College, University of Regina.

Strauss, Anselm (1977) *Mirrors and Masks: the search for identity*, London: Martin Robertson.

Thévenot, Laurent (1984) 'Rules and implements: investments in form', *Social Science Information*, 23, 1–45.

Thompson, E. P. (1967) 'Time, work-discipline, and industrial capitalism', *Past and Present*, 38, 56–96.

Thompson, Grahame, Frances, Jennifer, Levacic, Rosiland and Mitchell, Jeremy (eds) (1991), *Markets, Hierarchies and Networks: the coordination of social life*, London: Open University and Sage.

Thompson, John B., (1990) *Ideology and Modern Culture: critical social theory in the era of mass consumption*, Cambridge: Polity.

Traweek, Sharon (1988a) *Beamtimes and Lifetimes: the world of high energy physicists*, Cambridge, Mass.: Harvard University Press.

Traweek, Sharon (1988b) '"Feminist Perspectives on Science Studies": commentary', *Science, Technology and Human Values*, 13, 250–3.

Turkle, Sherry (1984) *The Second Self: computers and the human spirit*, New York: Simon and Schuster.

Weber, Max (1930) *The Protestant Ethic and the Spirit of Capitalism*, London: Unwin.

Weber, Max (1948) 'Science as a vocation', in Max Weber *From Max Weber: Essays in Sociology*, translated and edited with an Introduction by H. H. Gerth and C. Wright Mills, London: Routledge and Kegan Paul, 129–56.

Weber, Max (1978) *Economy and Society*, 2 vols, Berkeley: University of California Press.

Wieder, D. Lawrence (1974) 'Telling the code', in Roy Turner (ed.) *Ethnomethodology*, Harmondsworth: Penguin, 144–72.

Willis, Paul, (1977) *Learning to Labour*, Farnborough: Saxon House.

Wilson, Thomas P. (1971) 'Normative and interpretive paradigms in sociology', in Jack D. Douglas (ed.) *Understanding Everyday Life: toward the reconstruction of sociological knowledge*, London: Routledge and Kegan Paul, 57–79.

Winch, Peter (1958) *The Idea of a Social Science and Its Relation to Philosophy*, London: Routledge and Kegan Paul.

Winner, Langdon (1977) *Autonomous Technology: technics-out-of-control as a theme in political thought*, Cambridge, Mass.: MIT Press.

Winner, Langdon, (1986) *The Whale and the Reactor: a search for limits in an age of high technology*, Chicago: University of Chicago Press.

Wittgenstein, Ludwig (1953) *Philosophical Investigations*, Oxford: Blackwell.

Wittgenstein, Ludwig (1967) *Remarks on the Foundations of Mathematics*, 2nd edn, Oxford: Blackwell.

Woolgar, Steve (ed.) (1988) *Knowledge and Reflexivity: new frontiers in the sociology of knowledge*, London: Sage.

Woolgar, Steve (1991) 'Configuring the User: the Case of Usability Trials', in John Law (ed.) *A Sociology of Monsters? Essays on Power, Technology and Domination*, Sociological Review Monograph 38, London: Routledge, 58–99.

Wynne, Brian (1990) 'To believe or not to believe, is that the question? Expert credibility and the legitimation of science', Lancaster: University of Lancaster, Mimeo.

Young, Jock (1971) *The Drugtakers: the social meaning of drug use*, London: Paladin.

Index

as discourse a set of patterns
  2 discourse
  3 ordering <u>attempts</u>
  4 how performers embodied told
  5 how interact/change/fan
      extinction

<u>top</u>

top
remote control
displacement
abbreviation

(mode of order = style of thought
    ideology, discourse
    (159)

Enterprise · opportunism
              pragmatism }
              performance }

Administration · calkof + generates }
                  perfecto 6.

Vision · Charisma, grace, self mindedness,
          genius, transcence

Vocation · the proper character of
            certain kinds of work.